INDIA and CHINA

Comparative Economic Performance

INDIA and CHINA

Comparative Economic Performance

Surinder Kumar Singla

Assistant Professor,
Centre for South and Central Asian Countries,
School of Global Relations,
Central University of Punjab,
Bathinda, Punjab

New Century Publications
New Delhi, India

NEW CENTURY PUBLICATIONS
4800/24, Bharat Ram Road,
Ansari Road, Daryaganj,
New Delhi – 110 002 (India)

Tel.: 011-2324 7798, 4358 7398, 6539 6605
Fax: 011-4101 7798
E-mail: indiatax@vsnl.com • info@newcenturypublications.com
www.newcenturypublications.com

Editorial office:
LG–7, Aakarshan Bhawan,
4754-57/23, Ansari Road, Daryaganj,
New Delhi – 110 002

Tel.: 011-4356 0919

First Published: **July 2011**

ISBN: **978-81-7708-280-7**

Published by New Century Publications and printed at Salasar Imaging Systems, New Delhi.

Designs: Patch Creative Unit, New Delhi.

PRINTED IN INDIA

Affectionately Dedicated To
My Respected Parents
and
My Beloved Brother
(Late Shri Rajinder Kumar Singla)

About the Book

India's economic relations with China remained at low ebb after the Border War in 1962. However, economic ties between the two countries got a big boost when India initiated economic liberalization programme in early 1990s. India and China–with massive populations of 121 crore and 135 crore respectively–are the two fastest growing economies in the world. According to the much-publicised Goldman Sachs BRICS (Brazil, Russia, India, China and South Africa) Report, India is predicted to become the third largest economy in the world, after China and USA, by the year 2050, overtaking all other developed economies. Economic relations between the two emerging economic giants of the world need to be strengthened for mutual benefit.

The present volume provides a comprehensive analysis of economic relations between India and China in a disaggregative and comparative manner. Growth and composition of trade between the two countries has been examined through various trade related indices. Various dimensions of India's exports to China have been assessed in detail. Moreover, economic reforms and FDI inflows of the two countries have also been examined in a comparative perspective.

About the Author

Dr. Surinder Kumar Singla is Assistant Professor, Centre for South and Central Asian Countries, Central University of Punjab, Bathinda, Punjab. A Ph.D. from Punjabi University, Patiala, he has worked on three projects funded by National Foundation for India (NFI), New Delhi, Punjabi University, Patiala and Green Peace India Society, Bengaluru. He has also worked as Project Associate in Centre for South West Asia Study (Pakistan-Afghanistan). He has to his credit five research papers published in various journals of national repute.

Contents

Preface

India and China are two largest countries in the world in terms of their population, economic size and growth rates. These two countries together are home to the world's largest pool of skilled human resources and there is a general consensus that these two countries will continue to be the engines of global economic growth in the 21st Century.

Though India and China have a long history of economic and cultural exchanges, they established formal diplomatic relations in 1950 and signed their first trade agreement in 1954. However, all the agreements broke down in 1962 due to their border war. This attributed to the continuation of strain in their political relations and the restrictive trade practices followed by them towards each other. As a result of this syndrome, trade advantages emanating from geographical proximity and ethnic similarity have always remained elusive.

However, the economic and diplomatic relations between the two countries wee restored in the late 1970s. In 1984, both the countries offered Most Favoured Nation (MFN) status to each other, which paved the way for bilateral economic interactions. After that the high level officials' visits put a positive impact on their trade and economic relations. The bilateral trade got a big momentum only in early 1990s when India started its liberalisation process.

India-China relations are today conspicuous by the fast rise of their mutual trade. This is the result of deepening economic ties between the two that trade target of US$ 20 billion by 2008 was reached two years ahead of schedule. Today, India-China relations are conspicuous by the fast rise of trade, which has already crossed US$ 42 billion in 2009-10.

However, there exists a huge gap in the mutual dependence of the two countries. China, being the second largest trading partner of India, shares about seven per cent of India's overall trade. But India's share in China's global trade has been hovering just around one per cent. Further, India is also suffering from huge trade deficit with China. India's export basket to China is mainly dominated by primary and natural resource based products. The mutual investments between the two countries are also not very large.

Hence, there is definitely a strong need for both the countries to rectify all the hurdles in their mutual economic interactions and try to explore the fresh trade and investment opportunities. And, until both the sides open new vistas of economic cooperation, neither should under-estimate the value of rectifying imbalances that may otherwise add to factors that disrupt economic integration. Both have to work together to promote each others' contribution towards their bilateral and multilateral initiatives. Though recently their mutual trade has increased substantially but it remained at a lower level for a considerable period especially during 1950 to 1990. This period also consists the period of actually no trade of about 14 years. That is why no systematic and comprehensive studies are available focusing exclusively upon their economic relations. The existing literature mainly deals with the aspects other than economic particularly geo-strategic.

However, the academic interest pertaining to economic exchange between India and China at once got stimulated with the entry of the later into WTO. Numerous studies percolated by dealing with this dimension, i.e. the implications of China's entry into WTO for India. But, these studies remained partial and short period in data use and examined with greater emphasis on the sectoral implications. Thus, there has been a strong need to explore the economic relations between the two countries in the present milieu and futuristic perspective. The relevance of the study further increases by keeping in view the attempts by the two for building up the regional trading blocs. China has a strong presence in ASEAN, and India is more involved in SAARC. Further, India and China are in the midst to become the part of Asian Free Trade Area (AFTA), which will match the European Union (EU) and North America Free Trade Area (NAFTA). Besides this, both the countries are also members of Asia Pacific Trade Agreement (APTA-formerly known as Bangkok Agreement). All this will strengthen their mutual economic ties. Hence, the present study is useful keeping in view their economic ties in general and trade ties in particular.

It is hoped that this book would be of valuable help to government and non-government organisations, academicians, policy makers and scholars of the two countries to work towards strengthening and improving the economic ties between them.

I place on record my deep sense of gratitude to Dr. Jaswinder Singh Brar, Reader, Centre for Research in Economic Change, Punjabi University, Patiala, for his encouragement, co-operation and valuable comments at every stage of the completion of this work.

Thanks and respects are also due to my parents Shri Baldev Krishan and Shrimati Pushpa Devi who are guiding light of my life. I also express my sentiments towards my revered brother (late) Shri Rajinder Kumar Singla who, though miles apart, is always in my heart and thoughts. I owe special thanks to my wife Mrs. Monika Singla and daughter Saanvi Singla for providing some relaxed moments during the course of this tiresome work.

Bathinda   Surinder Kumar Singla
June 2011

1

India and China, 2006-10: Economic Ties and Trade

India and China share a long-standing friendly exchange history. Since the establishment of diplomatic relations, the two neighbouring countries achieved mutual understanding and support each other in the cause of maintaining sovereignty and independence, seeking development, and promoting world peace and prosperity. Although there have been twists and turns, under the care of several generations of leaders, India-China relations developed continuously through the tireless efforts of governments and people of both the sides. In recent years, the frequent high level exchanges between India and China improved mutual understanding and trust which laid a solid foundation for further deepening the bilateral economic and trade cooperation. During Chinese Premier Wen Jiabao's visit to India in 2005, India and China established the Strategic Cooperative Partnership, which indicates that India-China good neighbourhood and friendly relations ushered in a new stage of development. When Chinese President Hu Jintao visited India in November 2006, the two countries signed a joint declaration, which mainly focused on "Ten-Pronged Strategy" for deepening strategic cooperative partnership between the two sides (Gang, 2010).

Similarly Indian Prime Minister Manmohan Singh's visit to China in January 2008 also set up a new milestone for both sides' friendly partnership. Nearly a dozen memorandums of understanding were signed between the two countries. The two sides were convinced that it was time to look to the future in building a relationship of friendship and trust, based on equality, in which each would be sensitive to the concerns and aspirations of the other. The two sides reiterated that India-

China friendship and common development would have a positive influence on the future of international system.

The two sides believed that in the 21 Century, Panchsheel, the Five Principles of Peaceful Co-existence, should continue to constitute the basic guiding principles for good relations between all countries and for creating conditions for realizing peace and progress of the mankind. An international system founded on these principles will be fair, rational, equal and mutually beneficial and would promote durable peace and common prosperity, create equal opportunities and eliminate poverty and discrimination (Embassy of PRC, 2008). Thus, based on these propositions, both the countries are set to develop their mutual understanding in the areas of politics, economy, trade, culture and human welfare.

From a domestic perspective, both India and China constitute unprecedented stories of economic development. Owing to vibrant growth rates in the last decade, they have already reached heavyweight status in the global economy. Indeed, after adjusting for the price of non-tradables, India is already the fifth largest economy, just behind Japan, while China is the world's second largest economy, still behind the US but ahead of the Euro area (Bussiere and Mehl, 2008). Hence, India and China are two countries which are growing rapidly at the world juncture. However, their growth rates were slowed down due to the recent financial crisis. Though according to experts the impact of financial crisis on these two countries was not so severe but it is interesting to see how the two countries have borne the impact of this crisis.

Further, as two major emerging economies in the world, the bilateral economic and trade cooperation between India and China has witnessed a fast growth in the 21st Century. The economic and trade cooperation has become a bright spot for bilateral friendly cooperation. The bilateral trade volume is continuously breaking new records. According to Chinese customs statistics, even when bilateral trade volume showed a decline of 16.3 percent in the year of 2009 in the backdrop of global financial crisis, the two countries still witnessed a strong growth momentum of monthly trade volume, which made the two countries confident.

Moreover, the projects of cooperation in the area of infrastructural development have become a major part of their bilateral economic and trade cooperation. In recent years, Chinese enterprises in India have undertaken a large number of infrastructure projects including power plants, telecommunications, roads, metros, and bridges etc., and have effectively promoted the improvement of local infrastructure, created employment, trained a large number of skilled engineers, technicians and construction teams as well, and finally achieved the mutual benefit. Investment cooperation between the two countries has already taken off. Some well-known enterprises, such as Huawei Technology, ZTE Telecommunication, Sany Heavy Industry from China and TCS, Infosys, Wipro from India have invested in each other's country and continued to make progress. Even though the investment volume is still comparatively small and the areas invested are limited at present stage, the momentum of development is encouraging (Gang, 2010). Hence, India and China are doing well to strengthen their mutual economic and trade relations.

The present chapter examines the impact of financial crisis on the economic development of two countries as well as the growth of their mutual trade in the light of global slowdown. The chapter has been divided into two sections. First section deals with the origin of financial crisis and its impact on the Indian and the Chinese economy. Second section explores the mutual trade ties between India and China during 2006-10.

1.1 Financial Crisis of 2007

The global financial crisis, brewing for a while, really started to show its effects in the middle of 2007 and continue even after. Around the world, stock markets have fallen, large financial institutions have collapsed or been bought out, and governments even in the wealthiest nations have had to come up with rescue packages to bail out their financial systems. On the one hand many people are concerned that those responsible for the financial problems are the ones being bailed out, whereas on the other hand, a global financial meltdown has affected the livelihoods of almost everyone in an increasingly inter-connected world (Shah, 2010). The economies of India and China have also been feeling the heat of global slow down, which is an interesting topic to examine. But, before analysing the impact of financial crisis on Indian and the Chinese economy, it is important to view the origin of this financial crisis.

1.1.1 Origin of the Financial Crisis: The global financial crisis of 2007-08 is without a precedent by history's account even though economists tend to compare it to the Great Depression of 1929, the Russian Crisis of 1992 and the Asian one in 1997-98, etc. There is almost a universal agreement that the fundamental cause of the crisis was the combination of a credit boom and a housing bubble. This global financial crisis has already shocked the world economy. Since August 2007, financial markets and financial institutions all over the world have been hit by shattering developments that had started earlier with problems in the performance of sub-prime mortgages in the United States. A housing boom followed by a bust led to defaults, the implosion of mortgages and mortgage-related securities at financial institutions, and resulting financial turmoil. Financial institutions have written off losses worth billions of dollars and are continuing to do so. Liquidity has virtually disappeared from important markets and stock markets have plunged. Central banks have provided support with hundreds of billions, intervening not only to support the markets and provide liquidity but also to prevent the breakdown of individual institutions. Currently, governments in the United States and Europe are stepping in to support financial institutions at a massive scale (Lazarov, 2009).

In fact, during the 1990s, the U.S. economy went through

the longest cyclical expansion in its modern history, longer even than the one in the 1960s. The rise of the "new economy" with the explosion of computer science, the Internet and telecommunications, hand in hand with globalization and a bubble in financial markets, led some to argue, as always happens during long periods of expansion, that this was the end of economic cycles and crises. The housing bubble was part of the party. Between 1997 and 2006 alone, real estate prices shot up 93 percent, while in the previous 100 years, they had oscillated up or down between 10 or 20 percent, depending on the conditions of capital accumulation (Arturo, 2008).

While the immediate causes and development of the crisis are well-accepted, economists tend to diverge on the global causes, inherent in the system, which started a financial turmoil unknown by its scale. Krugman (2009) blames it on Greenspan's bubbles and especially lenient regulatory framework on the risk-taking financial institutions, leading the economy to a "magneto trouble" as said by Keynes. Even though Krugman had warned on various occasions about the fragility of a fairly liberal system, tolerating huge amounts of risks, he himself admits to be surprised by the effects of the failed banking shadow system. He quotes Tim Geithner on the risks of the rise of the shadow banking system:

"Once the investors in these financing arrangements–many conservatively managed money funds–withdraw or threatened to withdraw their funds from these markets, the system became vulnerable to a self-reinforcing cycle of forced liquidation of assets, which further increased volatility and lowered prices across a variety of asset classes. In response, margin requirements were increased, or financing was withdrawn altogether from some customers, forcing more de-leveraging. Capital cushions eroded as assets were sold into distressed markets. The force of this dynamic was exacerbated by the poor quality of assets–particularly mortgage-related assets–that had been spread across the system. This helps explain how a relatively small quantity of risky assets was able to undermine the confidence of investors and other market participants across a much broader range of assets and markets".

Indeed, the relatively small portion of sub-prime mortgages to other risky assets puzzled analysts as to why the system could not absorb the shock. Hellwig (2008), states that the share of sub-prime mortgages rose from around 9 percent of new mortgages in the early 2000's to above 40 percent in 2006. By the end of 2006, sub-prime mortgages accounted for some 14 percent of the total stock of outstanding securitized mortgage. It is important to remember that residential housing and real estate account for an important part of an economy's aggregate wealth in many countries, more important than the net financial assets.

If liquidity was the problem, then providing more liquidity by making borrowing easier and cheaper by the Federal Reserve would have been appropriate and the capital markets would have absorbed the losses, allowing the financial system to move forward. Crises of worse estimated losses have only caused hiccups in the system in the past. The difference between the other crises and the sub-prime mortgage crisis is not in the magnitude of the primary losses, but in the systemic linkages and repercussions. The biggest fault also lies in the fact that the big financial institutions ignored their own business model of securitization and chose not to transfer the credit risk to other investors.

The burst of housing bubble and the lack of down payments caused a shock regards the availability of funds for refinancing for the individual institution which on its own part needs funds to repay its short-term debt. Due to the lack of an alternative source of finance, the institution needs and must have a fire sale of its long-term assets which depresses the assets' prices in the market. The decline in the assets' prices puts pressure on all institutions that hold such assets and turns into a spiral or a domino effect. Observations of difficulties at one institution induce investors to be worried about other institutions and to withdraw funding from them. Such worries arise if one suspects that the other institutions may have followed similar strategies or if one suspects that the other institutions may be threatened by domino effects, through contractual relations or through asset prices.

Fears of such a domino effect forced the New York Fed rescue Long-Term Capital Management (LTCM) in 1998, which gained justification on the grounds that bankruptcy of LTCM and a quick liquidation of its portfolio would have created serious problems for some of its creditors (which included leading commercial banks and investment banks) and could have meant fire-sale prices for some of the assets to be sold as part of its liquidation. While the LTCM was a systematically insignificant institution and may not have caused repercussions on other institutions, the situation today causes acute fears of the domino effect. Fiscal measures are often cited as the main reason to why investors ran into a largely risky market such as sub-prime.

The government started the practice with the issuance of mortgage-backed securities but its share went from 76 percent in 2003 to 43 percent in 2006. At the same time, there was a relative decline in prime mortgage lending and a significant increase in sub-prime mortgage lending which did not meet the standards of the government-sponsored enterprises. The origins of Fannie Mae and Freddie Mac as government institutions led many investors to believe that, even though these institutions had been privatized, their assets were guaranteed by the government and, therefore, deemed to be reliable. The position of Fannie Mae and Freddie Mac in the system of housing finance in the United States is too important for the government to look aside when these institutions run into trouble. Thus, at a time when the system of mortgage-backed securities was developed, the neglect of moral hazard induced by securitization was at least partly due to a reliance of market participants on government guarantees (Lazarov,

2009).

In nutshell, globalization and financial innovation combined with the asymmetry of information are effectively the main reasons for this financial crisis. The financial system would have contained the effects from the housing bubble and there would be limited repercussions if there were not as much systemic risk in the system. The need for a new regulatory framework is the new paradigm which is being discussed across the world and which will shape the financial system in the decades to come.

1.1.2 Impact of Financial Crisis on Indian and Chinese Economy: The financial crisis began in August 2007 in the US and West European countries and spread out to the entire world economy. This section attempts to examine the impact of current global financial crisis on the emerging economies namely India and China. A critical analysis is important on this issue because these two countries together constitute more than one-third of the world's population. Moreover, since the adoption of neo-liberal economic reforms (also known as 'market-friendly' policies), both economies had experienced rapid economic growth and, thus, projected by the International Monetary Fund (IMF) and the World Bank as successful examples towards removal of unemployment and poverty (Winters and Yusef, 2007; Dyer, 2009; Bradsher, 2009). When the financial crisis started in the US, the mainstream economists and international financial institutions claimed that it would have marginal or no impact on the emerging economies, namely India and China because of the decoupling effects and also because these economies have adopted market reforms which had made them more efficient and competitive so that they could withstand such challenges (*The Economist,* 2008a; Wolf, 2008; Boothe, 2008).

The term "financial crisis" is a broad term that covers a range of events such as crashes in the housing market, banking sector and of course recession. The world economic crisis first surfaced in the US sub-prime mortgage market in August 2007 and soon spread to other areas both in US and other European countries. Within few months, a huge financial meltdown was witnessed (i.e. bankruptcies of banks and insurance firms) in many developed countries (*The Economist*, 2008b).

It is significant to understand the impact of current global crisis on Asian emerging economies because optimists pointed out earlier that these economies would act as shock absorbers that would act as a buffer for the Western economic slowdown. It was further suggested that a 'decoupled Asia' through its own growth and expanding domestic demand would ensure higher import demands for its growing economies and thus limit the economic slowdown in the developed economies. From the onset of the financial crisis, the optimists were of the view that Asian countries had undertaken market-friendly i.e. neo-liberal economic reforms which had strengthened these economies to withstand such situations. Asian economies so-called "success story" were crucial for the justification of the neo-liberal policies as it was said that adoption of these very policies had helped them to achieve higher growths. However, neo-liberal economic policies are losing credibility in Latin America and African countries (Siddiqui, 1990; Williamson, 1994; Patnaik, 2009).

Though economists suggested that India and China are among those countries which will not be affected much by the financial crisis, even then the growth of their GDP and per capita real GDP went down significantly. Due to the severe financial crisis of 2007, the growth of global GDP and per capita GDP went down sharply from 4.0 percent and 2.8 percent in 2006 to 2.2 percent and 1 percent in 2008 respectively. In 2009, the growth rate of both global GDP and per capita GDP went down to be negative i.e. -1.9 percent and -3.1 percent respectively. A similar trend was also seen in the case of India and China. The growth of India's GDP and per capita GDP went down from 9.7 percent and 8 percent in 2006 to 5.7 percent and 4.2 percent in 2009. During the period 2006-09, the annual average growth rate on these two aspects remained only 7.9 percent and 6.4 percent respectively. This sharp decline in the growth of India's GDP and per capita GDP was the result of financial crisis in the world economy. Though poor monsoon also had a negative impact but the financial crisis remained the major cause. On the other side, in China, the GDP and per capita GDP declined sharply from 13 percent to 12.3 percent in 2007 to 8.7 percent and 8.1 percent in 2009 (Table 1.1).

Table 1.1: Annual Growth Rate of Total and Per Capita GDP:
India, China and the World (percentage)

Years	India		China		World	
	Total GDP	Per Capita GDP	Total GDP	Per Capita GDP	Total GDP	Per Capita GDP
2006	9.7	8.0	11.6	10.9	4.0	2.8
2007	9.1	7.5	13.0	12.3	3.9	2.7
2008	7.3	5.8	9.0	8.4	2.2	1.0
2009	5.7	4.2	8.7	8.1	-1.9	-3.1
Annual Average GDP	7.9	6.4	10.6	9.9	2.1	0.9

Source: Handbook of Statistics 2009-10, UNCTAD.

During the period 2006-09, the annual average growth rate on these two aspects remained only 10.6 percent and 9.9 percent respectively. Thus, though the world economy had plunged down to negative growth of GDP and per capita GDP, yet India and China experienced positive growth rates. However, even during the financial crisis, the growth of China's GDP and per capita GDP remained well above that of India.

The economic crisis of 2007 spilled over to the Indian and Chinese economy by late 2008. This crisis had a cascading effect on three sectors of India and China. In India, the growth of agriculture declined sharply from 4.7 percent in 2007 to merely 0.2 percent in 2009. In case of China, the growth rate of agriculture sector remained quite fluctuating. During 2006-09, it oscillated between 3.7 percent and 5.4 percent. During the same period, the annual average growth rate of agriculture remained 2.6 and 4.8 percent for India and China respectively. The growth rate of India's industrial sector declined substantially from 12.7 percent in 2006 to 3.9 percent in 2008 but then it rebounded to 9.3 percent in 2009. In fact, there was a sharp decline in the flow of funds from American/global depository receipts (ADRs/GDRs) and external commercial borrowings; but the inflows of foreign direct investment (FDI) continued.

Domestically, the mobilization of resources by the private sector through the capital market, especially the equity route, saw a precipitous decline during 2008. However, bank credit to the industrial sector recorded impressive growth during 2009 and in some ways filled the gap due to the sudden shrinkage of other sources (Economic Survey, 2009-10).

On the other side, in China, the growth of industrial sector declined rapidly from 15.1 percent in 2007 to 9.9 percent in 2009. Thus, the global financial crisis dampened the growth of industrial sector in China also. During 2006-09, the annual average growth rate of industry in India and China remained at 9.4 percent and 12.7 percent respectively. Like the agricultural and industrial sector, service sector was also affected by the financial crisis.

The growth rate of service sector in India and China declined from 10.5 percent and 16 percent in 2007 to 8.5 percent and 9.3 percent in 2009 respectively. During 2006-09, the annual average growth of service sector in India and China remained at 10.3 percent and 13 percent respectively.

Thus, the impact of financial crisis on the three sectors of India and China is quite obvious. But it is interesting to note that even during the period of financial crisis, the annual average growth rate of all the three sectors remained higher in case of China vis-à-vis India (Table 1.2).

Table 1.2: Annual Growth Rate of Agriculture, Industry and Service Sectors: India and China

Years	Agriculture		Industry		Service	
	India	China	India	China	India	China
2006	3.7	5.0	12.7	13.4	10.2	14.1
2007	4.7	3.7	9.5	15.1	10.5	16.0
2008	1.6	5.4	3.9	9.9	9.8	10.4
2009	0.2	4.2	9.3	9.9	8.5	9.3
Annual Average Growth Rate	2.6	4.8	9.4	12.7	10.3	13.0

Source: Asian Development Bank: Key Indicators (Various Issues).

Table 1.3 shows the impact of financial crisis on savings and investment in India and China. Due to the financial crisis, gross domestic savings as percentage of GDP, both in India and China, declined slightly from 32.50 percent and 51.49 percent in 2008 to 30.36 percent and 51.21 percent in 2009 respectively.

Table 1.3: Saving and Investment as Percentage of GDP: India and China

Years	Gross Domestic Saving		Gross Domestic Capital Formation	
	India	China	India	China
2006	34.43	47.93	35.49	42.97
2007	36.41	50.52	37.71	41.74
2008	32.50	51.49	34.88	44.05
2009	30.36	51.21	35.04	47.66
Annual Average Share	35.32	53.49	37.97	47.08

Source: Asian Development Bank: Key Indicators (Various Issues).

During 2006-09, the annual average share of gross domestic savings in GDP remained at 35.32 percent for India and 53.49 percent for China. India's savings rate is high, but its total savings remain lower than that of other major countries due to its smaller economy–particularly when expressed at official exchange rates. India's total savings in 2008 was US$ 482 billion. This means China's total savings, i.e. finance available for investment, was almost five times than that of India in 2008 (Ross, 2009).

On the other side, in the case of gross domestic capital formation, an opposite trend could be seen. In fact, the share of gross capital formation, after declining in one year for both India and China, has shown a rising trend. During 2006-09, the annual average share of gross domestic capital formation in GDP of India and China remained at 37.97 percent and 47.08 percent respectively. Unlike those who advocate a reduction in investment and savings rates in India, Manmohan Singh, who is not only India's Prime Minister but an excellently trained economist, has constantly stressed the need to raise India's savings and investment rates and has made this a foundation of his economic policy–with considerable success, as has been seen, in terms of sustaining high growth rates. Manmohan Singh considered China's high savings and investment rates as the foundation for a superior economic performance. For example in 2003 when asked, 'is it legitimate to compare Indian and Chinese economies?' he replied: 'there is nothing wrong in the comparison. It is good to try and achieve the growth rate of China. But we must remember that the Chinese savings rate is 42 percent of the gross domestic product, whereas savings in India is hovering at 24 percent' (Ross, 2009).

Table 1.4 presents the annual percentage growth of exports and imports for both India and China. The impact of financial crisis on Indian and Chinese external trade is quite obvious from the table–as in 2009, the annual growth rate of exports and imports for both India and China remained negative. In 2009, the growth rate of both exports and imports remained -0.65 percent and -4.09 percent for India and -16.01 percent and -11.21 percent for China respectively.

However, it is interesting to note that the decline in growth rate of both exports and imports was sharper in case of China vis-à-vis India. This can be supported with figures–that during 2006-09, the annual average growth of India's exports and imports (i.e. 16.88 percent and 19.85 percent) remained higher than that of China's exports and imports (i.e. 13.58 percent and 11.99 percent). It may be due to the fact that a big portion of Chinese external trade is dependent on foreign direct investment. The fall in foreign direct investment caused a sharp decline in China's foreign trade.

**Table 1.4: Annual Percentage Growth of External Trade:
India and China**

Years	Exports		Imports	
	India	China	India	China
2006	25.28	27.17	27.27	19.93
2007	14.71	25.68	20.44	20.78
2008	28.19	17.48	35.77	18.47
2009	-0.65	-16.01	-4.09	-11.21
Annual Average Growth	16.88	13.58	19.85	11.99

Source: Asian Development Bank: Key Indicators (Various Issues).

Table 1.5 shows the volume of foreign direct investment (FDI) in India and China. As in case of exports and imports, the volume of total FDI inflow in India and China declined sharply from US$ 40418 million and US$ 108312 million in 2008 to US$ 34613 million and US$ 95000 million in 2009. In other words, the growth rate of FDI in both India and China remained negative. Thus, due to the severe financial crisis in the world economy, the growth of FDI in India and China was hit negatively.

Thus, from the above discussion, it is quite clear that India and China are among those emerging economies who were hit hard by the financial crisis. In other words, the deceleration in the growth rates in the developed countries due to financial crisis had a major impact on these two emerging economies, namely India and China. This is evident from the fact that during the last two years, India and China have experienced negative growth rates in GDP, per capita GDP, agriculture, industry, services, foreign trade and FDI.

**Table 1.5: Foreign Direct Investment Inflows:
India and China (US $ Million)**

Years	India	China
2006	20336 (1.67)	72715 (0.004)
2007	25001 (0.23)	83521 (0.15)
2008	40418 (0.62)	108312 (0.30)
2009	34613 (-0.14)	95000 (-0.12)
Annual Average	30092	89887

Note: Figures in parentheses show annual percentage change.
Source: World Investment Report, UNCTAD (Various Issues).

Notwithstanding the government claims made regarding India's GDP growth rates, the global economic prospect (GEP) has argued that the current growth rate will fall further. This will have further devastating impact on employment and a sharp fall in the growth rate will increase the levels of poverty in India with the GEP estimating that India is now only ahead of Sub-Saharan Africa in terms of population below the poverty line with over a quarter of Indians living in extreme poverty (Siddiqui, 2009).

For the last decade, the rapid increase in growth rates in the economies of India and China has given a lot of expectations both domestically and globally. Any decline in growth rates will not only increase unemployment but create explosive situation for instance, in terms of urban versus rural and regional differentiation as the growth slows down. Economic growth is precipitating social change and increasing internal tensions between people and regions. As the economy slows down, social unrest will increase. Some argue that China

can use the US\$ 2 trillion of foreign reserves to bail out
bankrupt US financial system (Winters and Yusef, 2007; Wolf,
2008).

However, these hopes are misplaced. China emerging as
an alterative engine of growth for the world economy is
unlikely to happen in the near future. This is mainly due to:
Chinese growth, which has pulled along with many other East
Asian countries is a production chain, has been largely export-
led. For example, the US, EU and Japan together account for
more than half of China's exports, and as recession deepens, it
is bound to affect both exports and economic activity in China.
It seems that the current global financial crisis has witnessed a
clear failure of the economic model of neo-liberalism. The
notion that market knows best, and that self-regulation is the
best form of financial regulation, have now been fully exposed
for how far they are from the real world and empirically wrong
(Siddiqui, 2009).

It will be useful to briefly summarize the East Asian
financial crisis of the 1997. During the 1997-98 Indonesian
financial crisis, the IMF advised that the country has to adopt
'market-friendly' policies, which was earlier given to most of
the countries in Latin America and Sub-Saharan Africa with
disastrous outcomes (Williamson, 1994). In order to pay off
debts, they were advised to privatize their national assets so
that foreign investors can buy it at lower prices in Indonesia.
At the same time, the interest rates were raised to slow down
their economy. This resulted in increasing the interest
payments for both domestic and international borrowings
which brought misery to a large section of the population.
During the financial crisis in East Asian countries, the IMF
advised that they should run budget surplus and the
government spending should be cut down.

However, the Western countries during their current
financial crisis were not following the similar policies, which
they imposed on East Asian economies in 1998. For instance,
the budget deficit in US is estimated at around 12 percent of

the GDP in 2009. Interest rates are reduced to almost zero to stimulate the economy. The governments are not privatizing, but are bailing them out. This clearly indicates a dual policy with one set of policy for poor countries, e.g. free market/monetarism, and while Keynesianism for rich countries (Siddiqui, 2009). In other words, Western countries follow Keynesian policies, while suggesting free market for the developing countries in similar economic crisis. Developing countries should learn from IMF's East Asian rescue plan and that is not to be in a situation where they were forced to turn to IMF for help. Therefore, they decided to accumulate massive amounts of foreign reserves as a defence mechanism.

1.2 Trade Ties between India and China during 2006-10

India and China are two rapidly emerging economies in the world. With their high growth rates and huge markets, these two Asian giants have attracted the attention of international business mangers to take a fresh look at the rapidly emerging opportunities in the two countries. After the Border War, the relations between these two countries remained depressed for a long time. However, since early nineties, both the countries started deepening their mutual economic relations. Today, India-China relations are conspicuous by the fast rise of trade, which has already crossed US$ 42 billion in 2009-10.

China has already become India's second largest trade partner after U.A.E. Since it is projected that, by 2050, India and China will be the two leading economies in the world, it is inevitable that bilateral trade between the two countries will be among the most important economic relationships in the world. It is quite obvious from the fact that the targets of bilateral trade set by the Prime Ministers of the two countries during the visit of Premier Wen Jiabao's to India in 2005 as US$ 20 billion by 2008 and US$ 30 billion by 2010 were met much ahead of the deadline. The target fixed during President Hu Jintao's visit to India in 2006 to increase the bilateral trade to US$ 40 billion by 2010 was also achieved well in advance. The current figures of India and China mutual trade could be more if it was not interrupted by the financial crisis. This section examines the growth and composition of India-China mutual trade during 2006-2009 and tries to analyse the impact of financial crisis on it.

1.2.1 Growth of India's Merchandise Trade with China during 2005-06 to 2009-10: Before analysing the mutual trade of India and China, it is important to have a look on the share of two countries in world trade. As is clear from Table 1.6, during 2006-09, the share of both the countries in world trade increased substantially. India's share in world exports and imports increased from 1.04 percent and 1.50 percent in 2006 to 1.50 percent and 2.22 percent in 2009. Similarly, China's share in world exports and imports increased from 8.35 percent and 6.66 percent in 2006 to 10.17 percent and 8.38 percent in 2009. Thus, though the developed countries of the world have been suffering with the heat of financial crisis but India and China are making their positions in world trade more and stronger.

Table 1.6: Percentage Share of India and China in World Exports, Imports and Total Trade

Years	Exports		Imports		Total Trade	
	India	China	India	China	India	China
2006	1.04	8.35	1.50	6.66	1.27	7.49
2007	1.11	9.24	1.61	7.03	1.36	8.12
2008	1.19	9.39	2.01	7.22	1.61	8.29
2009	1.50	10.17	2.22	8.38	1.86	9.27

Source: Calculated from UN Commodity Trade Statistics, United Nations.

During 1990-91 to 2004-05, the mutual trade between India and China increased by leaps and bounds, and this trend remained continue even during the period 2005-06 to 2009-10. As is clear from Table 1.7, India's exports to China increased continuously from ` 29,925 crore in 2005-06 to ` 54,714 crore in 2009-10, with one exception of 2008-09. During 2008-09, India's exports to China declined to ` 42,661 crore from previous year's ` 43,597 crore. It happened mainly due to the sharp decline in exports of cotton; ores, slag and ash; organic chemicals; plastic; etc. Like Indian exports to China, Indian imports from China also increased continuously from ` 48,117 crore in 2005-06 to ` 1,4,7606 crore in 2008-09 and then declined to ` 1,46,049 crore in 2009-10. This decline was experienced due to fall in Indian imports of iron and steel; mineral fuels and oils; natural or cultured pearls, precious or semiprecious stones; etc.

**Table 1.7: Value of India-China Merchandise Trade
(` Crore)**

Years	Exports	Imports	Balance of Trade	Total Trade	Annual Percentage Change
2005-06	29925	48117	-18192 (8.92)	78042	36.61
2006-07	37530	79009	-41479 (15.44)	116538	49.33
2007-08	43597	109116	-65519 (18.38)	152713	31.04
2008-09	42661	147606	-104944 (19.66)	190267	24.59
2009-10	54714	146049	-91335 (17.63)	200763	5.52

Note: Figures in parentheses show the percentage share in India's overall negative balance of trade.
Source: Calculated from Monthly Statistics of Foreign Trade of India, DGCIS; Kolkata, (Various Issues).

Though, during 2005-06 to 2009-10, Indian exports to and imports from China declined once, however, the total trade between these two countries increased continuously from ` 78,042 crore in 2005-06 to ` 2,00,763 crore in 2009-10.

However, the pace of this rise in total trade slowed down from 49.33 percent in 2006-07 to 5.52 percent in 2009-10. This decline in India's trade with China was partly due to the global slow down in international market.

Though, the value of India's exports to and imports from China remained quite phenomenal, however, one major problem from India's point of view was its rising trade deficit with China. Since 1993-94, India suffered unfavourable balance of trade with China. During 2005-06 to 2009-10, this trade deficit remained very high and increased from ` 18,192 crore in 2005-06 to ` 1,04,944 crore in 2009-10. Further, the trade deficit with China accounted for only 0.29 percent of India's overall trade deficit in 1990-91, which rose to its maximum i.e. 19.66 percent during 2008-09, and then slightly reduced to 17.63 percent during 2009-10. A senior Indian government official said that the government is closely monitoring the Chinese response to its concerns over the widening trade gap. He further said that if China fails to take adequate steps to reduce the deficit and move towards more balanced trade ties, India would take retaliatory measures (The Economic Times, 2010).

The relative importance of India as China's trade partner and that of China as India's trade partner is depicted in Table 1.8 and Table 1.9 respectively.

Table 1.8: India's Percentage Share in China's Exports and Imports

Years	Exports	Imports	Total Trade
2006	1.50	1.30	1.41
2007	1.97	1.53	1.78
2008	2.21	1.79	2.02
2009	2.47	1.36	1.97

Source: Calculated from UN Commodity Trade Statistics, United Nations.

It is clear from the Table 1.8 that during 2006-09, India

has made a strong position in China's global trade. Though, during the nineties, India's share in Chinese global trade remained insignificant but, after the Chinese accession to the WTO in 2001, India emerged as important trade partner of China. India's share in China's global trade increased from 1.41 percent in 2006 to 2.02 percent in 2008. However, in 2009, it declined slightly to 1.97 percent. The similar trend can also be seen in case of exports and imports with one exception, that the share of India in China's global exports increased even during the financial crisis and reached its ever maximum point, i.e. 2.47 percent in 2009.

**Table 1.9: China's Percentage Share in
India's Exports and Imports**

Years	Exports	Imports	Total Trade
2005-06	6.56	7.29	6.99
2006-07	6.56	9.40	8.25
2007-08	6.65	10.78	9.15
2008-09	5.07	10.74	8.59
2009-10	6.47	10.71	9.09

Source: Calculated from Monthly Statistics of Foreign Trade of India, DGCIS; Kolkata (Various Issues).

Table 1.9 depicts China's position in India's overall trade. China's share in India's total trade increased from 6.99 percent in 2005-06 to 9.15 percent in 2007-08. It declined to 8.59 percent in 2008-09 and again revived to 9.09 percent in 2009-10. During 2005-06 to 2009-10, China's share in India's global exports remained more than 6 percent, except in the year 2008-09, when it declined to 5.07 percent. On the other side, China's share in India's global imports increased from 7.29 percent in 2005-06 to 10.78 percent in 2007-08, but then declined continuously in the subsequent years and reached 10.71 percent in 2009-10. Thus, it can be said that the Chinese accession to the WTO has laid the foundation for the deepening of trade ties between the two Asian powers. Though the recent crisis has curtailed the pace of their mutual trade, even then the two countries are emerging as dominant trade partners for each other.

1.2.2 Composition of India's Trade with China during 2005-06 to 2009-10: The usefulness of foreign trade depends upon the structure and pattern of trade which is determined by the nature of commodities exported and imported by a country. Hence, to explore the usefulness of India's trade with China, it is important to examine the composition of India's exports to and imports from China.

(a) Composition of India's Exports to China: There were not much changes in the composition of India's exports to China over the period 2005-06 to 2009-10. One commodity, namely ores, slag and ash plays a crucial role in India's exports to China. The value of this commodity increased sharply from ` 15,341 crore in 2005-06 to ` 24,798 crore in 2007-08. However, it declined to ` 21,905 crore in 2008-09. This is primarily attributed to the fact that the Chinese ports were piled up with the previous stocks. In fact, even the demand hampered, as several steel mills closed down in accordance to the Middle Kingdom's reduced industrial operations to bring down the pollution level for the Summer Olympics.

However, after the reopening of steel mills in China, demand for ores, slag and ash surged again and reached to ` 26,151 crore in 2009-10. Further, the incentives announced by the Indian government to increase the overseas shipments also pushed up the exports. The government announced to cut the export duty on iron ore, bringing it to zero percent, whereas duty on lumps was reduced from 15 percent to 5 percent. This boosted the Indian exports of ores, slag and ash to China. Reduction in railway freight was also announced by the Indian government, which further added to the growth of India's iron ore exports (RNCOS, 2009).

Besides ores, slag and ash, the value of one more commodity namely cotton, increased sharply from ` 2,279 crore in 2005-06 to ` 4,350 crore in 2007-08 but then declined sharply to ` 1,738 crore in the subsequent year. This was the result of a sharp rise in Minimum Support Price (MSP) of cotton in the domestic economy. The government had raised the MSP of long staple cotton to ` 3,000 per quintal from ` 2,030 and the medium staple to ` 2,500 from ` 1,800 per quintal (The Economic Times, 2008). But, the MSP was not hiked in 2009-10 and due to that, the value of India's export of cotton to China rose sharply to ` 5,888 crore. Besides ores, slag and ash and cotton, organic chemicals, copper, plastic, iron and steel etc. also play a crucial role in India's exports to China.

The share of selected fifteen commodities in India's total exports to China decreased from 93.04 percent in 2005-06 to 79.66 percent in 2008-09 and then rose to 85.12 percent in 2009-10. It is discernible to note that during 2005-06 to 2009-10, one single commodity namely ores, slag and ash dominated Indian exports to China, as its annual average share in India's total exports to China remained more than fifty percent. In other words, more than half of Indian exports to China were dominated by ores, slag and ash. Hence, this export item was the actual export driver for enhancement of India's export trade with China. In fact, the rapid depletion of China's iron ore reserves has made its front-running steel industry dependent on imports from India to meet the growing demand for steel for its construction and defence industries. Besides ores, slag and ash, annual average share of cotton also remained high i.e. 8.29 percent followed by organic chemicals (5.50 percent); iron and steel (4.15 percent); copper (3.57 percent); plastic (3.12 percent); etc.

During 2005-06 to 2009-10, China's demand for ores, slag and ash remained extremely high. In fact, the annual average share of China in India's global exports of ores, slag and ash remained at 83.20 percent. Now, one question comes in mind that why India is exporting too much volume of ores, slag and ash to China alone? The answer is that China is paying higher price (i.e. unit value) for this commodity to India than rest of the world. China's share in India's global exports of prepared feathers and down also remained very high (i.e. 51.96 percent) followed by inorganic chemicals (27.03 percent); salt, sulphur, earths and stone (19.61 percent); cotton (19.36 percent); etc.

One thing noteworthy here is that India's exports to China were mainly dominated by raw materials and semi-manufactured products like iron ores. Though, India's overall exports of manufactured items have increased but not in the case of China. It is still exporting a great extent of raw materials to China.

(b) Composition of India's Imports from China: During the liberalisation era, Indian dependency on Chinese items increased rapidly and this dependency strengthened further during the first decade of 21st Century. In fact, due to the cheap prices of Chinese products, Indian imports from China increased at a tremendous pace. Indian imports from China exhibited some changes over the period 2005-06 to 2009-10. It is interesting to note that these three commodities cover more than half of the value of India's total imports from China. Thus, it can be said that like Indian exports to China, Chinese exports to India are also getting concentrated around few commodities. But the difference is that Indian exports to China are concentrated around raw materials and natural resource-based products while Chinese exports to India are concentrated around high value added manufactured items.

The high amounts of such imports from China are giving birth to fear among Indian industry dealing in electrical equipment. Associated Chambers of Commerce and Industry of India (ASSOCHAM) had accused China for providing incentives for export of power equipment by completely exempting them from internal duties. According to the spokesman of ASSOCHAM, this is one of the reasons why import of such equipment is much cheaper. He further stated that the Chinese government provides incentives and rebates of 14 percent to its power plant manufacturers for exports and at the same time when such power equipment is imported into India, it does not suffer from customs duty or countervailing duty (CVD) and special CVD etc. On the other hand, Indian manufactured equipment attracts duties and taxes to an extent of nearly 6 percent of the equipment cost.

Therefore, export benefits offered to Chinese manufacturers by their government, compounded by taxation on Indian manufacturers for domestic supply, has resulted in an unfairly competitive advantage of Chinese manufacturers in the Indian market (Machinist.in, 2009). Besides these three commodities, the value of mineral fuels and oils; projected goods; iron and steel; optical, photographic and cinematographic products; impregnated, coated, covered or laminated textile fabrics; etc. has also increased rapidly.

The total share of selected commodities in India's total exports to China hovered around 80 percent. The share of two commodities namely electrical machinery and equipment; and nuclear reactors and boilers in India's total imports from China improved quite surprisingly. During 1990-91, the share of these two commodities was just 1.64 percent and 2.16 percent respectively. However, during 2005-06 to 2009-10, the annual average share of these two commodities peaked to 28.05 percent and 18.68 percent respectively. Thus, these two commodities constitute nearly half of India's total imports from China. This rise may be the result of an increasing demand in Indian consumer market for cheap Chinese electrical equipment. During the same time period, the average annual share of some other commodities namely mineral fuels and oils; iron and steel; articles of iron and steel; projected goods; etc. also remained healthy, while the share of all the other commodities remained very low.

During the mentioned time period, Indian dependency on Chinese silk remained tremendously higher. During 2005-06 to 2009-10, the annual average share of China remained 96.87 percent in India's global imports of silk. It is interesting to note that Varanasi, the famous Indian city for making silk saris by hand, has lost 60 percent of its handloom industry since 2003 due to import of cheap imitation saris from China. In 2007, reports emerged of weavers in Varanasi selling their blood to make ends meet as Chinese imitation saris flooded the market, costing about ` 2,500 compared with at least ` 4,000 for an original one (Hindustan Times, 2011).

Though, the official import figures for saris from China are low, but much of the material is imported as fabric, not as tailored saris, and a lot makes its way into India as contraband via Nepal. Hence, there is an urgent need that Indian government should use tariff and non-tariff barriers to save the interest of their home industry. China's share in Indian imports of some other commodities, i.e. impregnated, coated, covered or laminated textile fabrics; man-made filaments; electrical machinery and equipments; projected goods; articles of iron and steel; organic chemicals also remained high. However, in case of other commodities, China's share remained quite unstable and low.

To sum up, during 2006-10, trade and economic relations between India and China have developed at its own momentum and dynamism. There is a strong political impetus on both sides to advance trade and economic ties further. Both the countries have decided to move faster on the track of economic relations. In 2008, the governments of two sides revised the trade target to US$ 60 billion for 2010, rather than US$ 40 billion (fixed in November 2006). However, this target could not be achieved due to global slowdown and country-specific reasons. But, both the countries are now trying to get rid of all the hurdles in the way to further extend their mutual trade ties.

The institutional framework of bilateral cooperation, including the Joint Economic Group, Joint Working Group and other sector-specific mechanisms, is being strengthened and expanded to cover new areas. Business exchanges are intensifying and the flow of delegations between the two countries is consistently increasing. Both the countries are also making efforts to expand areas of economic linkages that could further boost and broaden bilateral trade ties.

However, one major problem, from the Indian perspective, is its rising trade deficit with China. Almost all the years, India experienced adverse balance of trade with China and the deficit of trade widened substantially due to the higher growth rate of her imports. According to the Ministry of Commerce and Industry, Government of India, during the year 2008-09, India's trade deficit with China was over US$ 20 billion, which is likely to surge further in the coming years, if corrective steps are not taken (GOI, 2009). Though Indian government has put its concerns in front of the Chinese government, but till now no comprehensive steps have been taken.

India has proposed a number of measures for increasing its exports to China such as the removal of tariff and non-tariff barriers, restricting import of power plant equipment, and removal of restrictions on imports of basmati rice, fruits and vegetables. It also sought higher export of Information Technology (IT) and Information Technology Enabled Services (ITES) from India, landing rights for Indian TV channels in China, and export of Indian films. Removal of procedural bottlenecks including time-consuming licensing procedures being faced by Indian drugs and pharmaceuticals industry is also high on India's wish list. Now, it will be interesting to see how Chinese government will entertain Indian demand for balanced trade.

China has already emerged as one of major trading partners of India. China's share in India's merchandise trade has increased rapidly since the mid nineties and that is why China has emerged as the second largest trading partner of India after U.A.E. However, India's share in China's global trade though increasing yet is very low. In fact, India has failed to grab a big share in the Chinese market. Though India's exports to China rose rapidly during the recent few years, yet there exists a vast potential to enhance them further by improving their competitiveness. There is a need to control the unit values of major exports to China, so that India can get maximum market share in Chinese world imports. Further, by promoting higher FDI inflows; reducing the intensive industrial reservation; and improving the quality of public infrastructure, India can reduce the cost and improve the quality of its exports. Then, India would be in position to grasp the higher market share for a large range of commodities in Chinese economy as well as in the world economy.

The other major problem, with India-China trade, is the narrowness of trade basket. From the above analysis, it has been found that during 2005-2006 to 2009-10, India-China mutual trade remained highly concentrated around one or two commodities. More than half of India's total exports to China were constituted by one single commodity namely ores, slag and ash. Similarly, in case of imports, nearly half of the value was constituted by two commodities namely electrical machinery and equipment and nuclear reactors and boilers. Thus, it is not wrong if we say that India-China trade is driven by one or two commodities.

However, it is noteworthy here that India is exporting raw materials to China, whereas it is importing mostly high value-added goods. This is not the trade structure one would expect between the two developing countries. This is a situation well known from the time of English colonialism in India. It is obvious that India is not pleased by this structure of bilateral trade and demands concessions from China. Unless the imbalance in trade volume and structure is not redressed, it is unlikely that India will comply with a Free Trade Agreement (FTA) with China.

Hence, India and China are only beginning to discover the full scope and opportunities for expanding trade and economic cooperation at the regional and international levels. If coordinated well, the combined market size of India and China can provide significant leverages to both countries in regional and global trade across a range of product categories. The complementarities inherent in the economies of the two countries could be harnessed to propel trade and economic cooperation between India and China to greater heights. There is yet another area where India and China can learn from each other, viz. functioning of special economic zones (SEZs). SEZs in India seek to promote value addition component in exports, generate employment and mobilize foreign exchange. SEZs when operational are expected to offer high quality infrastructure facilities and support services, besides allowing for the duty free import of capital goods and raw materials. Additionally, attractive fiscal incentives and simpler customs, banking and other procedures are offered in such zones. Setting up of SEZs is also treated as an infrastructure development activity and offered same incentives. SEZs in India closely follow the Chinese model.

SEZs are intended as engine for economic growth supported by quality infrastructure, with minimum possible regulations, and an attractive fiscal package, both at the level of Central and State Governments. The SEZ Act, 2005, supported by SEZ Rules, came into effect on February 10, 2006.

Chinese SEZs are like townships. India has not gone that far, but it is heartening that realising that size does matter, the government has decided to have large-sized SEZs. According to the guidelines, the area of an SEZ should be 1,000 hectares. This reflects a sea change in the Government's perception.

The customs regime in Chinese SEZs provides tremendous operational ease. The customs regulations designed for Indian SEZs also seem to be far less cumbersome than those for EPZs. The entrepreneurs will be free from routine inspections of import-export cargo. Procedures for operations such as record keeping, inter-unit transfer, sub-contracting and disposal of obsolete material and waste and scrap will be simpler. Enterprises will be allowed to utilise duty free raw materials over five years. These changes will definitely make the customs regime investor friendly.

The incentive package in India is quite liberal and may

even be a shade better than that for Chinese SEZs. In fact, it is more or less on par with the package for the existing EPZs. Duty free import of capital goods and raw materials, reimbursement of Central sales tax, tax holiday for specified period, 100 per cent repatriation of profits for subcontracting facilities are allowed. The Government has done well by extending incentives for the infrastructure sector to zone developers and the units as well. This can attract foreign direct investment for providing internationally competitive infrastructure.

Thus, so far as the size of SEZs, their customs regime and incentive package are concerned, the Indian policy compares quite favourably with the Chinese policy framework. However, in relation to the regime of labour laws, and decentralisation of powers in favour of State Governments, it falls short of expectations.

2

India, China and Globalization

The world economy has changed rapidly both in horizontal and vertical spectrum. These changes in the world economy have established clearly that no nation can isolate itself completely from the rest of the world and survive for long (Agarwal, 2002). The recent explosion of the information technology has amazingly reduced the cost, time and space in communication among the economic agents. This revolution of communication technology has generated new waves of dynamism and reduced virtually the whole world into a global village. This process of increasing economic integration and growing economic interdependence among the nations of the world is widely known as globalization (Singh, 1999).

Globalization of the world economy over the last two decades of the twentieth century and its robust continuation in the twenty-first century has been hailed as a major development ushering in the era of economic prosperity for all. The effect of this process on policy makers, various governments, academia, and on business all over the world has been phenomenal. This is particularly so in the developing countries. However, globalization has drawn mixed reactions. Some found it as a boon while others a curse (Chishti, 2002).

Whatever the arguments regarding the globalization or apprehensions over the WTO or the opening-up of developing economies are, it cannot be denied that it has offered newer opportunities and scope for unconventional alliances in the sphere of world trade and commerce. The emergence of India and China as prominent global economic players in a short span of about fifteen years is a proof enough. Most of the developing world and Newly Industrialised Economies (NIEs) have achieved faster expansion in their external trade since the beginning of the nineties, and Asia is right at the centre of such phenomenon (Singh, 2000).

In Asia, India and China are emerging as economic powerhouses. With their high growth rates and huge markets, these two Asian giants have attracted the attention of international business mangers to take a fresh look at the rapidly emerging opportunities in the two countries (Javalgi, et al., 1997). Given the emerging strength of India and China, as well as their possible competition for dominance as the leading Asian economic power, it is important to analyse their economic performance as well as their mutual economic relations in a comparative framework.

India and China are the two largest countries in the world in terms of their population, economic size and growth rates. These two countries together are home to the world's largest pool of skilled human resources and there is a general consensus that these two countries will continue to be the engines of global economic growth in the 21st Century (GOI, 2005).

It is held that with the rapid growth of India and China, Asia is expected to regain its place as a centre of gravity of the world economy. It is held that 'Asia is on its way to regain its lost share in the world economy by 2050, by which time India and China will be among the top three economies in the world along with US, and the combined share of India, China and Japan in the world economy would be about 57 percent' (Kumar, 2005b).

India and China established formal diplomatic relations in 1950 and also signed the first trade agreement in 1954. But, all the agreements between the two neighbours were broken down in 1962 due to the Border War. This attributed to the continuation of strain in their political relations and the restrictive trade practices followed by them towards each other. As a result of this syndrome, trade advantages emanating from geographical proximity and ethnic similarity have always remained elusive. However, the economic and diplomatic relations between the two countries were restored in the late seventies. In 1984, both the countries offered Most Favoured Nation (MFN) status to each other, which opened up the boundaries of the two countries for their economic interactions. After that, the high level officials' visits had a positive impact on their trade and economic relations. However, their trade got a big momentum since early nineties, when India started its liberalisation process (ITPO, 2003).

India-China relations are today conspicuous by the fast rise of trade, which crossed US$ 25 billion in 2006. Thus, the mutual trade target of US$ 20 billion by 2008 was already been reached two years ahead of schedule. The revised target of US$ 40 billion by 2010 has already been achieved ahead of the schedule. That is why, during the visit of Indian Prime Minister to China in January 2008, the mutual trade target between the two countries was further revised to US$ 60 billion by the year of 2010. Both the countries have also agreed to encourage and promote greater investment flows (Strategic Digest, 2008).

The resumption of border trade through Nathula La Pass in 2006 is of great importance. To strengthen the border trade with China, India has also proposed to open two more border trade points: Demchok in Ladakh and Bumla in Arunachal Pradesh (Kazi, 2007). The institutional framework of bilateral cooperation, including the Joint Economic Group, Joint Working Group and other sector specific mechanism, is being strengthened and expanded to cover new areas of economic cooperation. Both countries are also making efforts to expand the areas of economic linkages, which could further boost and broaden their mutual trade.

China has become a full-fledged member of WTO with effect from December 11, 2001. China's accession to the WTO has presented both opportunities and challenges for the Indian economy. It has also offered a suitable entourage for the growth of the mutual trade and economic cooperation between India and China. However, there exists a huge gap in the mutual dependence of India and China. China, being the second largest trading partner of India, shares about seven percent of India's overall trade. But the share of India in China's global trade has been hovering just around one percent. Further, India is also suffering from huge trade deficit with China. India's export basket to China is mainly dominated by primary and natural resource based products. The mutual investments between the two countries are also not very large (Peiyong, 2004).

Hence, there is definitely a strong need for both the countries to rectify all the hurdles in their mutual economic interactions and try to explore the fresh trade and investment opportunities. And, until both the sides open new vistas of economic cooperation, neither should under-estimate the value of rectifying imbalances that may otherwise add to factors that disrupt economic integration. Both have to work together to promote each others' contribution towards their bilateral and multilateral initiatives.

2.1 India-China Economic Interactions

There are possibly few issues that academicians, policy makers and market participants regard as new chapters in the history. The emergence of India and China is probably one of them. From a domestic perspective, both constitute unprecedented stories of economic development. Owing to vibrant growth rates in the last two decades, they have already reached heavyweight status in the global economy. However, their mutual economic interactions have remained at a lower level for a considerable period especially during 1950 to 1990. This period also consists the period of actually 'no trade' for about 14 years. That is why no systematic and comprehensive studies are available focusing exclusively upon their economic relations.

The existing literature mainly deals with the aspects other than economics, particularly geo-strategic. For a long period, Chinese economy remained and functioned in a close environment with strong inward-orientation. The things changed with the introduction of the reforms in 1978. For a considerable period, China has not joined the multilateral framework for the conduct of its external sector. However, the decade of 1990s proved to be a great watershed for both India and China and their entire course of economic policy-making witnessing a drastic transformation. This period has also been co-terminated with the post-Cold War dispensation. Both have been moving inherently in the same direction though the intensity of the reforms between the two entities varies. This process will generate the areas of similarities, complementarities and, of course, competition also. The need is to identify the commonality of both economic and non-economic interests.

The last one and half decade has witnessed the opening up and strengthening of economic and trade cooperation between the two and, with every passing year, newer dimensions have been attached to this cooperation. Number of trade, technology, capital and service sector related agreements and protocols have been signed. During this period, understanding in the areas of politico-diplomatic spheres also strengthened between these two nuclear neighbours. All this has drawn the attention of researchers and policy makers. But, up till now no comprehensive and inclusive study related to their economic exchange is available which can explain this period.

However, the academic interest pertaining to economic exchange between India and China at once got stimulated with the entry of the later into WTO. Numerous studies percolated by dealing with this dimension, i.e. the implications of China's entry into WTO for India. But, these studies remained partial and short period in data use and examined with greater emphasis on the sectoral implications. Thus, there has been a strong need to explore the economic relations between the two countries in the present milieu and futuristic perspective. The relevance of the study further increases by keeping in view the attempts by the two for building up the regional trading blocs.

China has a strong presence in ASEAN, and India is more involved in SAARC. Further, India and China are in the midst to become the part of Asian Free Trade Area (AFTA), which will match the European Union (EU) and North America Free Trade Area (NAFTA). Besides this, both the countries are also members of Asia Pacific Trade Agreement (APTA-formerly known as Bangkok Agreement). All this will strengthen their mutual economic ties. Hence, the present study is useful keeping in view their economic interaction in general and trade interaction in particular.

The main objectives of the study were as follows:

1. to explore the evolution of trade and economic interactions between India and China;
2. to comparatively examine the various dimensions of economic reforms in India and China;
3. to investigate the implications of China's accession to the WTO for Indian economy and particularly to their mutual trade;
4. to make a comparative analysis of FDI inflows and service trade of India and China;
5. to analyse the growth, direction, and composition of the mutual trade between India and China;
6. to study the gains from their mutual trade; and
7. to estimate the instability, competitiveness, and comparative advantage of India's exports to China.

2.2 India-China Trade Indices

India and China, at present, fall in the category of fast growing developing countries, vigorously following the process of market-based economic reforms and adjusting their external trade in the multilateral framework as enshrined by the WTO and other global institutions. The two nuclear neighbours have been aspiring for greater economic and politico-strategic voice in global affairs. The management of their mutual economic concerns with greater maturity would be very crucial in such an endeavour. The two countries have their strong standing in the world market in a number of areas covering goods, services, technology, finance and human resources. The complementarity at the level of production, distribution and consumption between the two actually holds the key for the strengthening of each other's position. Among the economic interactions, the mutual trade between the two countries has grown tremendously during the nineties and further boosted by China's accession to the WTO in the initial years of 21st Century.

In 2005, China emerged as the second largest trading partner of India, only after USA. Hence, the over-riding goal of the study is to examine the trade interactions between India and China. An attempt has been made to present a comprehensive picture of their economic exchange by putting the things in a most disaggregative and comparative manner. The direction and composition of their mutual trade have been analysed with the use of percentage and ratio methods by taking into account the yearly and over period change in trade flows. Trade growth has been assessed by the use of trend growth rates. Further, the various trade-related indices have also been computed such as Trade Intensity Index, Trade Integrity Index, Concentration Index, Intra-Industry Trade Index, Export Specialisation Index, Complementarity Index, Trade Overlap Index, Economic Distance Index, etc. The gains from the trade have been assessed by using Net Barter Terms of Trade (NBTT) Index and Relative Terms of Trade Index (RTTI). For this purpose, export and import unit values have been used as proxy for prices. A representative bundle of commodities has been selected by taking into account their weight in the foreign trade and continuous trade presence.

To assess the stabilisation effect of India's exports to China, Coppock's Instability Indices have been calculated. The competitiveness of India's exports to China has been examined with the help of relative market shares and unit values. Further, the total change in India's exports to China has been decomposed into three effects, namely demand effect, competitiveness effect and product-diversification effect. The comparative advantage of the two countries, in different sectors, has been computed by using Balassa's Revealed Comparative Advantage (RCA) index. Economic reforms, FDI inflows and service trade of the two countries have also been examined in a comparative perspective.

3

Evolution and Growth of Economic Relations

The history of India-China interaction is almost as old as the two civilisations themselves (Acharya, 2000). Even today, these two emerging world powers and close neighbours are very keen to strengthen their overall relations, especially economic relations. This is the result of the respective government's concerted efforts that the value of their mutual trade increased quite fabulously, i.e. 594 times over the period 1991-2005. Similarly, the mutual investment between the two countries has also been increasing. The economic integration between these two countries is a major driver of their overall relations.

However, this growing economic integration between the two did not remain the same in the past, as it was negatively affected by their political hangover, time to time. Hence, it is very essential to examine that how the bilateral economic relations between these two countries grew in the past. This chapter is an attempt to analyse the existing literature available on evolution and growth of India-China economic relations. For this purpose, the chapter has been divided into two parts. First part deals with the brief analysis of India-China economic relations in the historical context. The second part explores the ups and downs in the economic relations of the two countries since 1950. Further, since 1950, India's economic relations with China are analysed under four broad phases, viz. first phase (1950-1962); second phase (1962-1976); third phase (1976-1991); and fourth phase (1991-2005).

3.1 India-China Economic Relations: Historical Context

India and China are two ancient civilisations in the world.

The traditional friendship between the Chinese people and the Indian people dates far back in the history. The Himalayas is the highest mountain in the world, but it cannot severe communication between the two great civilisations (Ruixiang, 2000). Economic relations between India and China, in the fields of trade, dates back to very ancient times when merchant adventures used to cross the barriers of mountains, seas and deserts in search of markets in either countries (Ganguli, 1956).

It is generally accepted that contacts between India and China began as early as 400 B.C., although there is yet no definite record to establish this. The most significant aspect of ancient contacts was the establishment of Buddhism in China. The Chinese had responded with great enthusiasm to the arrival of Buddhist missionaries and, thereafter, initiated a wave to bring Indian Buddhist monks and scholars to help teach, explain and to establish Buddhism firmly in China (Swamy, 2001). The dominance and firm grip that Buddhism came to acquire in China was of course the result of a long lasting process of considerable interaction and exchange with India. Indian monks acted like honey bees carrying cultural pollen to China and apart from the development of religion and philosophy, they promoted the advancement of phonology, astronomy, medicine, chemistry and physical exercise in China (Acharya, 2000). Thus, historically, economic interactions between India and China have been of much less importance than that of the cultural interactions.

Trade and commerce along cultural contacts flourished between the two countries via "Silk Route". This route has played an important role in reconstructing the history of cultural and economic affinity between India and China. Thanks to Silk Route, silk fabrics and tea from China had been the two pillars of commerce and foreign trade between the two nations. China learnt from India how to make sugar from cane; how to decorate customs and living spaces with beads; how to weave gold and silver threads into fabrics; how to enrich

Chinese cuisine with black pepper; and how to make medicines from aromatic woods and tropical herbs. India also learnt papermaking and the use of compass, in addition to sericulture and silk industry from China and gained from such Chinese inventions like tea, gunpowder and printing. This extensive road network, known as Silk Route, facilitated all these interactions. Chinese merchants used Silk Route to sell silk, tea, porcelain and other goods to India, and took from India pepper, perfume, jewels, horses, etc. (Singh, 2005).

However, the decline of Buddhism in India led to weakening of contacts between the two countries. Over the next two centuries, trade and commerce between India and China also declined on account of a number of economic and political developments and gradually, whatever little residual contacts existed, faded with the advent of colonial and imperialist era in Asia (Swamy, 2001). During this imperialist era in Asia, the evolution of the colonial economic pattern in the countries of this region resulted in such a re-orientation of their trade that the internal trade within the region was reduced to the minimum, and these countries became isolated from the point of view of their trade relations (Ganguli, 1956).

If anything, it was the opium trade that became the epitome of India-China trade during colonial period. The disputes over trade in opium in China ultimately resulted in the waging of Opium War of 1840-42. Under the treaty of Nanking of 1842, China agreed to open five ports–Canton, Shanghai, Amoy, Ningpo and Foochow–for foreign trade, which was virtually opium trade. Following China's defeat in the second Opium War of 1858 at the hands of the British, more ports were opened for trade. This was to open an entirely new (and totally negative) phase of China's trade with India, i.e. British India (Singh, 2005). This opium trade and opium wars were not only to become symbols of China's anti-colonial sentiment but also greatly undermined the long-standing positive India-China equations since ancient times.

The exploitation and domination by the imperialist and

colonial powers that India and China experienced, and their struggles against them, did not however bring the two countries together. India won her freedom from British in 1947 and Communist Party of China (CPC) had won the Civil War in 1949 and came to power in the newly proclaimed "People's Republic of China". The world, in which India awoke "to life and freedom" and China achieved "liberation", was already sharply divided into two ideologically opposed blocs: the socialist bloc led by USSR and the democratic anti-communist bloc led by the United States (Swamy, 2001).

3.2 India-China Economic Relations since 1950

Since 1950, India's economic relations with China could be divided into four phases: (a) First Phase (1950-1962); (b) Second Phase (1962-1976); (c) Third Phase (1976-1991); and (d) Fourth Phase (1991-2005).

3.2.1 First Phase (1950-1962): Planned efforts of India and China towards development started almost during the same periods. Former's political freedom and latter's revolution occurred in the second half of the 1940s. The first decade of relations between the People's Republic of China and the newly independent India was peaceful and harmonious. Both sides played up the spiritual kinship between the two great civilisations that had just come to assert their national independence after suffering foreign dominance for a century or more. United by their anti-imperialist perspective, the two countries cooperated well (Shirk, 2004).

In early fifties, both the countries were at a similar stage of development and also adopted similar development strategies, which were heavily influenced by the Soviet Union's development strategy. Srinivasan (2004) has made a comparison of economic development strategies and performance of both the countries since the early fifties.

The development strategy of Soviet Union, which was emulated by India and China, emphasised investment in heavy industry. Both, India and China implemented their industrialisation programmes through state controls on investment and foreign trade.

India became the first non-socialist country to establish diplomatic relations with People's Republic of China. In fact, the 1950s saw a rapid growth of India-China mutual relations and, as a result, well known Five Principles of Peaceful Coexistence (Panchsheel) came into existence on 29 April, 1954. These principles were: (i) mutual respect for each other's sovereignty and territorial integrity; (ii) mutual non-aggression; (iii) mutual non-interference in each other's internal affairs; (iv) equality and mutual benefits; and (v) peaceful coexistence. These principles were in line with the aims and principles of UN charter, which had received popular support amongst the third world countries and had become guiding principles of international relations (Acharya, 2000). Thus, by then, the mutual relations between India and China including economic relations had reached at the highest stage of mutual understanding and peace.

Further, in 1954, the two countries also signed the Sino-Indian Agreement on Trade. This was the first ever trade agreement, which was signed between People's Republic of China (PRC) and independent India. With this, the mutual trade between the two countries rose steadily. According to Ganguli (1956), India's trade with China during this period has reflected the changes in the political and economic structure of new China. The general trade policy of the People's Republic of China was to promote exports and reduce imports so as to build up foreign exchange reserves.

However, this policy was not evidently implemented in the case of her trade with India. India's trade with China increased considerably during 1950-51 and 1951-52. Peiyong (2004) stated that the trade between India and China rose rapidly during the 1950s. The trade volume increased from ` 41.3 million in 1950 to ` 126.7 million in 1959. This was the sweet phase of India-China economic and trade relations which was strengthened by the "Panchsheel" and the phrase "Hindi-Chini

Bhai-Bhai". However, this sweet phase of India-China relations was short lived. After 1959, their mutual trade declined every year steadily and reached to only ` 11.3 million in 1962, which accounted for only 9 percent of that of the year 1959-60. All the agreements between the two countries got expired in 1962, due to India-China war (Deepak, 2001).

3.2.2 Second Phase (1962-1976): After the Border War in 1962, India-China relations suffered a serious setback. The mutual trust and sympathy was lost in no time. Biyum (2005) argued that the relationship between India and China was also overshadowed by the Cold War. So, the two countries drifted apart and became increasingly estranged. Competing in non-comparative way, both India and China missed many opportunities for cooperation. The mutual trade ties were almost broken down for 14 years, from 1962 to 1976. Neither of the two countries developed fast during that time.

The shadows of the Border War put a critical and long lasting impact on the studies relating to India-China economic relations. Notwithstanding this, in all terms till the seventies, very little serious and systematic work on India and China was done. The decade of sixties was almost wholly taken up by post-mortems on the war from every conceivable standpoint. The seventies saw the emergence of comparative works in a modest but determined way. However, the economic aspect appears to be almost obsessive (Deshpande and Acharya, 2001). Therefore, all the studies on India-China relations during that period were mainly related to political aspects.

3.2.3 Third phase (1976-1991): The bilateral relations improved gradually since 1976 when diplomatic relations were restored. Al-Rfough (2003) stated that the leadership in China under Deng Xiaoping embarked an ambitious programme of modernisation and economic development. In order to boost its programme of domestic economic development, China badly needed a peaceful external environment. Therefore, China tried to normalise relations with her neighbours and it established diplomatic relations with India. These diplomatic relations paved the way for the economic cooperation between the two countries.

During this period, China marched ahead on front of economic reforms and drastically changed her foreign trade and investment regime (Tseng and Zebregs, 2003). Though India had also liberalised its economy to a limited extent in 1980's, yet it did not show superb results like China (Srinivasan, 2004). Economic reforms greatly promoted the development of China's foreign trade, which, in turn, contributed to rapid economic development in the country (Yin, 2004). With the trade reforms, China also attracted a huge amount of FDI, during this period. China welcomed the FDI with open hands, which further boosted her economic development. The infusion of massive flow of FDI won the worldwide acclaim (Ghosh, 2005).

Purushottam (1999) argued that the reform process in China has relevance for India, which is also trying to attain high economic growth rates, to eliminate poverty and to improve standard of living of its people. Greater cooperation with China could help India to understand its problems and seek their solutions better. The future options may be different, both because of systematic differences and because the resource endowments of the two countries are now different. However, both countries face the same task of removing obstacles to growth, ensuring optimum development of resource and correcting the earlier misallocations. Consequently, both have a lot to learn from each other. India can imbibe Chinese pragmatism and dynamism in the development process and Chinese can study India's institutional structure and reforms.

Banerjee (1994) stated that the planned development in India and China, in the last few years, was tremendous. There exists a great potential for both the countries to learn from each other's experience of planned development. The management techniques of China have their own uniqueness, which can play a critical role in the development issues of

India. Similarly to China, India is combining a market economy with planned development though their relative combinations are different.

Peiyong (2004) stated that the resumption of diplomatic relations in 1976, Sino-Indian economic and trade relations proceeded rapidly. The trade volume soared from ` 25.6 million in 1977-78 to ` 1.06 billion in 1980-81. During this period, frequent visits of high level officials between the two nations strongly boosted the development of mutual trade.

During the period from 1977-78 to 1987-88, the total trade turnover between India and China had increased by 29.3 percent. India and China's relations got intensified in August 1984 with the extension of principle of Most Favoured Nation (MFN). Thus, this phase (1976-1991) showed a gradual development of India-China economic relations, primarily due to the opening up of Chinese economy to the outside world. But, one major problem with India-China trade in 1980s was the growing trend in India's trade deficit, a phenomenon that seems to have been accentuated since China introduced the reforms (Debroy, 1989).

3.2.4 Fourth Phase (1991-2005): The end of the Cold War and the emergence of a vibrant Asian economy had altered the global balance of power during the nineties (Javalgi, et al., 1997). After more than a decade's experience of economic reforms and opening up, China entered in the nineties as one of the fastest growing economies in the world. While on the other side, in 1991, India suffered from a serious balance of payments crisis, which compelled her to adopt the policies of globalisation and liberalisation. Thus, with the opening up of both the economies, the bilateral trade grew rapidly during 1991-2005 (ITPO, 2003). In fact, this phase proved as a spree time for the economic relations between India and China, except the year 1998 when the bilateral trade got negatively affected due to their nuclear considerations. However, except this year, India and China tried to deepen their economic relations.

During this period, India and China signed a lot of bilateral agreements, which made a watershed impact on their economic relations. The high level officials visited in each other's country to further strengthen their economic and political relations. Hence, during this phase, the mutual trade between the two countries recorded an impressive growth as their trade rose from ` 96.17 crore in 1990-91 to ` 7894.91 crore in 1999-00 (Kwatra, 2005). China's entry into the WTO further strengthened their economic relations. In fact, China, along with India, was among the founding members of GATT, but in 1950, due to Taiwan's unilateral withdrawal, China ceased to be a member of GATT. Negotiations for China's entry begin in 1986 and, finally, it became a full fledged member of the WTO with effect from December 11, 2001. China's accession to the WTO coincided with rapid rise of India-China bilateral trade.

According to Bhat, et al. (2006), during 2000-04, the two-way trade grew over twenty five percent per annum. Indian exports to China increased by twenty six percent and import from China increased by twenty four percent per annum. However, India's share in China's global imports remained around one percent while China's share in India's global imports remained over five percent. Thus, for India, China was an important export destination but it cannot be said for China. Further, Indian exports were mainly dominated by primary and resource based products, while Chinese exports to India were more diversified and included resource-based manufactures and low and medium technology based products. Major change in product composition of China's exports to India occurred in 2003 with the entry of a large number of electric and electronic products. Therefore, it appears that Chinese exports to India were more sustainable than that of Indian exports to China.

According to Fude (2004), WTO presented both opportunities and challenges for the mutual economic cooperation between India and China. Author argues that to enhance their economic and trade cooperation and to boost their economic development, both the countries should seize the opportunities and overcome challenges. On the other hand, as being large, poor and labour abundant developing countries, they would find much common ground in their negotiating positions (Pappu and Kumar, 2002; Srinivasan, 2004; and Peiyong, 2004).

Agrawal and Sahoo (2003) also evaluated the implications of China's accession to WTO in terms of its impact on country's exports, imports and foreign investment inflows and also discussed the likely impact of these developments for the Indian economy. They argued that with the accession to WTO, the economic activity in China was stimulated which resulted in the higher GDP growth of the country. Authors suggested that for India, the Chinese challenge can be met only by strengthening the competitiveness of the economy; by undertaking additional reforms; and by improving the infrastructure.

Opening up of the economy to trade and foreign direct investment proved a main driving force behind the exceptional growth performances of India and China during the last fifteen years. Indeed, attracting FDI become a pillar of the policies of the two countries to increase their openness to the world economy, and resulted in both the countries becoming the major recipients of FDI among the developing countries. However, Indian policies for FDI inflows remained somehow restrictive than China. And, that's why in attracting FDI inflows the later out-stepped the former by big margin (Tseng and Zebregs, 2003).

Chittle and Kim (1999) also examined the Foreign Direct Investment (FDI) in India and China during the mid-nineties. The policies of economic liberalisation including foreign trade and investment policies, macro-economic stabilisation, economic growth and infrastructural improvements in both the countries encouraged the inflows of foreign capital, especially FDI. According to Guha and Ray (2000), the sources of FDI in the two countries were very different. Chinese FDI was dominated by East Asian sources, particularly Hong Kong and Taiwan and mostly from expatriate Chinese population, whereas NRI investment in India was abysmally low. In both the countries, MNC responses were delayed. In China, it has by now acquired substantial momentum but it is yet to take off in India. However, both these countries have a vast potential to attract foreign investment to serve the local market and to become a more important part of the global integration that is taking place.

Though, during 1991-2005, the FDI inflows in India and China grew rapidly, but the mutual investments between the two countries remained vestigial. Mitra and Roy (2005) stated that China is not only a magnet for FDI, but it is also a source of FDI. By contrast, China has made virtually no direct investment in India. There is no doubt that China will be an even bigger foreign direct investor in the years to come. India needs to do a lot of homework to attract a larger slice of the Chinese investment dollar. For adding mutual investment between the two countries, Yang (2005) suggested three major issues: strengthening the mutual investment, improving the investment environment, and strengthening the mutual cooperation. Along with the enhancement of mutual understanding, it will be most important for the two countries to develop economic interests jointly. Inevitably, this will strengthen cooperation in mutual investment and promote development in the two countries.

According to Biyun (2005), the advantages and mutual complementarities of economic cooperation and partnership between India and China should be self-evident. India is viewed as 'world office' and China as 'world manufacturer'. Therefore, their rise as world economic great powers is an inevitable trend. The economic cooperation of the two countries has had a favourable beginning. So long as both the governments carry out their friendly policies; the respective chambers of commerce and industry adopt various promotional measures; and enterprises strengthen the communications links, one can anticipate a bright future in terms of business opportunities. Similarly, Singla and Singh (2008) argued that India and China are only beginning to discover the full scope and opportunities for expanding trade and economic cooperation at the regional and international levels. If coordinated well, the combined market size of the two can provide the significant leverages to both countries in regional and global trade across a range of product categories.

Thus, it can be said that the key to development of India-China economic relations rests in good neighbourly relations and mutual understanding. As long as both countries adhere to Five Principles of Peaceful Coexistence and continue to develop mutual cooperation and trust, their economic relations will be further developed and strengthened. The two countries should grasp the opportunities for development; eliminate obstacles; act in close coordination; and together strive for twining the twenty-first century into the Asian one. And, hence, it is hoped that India and China through their friendly cooperation could work towards a better future for their economies.

4

Economic Reforms and WTO

India and China, the two most populous countries of the world and among the poorest, have been attempting to develop economically through similar development strategies, under vastly different political frameworks, namely a multiparty democracy in India and a single-party (communist) authoritarian rule in China (Srinivasan, 2004). India began relaxing its rigidly controlled economy in a piecemeal fashion in the later part of 1980s, but its significant opening to the world economy and deeper domestic reforms did not begin until the severe macro-economic crisis of 1991. On the other side, China began its economic reforms and opening up to the world economy in 1978. With the experience of economic reforms and globalisation for nearly eighteen years in India, and thirty years in China, much more information and critical analyses have become available. This chapter is devoted to a comparative analysis of economic reforms, development strategies, and their results for Indian and Chinese economy. The chapter concludes by examining the background of China's entry into the WTO and its implications for the Indian economy.

4.1 Economic Reforms

India and China have been perceived as leaders amongst the developing countries with immense potential and prospects emerging as global players in economic and diplomatic spheres in the foreseeable future. There have been continuing differences in their political and economic structures and the underlying and governing political and economic perceptions, principles, philosophies and ideologies. Besides these differences, however, it is also held that any comparison between these two countries in terms of economic reforms and their impact on these countries may have at best limited validity (Saksena, 2005). However, before comparing the results of economic reforms for both the economies, it is important to view the origin of these reforms in both countries.

4.1.1 Origin of Economic Reforms: India: It is only from 1991 onwards that India really initiated its meaningful process of economic reform. The pre-reform economy in India was essentially state guided with public sector enterprises (PSEs) occupying the commanding heights. The controlled prices, exchange rates and investment were directed by the planned objectives (Guptaand Singh, 1995). Until the early eighties, India's macro-economic policies were considered conservative and inward oriented. The current revenues of the central government exceeded current expenditures and a surplus was available to finance in part the deficit in the capital account.

In the early eighties, because of lax fiscal policies, current revenue surpluses turned into deficits (Srinivasan, 2004). The widening gap between the revenue and expenditure of the government resulted in growing fiscal deficits which had to be met by borrowing at home. Further, the steadily growing difference between the income and expenditure of the economy as a whole resulted into a large current account deficits in the balance of payments which were financed by borrowing from abroad. The revenue deficit had risen from 0.2 percent of GDP in 1981-82 to 3.3 percent of GDP in 1990-91. But, the most disquieting development was a steep rise in the gross fiscal deficit which rose from 5.7 percent of GDP in 1980-81 to 6.6 percent of GDP in 1990-91. Since this fiscal deficit had to be met by recourse to borrowings, the internal debt of the central government rapidly rose from 35 percent of GDP in 1980-81 to 49.8 percent of GDP in 1990-91. Further, interest payments on these debts also rose rapidly. This naturally made the burden of servicing the debt onerous (Mishra and Puri, 2007).

The Gulf War of 1990 and the political instability at the turn of the decade, further, contributed towards the collapse of international confidence in the Indian economy and the result was the balance of payments crisis of 1991. Inflation was rising, industrial production was declining, foreign exchange reserves at one billion US dollars were at the lowest level ever, and the possibility of international default was real (Ahluwalia, 1999). The expectations of the devaluation of the rupee and the decline in the confidence led to the withdrawal of deposits in the Indian banks by non-resident Indians and to the withdrawal of capital by other external investors. Foreign exchange reserves dwindled to a level that was less than the cost of two weeks' worth of imports. The spectre of default on short-term external loans loomed large and led to a downgrading of India's credit rating (Gupta and Singh, 1995).

In response to the crisis situation of 1990-91, the government decided to introduce widespread economic reforms. The major thrust of the reforms of 1991 addressed the macro-economic and balance of payments crisis through fiscal consolidation and limited tax reforms, removal of controls on industrial investment and on imports, reduction of import tariffs and creation of a more favourable environment for attracting foreign capital (Srinivasan, 2004). The reforms also included an initial devaluation and subsequent prudent management of movements in the exchange rate while allowing market forces to play a major role in its determination, making the rupee convertible for current account transactions, and finally, opening the energy and telecommunication sectors for private investment (Ghosh, 2005).

4.1.2 Origin of Economic Reforms: China: The story of China's new transformation started since the beginning of its economic opening up and reforms in the late 1970's. This period was aptly described by China's paramount leader, Deng Xiaoping, as their "Second Revolution" with the first one being their political liberalisation in 1949 (Singh, 2005).

However, the situation in 1949 was quite stark, when China emerged from decades of war and civil strife with a shattered economy, with a very low level of development. Around ninety percent of the population lived in rural areas and industry accounted for only 12.6 percent of the national income (Ruisheng, 1999). The leaders of China chose to develop heavy industry, influenced by the Soviet model and the prevailing intellectual wisdom, which favoured a heavy industry development strategy to ensure self-reliance.

China's leadership selected central planning, through which resources could be mobilised administratively to enable speedy industrialisation. The major part of the resources was allocated to heavy industry, ignoring China's comparative advantage in labour-intensive sectors of light industry and agriculture. Estimates are that during 1953-80, nearly 80 percent of total Chinese investment was directed towards heavy industry. Private firms were fully collectivised by 1958, to be replaced by state procurement and distribution, according to centrally fixed targets. All private firms were also nationalised by the end of 1957. Foreign investment was prohibited and the private sector phased out of existence (Purushottam, 1999).

Further, the turmoil of Great Leap Forward (1958-62) and Cultural Revolution (1966-76) severely dislocated the economy and it would have been natural for those who came to power after death of Mao to focus on economic recovery (Srinivasan, 2004). The first sure signs of China's economic opening up and reforms were to come two years after Mao's death when Deng Xiaoping managed to persuade the Communist Party of China (CPC) to shift the focus from revolution and ideology to economic development of the country. De-collectivisation in rural sector and the Special Economic Zones (SEZs) in coastal cities were to become the first two priorities for China's second generation leaders and these were to begin showing results by early 1980s (Singh, 2005).

Till the very last years of Mao regime and even till the end of 1970s, China had been the world's most isolated economy in all respects. However, this situation changed completely with Deng's two fold policy initiatives–first was the shift in allocation mechanism from central planning to market-forces and second the shift of development strategies from an inward to an outward-orientation. The major goal of Chinese economic reforms was to generate sufficient surplus value to finance the modernisation of the Chinese economy. The initial reforms in the late 1970s and early 1980s consisted of opening trade to the outside world and instituting the contract responsibilities system in agriculture, by which farmers could sell their surplus crops and place them in the market (Hu, 2005). The huge response of rural China to the reformed incentives cemented political support for reforms. Farm output grew prodigiously and farm incomes more rapidly still. A high proportion of the increase in income was saved; and the new policies allowed the saving to be reinvested profitably in rural areas in townships and village industries, rapidly expanding off-farm employment and incomes.

Further, to speed up the transition from a centrally planned economy to a market economy and to attract foreign capital, technology and management skills, China established four major SEZs (Shenzhen, Zhuhai, Shantou and Xianan) in 1980. Similarly, Coastal Open Cities (COCs) were instituted along the coastal region of China in 1984 (Ruisheng, 1999). As a result, the exports of the country rose sharply; primary products were replaced by labour-intensive manufactures as the main exports; and, in the 1990s, foreign direct investment became an important source of capital formation and technological upgrading (Garnaut, 1999).

So, over the two decades of reforms, the Chinese economy achieved world-shaking changes. The market (the invisible hand) became a basic way of allocating resources, while enterprises played a key role in the development of economic activities. In the past, before China's economic reforms, only the government played an important role in economic activities; now there were enterprises that did so (Hu, 2005).

4.1.3 Results of Economic Reforms in India and China: A Comparison: As is clear from the above discussion, both India and China initiated the process of economic reforms to bring out their economies from the socio-economic crisis. But, the performance of both the countries was not equal. In fact, China had transformed and developed more rapidly as comparison to India. This may be proved with the results of economic reforms undertaken by both the countries.

(i) GDP and Per Capita GDP: During the reforms period, both India-China substantially improved the pace of their Gross Domestic Product (GDP) and per capita GDP. As is clear from the Table 4.1, during the period 1980-2005, China outperformed India and the world in the growth of total and per capita GDP.

Table 4.1: Average Annual Growth Rate of Total and Per Capita Real GDP

Country	1980-90		1990-00		2000-05		1980-2005	
	T GDP	PC GDP	T GDP	PC GDP	T GDP	PC GDP	T GDP	PC GDP
India	5.8	3.4	6.0	3.9	6.7	5.0	5.7	3.6
China	10.3	8.8	10.6	9.5	9.6	8.8	8.1	8.7
World	3.1	1.3	2.8	1.3	2.8	1.5	2.7	1.1

T = Total; PC = Per capita.
Source: Handbook of Statistics 2006-07, UNCTAD.

During this period, the average annual growth rate (AAGR) of China's GDP and per capita GDP (i.e. 8.1 percent and 8.7 percent respectively) remained well above that of India (i.e. 5.7 percent and 3.6 percent respectively) and the world (i.e. 2.7 percent and 1.1 percent respectively). Similarly, during all the sub-periods, the AAGR of China's GDP and per capita GDP remained higher than that of India's and world's. The factors which made the high growth rates of GDP and per capita GDP possible for China were–a sustained high rate of domestic savings and foreign capital inflows which made a continuous higher investment rate possible and a higher growth rate of industrial production, particularly manufacturing and booming exports. Similarly, the growth of per capita GDP was also strengthened by China's remarkable success in the management of population growth.

(ii) **Sectoral Composition:** In both the countries, economic reforms had differential impacts on different sectors of the economy. In China, the initial thrust of the reforms was on agricultural sector. The introduction of the household responsibility system, the reduction in compulsory deliveries to the state, and increase in the proportion of output that could be sold in the market provided effective incentives for farm households to increase output. In India, on the other side, distortions prior to reforms were more pronounced in industry and foreign trade and the reforms were aimed at removing those distortions. However, in China, the growth of agricultural and service output slowed markedly and that of manufacturing output increased rapidly in the nineties compared to the eighties. In India, on the other side, the growth of manufacturing output slowed significantly and that of services rose sharply (Srinivasan, 2004). Thus, the sectoral composition of output growth in the two countries reflects not only the differing targets of reform but also the lingering effects of pre-reform policies. On the whole, during 1986-2005, the AAGR of all the three sectors (namely agriculture, industry and service) of China (i.e. 3.99 percent, 11.70 percent and 9.81 percent respectively) remained higher than that of India (3.17 percent, 6.53 percent and 7.53 percent respectively) (Table 4.2).

Table 4.3 shows the share of all the three sectors in the GDP of both the countries. The table reveals that the share of agriculture in both India and China's GDP declined substantially. This declined share of agricultural sector in both the countries was mainly absorbed by the service sector. However, during the period 1986-2005, the service sector accounted for nearly half of India's GDP (i.e. 46.90 percent), while, in China, nearly half of GDP was accounted by industrial sector (i.e. 45.22 percent). Thus, it can be said that the major driver of India's economic development was its service sector, while that of China's economic development was its industrial sector.

Table 4.2: Average Annual Growth Rate of Agriculture, Industry and Service Sectors: India and China

Years	Agriculture		Industry		Service	
	India	China	India	China	India	China
1986-90	4.03	4.40	7.67	8.80	6.96	8.82
1991-95	2.41	4.16	6.05	17.46	6.71	10.82
1996-00	3.23	3.46	5.09	9.80	7.97	9.48
2001-05	3.01	3.94	7.30	10.74	8.48	10.12
1986-2005	3.17	3.99	6.53	11.70	7.53	9.81

Source: Asian Development Bank: Key Indicators (Various Issues).

Table 4.3: Average Annual Percentage Share of Agriculture, Industry and Service Sector in GDP: India and China

Years	Agriculture		Industry		Service	
	India	China	India	China	India	China
1986-90	30.77	26.26	27.80	43.25	41.43	30.49
1991-95	28.52	20.95	26.48	45.11	45.01	33.94
1996-00	25.57	17.19	26.27	46.59	48.16	36.22
2001-05	20.42	13.17	26.59	45.93	52.99	40.90
1986-2005	26.32	19.39	26.78	45.22	46.90	35.39

Source: Asian Development Bank: Key Indicators (Various Issues).

(iii) Savings and Investment: The simple and most obvious reason for China's consistently much higher real GDP growth rate than India's was the much higher rate of investment or capital formation in China made possible by almost equally high rates of domestic savings. Table 4.4

reveals that the average annual share of gross domestic savings in GDP grew more rapidly in China vis-à-vis India. For the period 1986-2005, the average annual percentage share of gross domestic savings and gross domestic capital formation in Indian GDP was 23.97 percent and 25.19 percent respectively, the corresponding figures for China being 38.81 percent and 38.77 percent respectively. Hence, this difference in the growth of gross domestic savings and gross domestic capital formation of the two countries was the major reason for the difference in the growth of GDP of the two.

Table 4.4: Average Annual Percentage Share of Saving and Investment in GDP: India and China

Years	Gross Domestic Saving		Gross Domestic Capital Formation	
	India	China	India	China
1986-90	21.11	36.08	24.06	36.81
1991-95	22.70	37.66	23.86	40.43
1996-00	23.45	38.43	24.55	37.47
2001-05	28.62	43.05	28.29	40.37
1986-2005	23.97	38.81	25.19	38.77

Source: Asian Development Bank: Key Indicators (Various Issues).

(iv) Goods and Services Trade: During the reforms period, there was a considerable expansion of goods trade and services trade in both the countries. During the period 1981-2005, the goods exports constituted nearly 3/4th of India's total exports while the remaining 1/4th was constituted by service exports. However, in China, as compared to India, service exports remained at lower levels and grew more slowly. Overall, Chinese goods exports accounted for approximately 90 percent of its total exports while the remaining 10 percent was accounted by service trade (Table 4.5). The same was the case with imports. All this suggests that China's exceptional integration into the world economy was mainly driven by goods trade (Kowalski, 2008), which was mainly due to the considerable increase in FDI inflows into the country.

(v) Merchandise Trade and Balance of Payments:
During the reforms period, both India and China dramatically
reformed their foreign trade regime, which greatly promoted
the development of their foreign trade and contributed to their
rapid economic development (Yin, 2004). However, in terms
of both merchandise exports and imports, China grew very
rapidly, at the rates far exceeding the growth rates of India's
merchandise exports and imports, due to which China has now
emerged as a major player in the international market.

**Table 4.5: Average Annual Percentage Share of Goods and
Service in Total Exports and Imports: India and China**

Years	Exports				Imports			
	Goods		Services		Goods		Services	
	India	China	India	China	India	China	India	China
1981-85	75.07	89.33	24.93	10.67	79.89	90.70	20.11	9.30
1986-90	78.30	89.07	21.70	10.93	79.34	92.71	20.66	7.29
1991-95	80.61	87.57	19.39	12.43	78.23	86.83	21.77	13.17
1996-00	76.08	88.37	23.92	11.63	76.84	84.21	23.16	15.79
2001-05	69.61	89.99	30.39	10.01	72.77	87.07	27.23	12.93
1981-2005	75.93	88.86	24.07	11.14	77.41	88.30	22.59	11.70

Source: Balance of Payment Statistics Yearbook, IMF (Various
Issues).

Due to much less value of exports than that of imports in
all the sub-periods, India experienced a negative trade balance.
India had a large negative current account balance also in all
the sub-periods, except the last one, i.e. 2001-05. During this
period, India's service exports rose sharply which turned the
negative current account balance into positive. During 1986-
90, India's average annual overall balance of payments was
also negative (i.e. US$ -399 million). This had happened
mainly due to the balance of payments crisis of 1990.
However, afterwards the policies of globalisation and
liberalisation were initiated which enhanced India's capital
receipts and, therefore, the balance of payments turned out to

be positive. On the other hand, because of larger value of merchandise exports China had large trade surpluses during all the sub-periods, except first one (i.e. 1986-90) and the same happened with China's current account balance. During all the sub-periods, China's balance of payments remained positive and well above that of India. Hence, in the development of foreign trade regime, China outperformed India by a big margin.

Similarly, China's foreign trade, in contrast to India's, constituted a major share of its GDP. The corresponding figures for India, during the same period, were 8.12 percent and 10.99 percent respectively. Due to India's negative trade balance and current account balance, during all the sub-periods, their average annual percentage share in GDP also remained negative (except 2001-05, where the share of current account balance in GDP was positive, i.e. 0.57 percent per annum). However, India's balance of payments, except first sub-period, remained positive and hence its share in India's GDP also remained positive and increased continuously. On the other hand, China suffered negative trade balance and current account balance only in the first sub-period, otherwise both the components constituted positive and healthy average annual percentage share in China's GDP. Similarly, China's balance of payments also constituted major share in its GDP. Thus, it can be said that during the reforms period, Chinese economy remained more foreign trade oriented as compared to the Indian economy.

(vi) Trade Openness: It may be useful to compare the trade policy openness in both India and China. In India, the biggest tariff reduction occurred in the immediate aftermath of 1991 balance of payments crisis and the trend towards reduction in average tariffs was reversed in 1998. This is largely the result of conversion of quantitative restrictions or non-tariff barriers to tariff barriers, required because of GATT's Article XI (Bhat, et al., 2006). On the other side, China started reducing its tariff rates in the early eighties and after its accession to WTO, tariff rates went down more rapidly.

A simple unweighted tariff comparison suggests that India is much more restrictive to trade as compared to China. The simple average Chinese tariff rates on agricultural and non-agricultural products were reduced from 46.58 percent and 41.39 percent in 1992 to 14.96 percent and 8.96 percent in 2005 respectively, while that of India decreased from 82.87 percent and 82.17 percent in 1990 to 37.57 percent and 15.00 percent in 2005 respectively. However, these differences in tariff rates of the two countries became sharper in terms of weighted mean tariffs and standards deviation of tariffs. Further, during the whole period, maximum tariff rate of India was very high as compared to China. Hence, it can be concluded that Chinese economy is relatively more open as compared to Indian economy.

(vii) Foreign Direct Investment Inflows: During the reforms period, both India and China put their doors wide open for the Foreign Direct Investment (FDI) inflows. However, China succeeded in attracting huge amounts of FDI inflows as compared to India. As is clear from Table 4.6, during the study period, the average annual FDI inflows of China remained very high as compared to India. The difference is clear from the figures that during 1981-2005, the average annual FDI inflows of China amounted to US$ 25337 million while that of India amounted to US$ 1904 million.

In fact, India did not seek higher share of relatively more stable FDI and instead opted for more volatile Foreign Portfolio Investment (FPI). The reason was that in India, since the Independence days, an influential class of private capitalists was present which received protection from stringent import control regime for forty years till 1990-91 and this class of capitalists did not want FDI in competing areas but advocated it mostly through the joint venture route and in areas like physical infrastructure where it would be complementary (Tendulkar and Bhavani, 2007). However, since the mid-eighties, the average annual growth rate of India's FDI inflows remained well above than that of China's. It suggests that though India's FDI inflows are still low but they are increasing rapidly.

Table 4.6: Average Annual Growth of Foreign Direct Investment Inflows: India and China

Years	India[1] (US$ Million)	Average Annual Growth	China[1] (US$ Million)	Average Annual Growth
1981-85	59	118.98	997	126.59
1986-90	182	40.89	2926	12.98
1991-95	797	96.54	22835	72.22
1996-00	2906	16.23	42696	1.96
2001-05	5574	16.29	57232	12.37
1981-2005	1904	57.79	25337	45.22

Note: 1. Figures are in average.
Source: World Investment Report, UNCTAD (Various Issues).

(viii) External Debt and Debt Services: During the balance of payments crisis, India took a huge amount of external debt. For the period 1986-2005, India's external debt as percentage of GNI remained 24.35 percent per annum which was higher than that of China's, i.e. 14.10 percent per annum. Most of the external debt had been long term in both India and China, however, during 1986-2005, India's average annual percentage of long term debt to total debt (i.e. 91.05 percent) was higher than that of China (i.e. 75.69 percent). However, China had been allowing relatively larger inflows of short-term capital due to greater resilience of their economy and far superior foreign trade performance (Saksena, 2005). Therefore, during 1986-2005, China's average annual percentage of short term debt to total debt (i.e. 23.62 percent) was much higher than that of India (i.e. 6.43 percent). The debt services as percentage of exports of goods and services for both the countries declined considerably during the whole study period. However, because of much higher exports, during 1986-2005, debt services as percentage of exports of goods and services remained much lower in China (i.e. 9.03 percent per annum) than in India (i.e. 24.47 percent per annum).

(ix) **International Reserves:** During the period 1986-90, India suffered a serious fall in total reserves and foreign exchange reserves and their average annual growth rate remained -2.99 percent and -22.26 percent respectively. But after that they turned out to be positive. However, during the whole study period, China's average annual international reserves (i.e. US$ 144650 million) and foreign reserves (i.e. US$ 141350 million) remained well above that of India (i.e. US$ 31967 and US$ 29165 million respectively).

Similarly, during the whole period, average annual percentage of China's foreign exchange in total reserves remained above 90 percent while that of India crossed 90 percent mark only once (i.e. 95.37 percent per annum during 2001-05). Hence, during 1982-2005, the average annual percentage of India's foreign exchange reserves in total reserves (i.e. 81.38 percent) remained lower than that of China's (i.e. 94.92 percent).

(x) **Consumer Price Index:** During 1986-95, both India and China experienced high inflation rates in terms of rise in consumer price index. In India, the inflation rate in terms of annual percentage change in consumer price index reached to its peak in 1991, i.e. 13.8 percent. Similarly, in China, inflation rate in terms of rise in consumer price index was as high as 18.8 percent in 1988, which further rose to 24.1 percent in 1994.

Thus, these figures made the annual average growth of consumer price index much higher in the second sub-period for both the countries (i.e. 10.48 percent for India and 13.13 percent for China). However, since the mid-nineties, both the countries succeeded in reducing the rate of inflation. But, here once again, China did well as compared to India. On the whole, during 1986-2005, China experienced 6.77 percent inflation rate in terms of annual percentage change in consumer price index, while the corresponding figure for India remained 7.67 percent (Table 4.7).

Table 4.7: Average Annual Percentage Change in Consumer Price Index: India and China

Years	India	China
1986-90	8.61	10.74
1991-95	10.48	13.13
1996-00	7.61	1.86
2001-05	3.98	1.36
1986-2005	7.67	6.77

Source: Asian Development Bank: Key Indicators (Various Issues).

(xi) Total Population and Density of Population: Another very important factor which accounts for China's remarkable economic performance is her population control. Table 4.8 reveals that during all the sub-periods, the AAGR of population and population density for China remained below that of India. During the period 1986-2005, the AAGRs of China's population and population density were 1.10 percent and 1.06 percent respectively and that of India was 1.93 percent (same for both). A higher rate of population growth, or the failure to sufficiently reduce the population growth rate, not only depressed India's per capita GDP growth rate, but also its savings rate and necessitating pre-emption of a larger proportion of the country's resources for providing basic health and child care facilities (Saksena, 2005).

(xii) Human Development Index: During the reforms period, China remained ahead of India in terms of Human Development Index (HDI)–which is a summary measure of life expectancy, school enrolment, literacy and income. In 1980, India's rank was 94 among all nations in terms of HDI and its value was 0.45. The corresponding figures for China were 78 and 0.56. However, India went down to 128th rank in spite of rise in HDI value to 0.62 in 2005. Similarly, China also slightly went down to 81st rank even with the improvement in HDI value, i.e. 0.78 in 2005 (Table 4.9).

Table 4.8: Average Annual Growth of Population and Density of Population: India and China (Million)

Years	Population		Population Density	
	India	China	India	China
1986-90	802 (2.13)	1101 (1.55)	244 (2.13)	116 (1.55)
1991-95	887 (2.00)	1178 (1.20)	270 (2.00)	123 (1.16)
1996-00	973 (1.68)	1241 (0.94)	297 (1.94)	130 (0.91)
2001-05	1069 (1.90)	1292 (0.70)	325 (1.65)	135 (0.60)
1986-2005	932 (1.93)	1203 (1.10)	284 (1.93)	126 (1.06)

Note: Figures in parentheses show average annual percentage growth rates.
Source: Asian Development Bank: Key Indicators (Various Issues).

Table 4.9: Value and Rank of Human Development Index (HDI): India and China

Years	India		China	
	Value	Rank	Value	Rank
1980	0.45	94	0.56	78
1985	0.49	96	0.60	81
1990	0.52	104	0.63	90
1995	0.55	104	0.69	84
2000	0.58	102	0.73	76
2005	0.62	128	0.78	81

Source: UNDP: Human Development Report (Various Issues).

As is clear from the above discussion, since the 1980s, China had far outstripped India in economic performance in terms of growth, living standard of its population and integrating its economy with the world. The fact that China initiated reforms more than a decade earlier than India explains only a small part of this difference, since India also liberalised its economy to a limited extent in the 1980s. It is argued that China's success in achieving such high economic growth is due to the huge investments of overseas Chinese (Chandra, 1999), an advantage that India does not have as its NRIs are mostly professionals.

Further China, being an authoritarian government, did not respond to the pressure groups that stood to gain or lose from reforms. The dominance of communist party also helped in keeping the bureaucratic apparatus intact and reasonably efficient while the pro-market policies of its paramount leader, Deng Xiaoping, took hold. Of course, the heavy investment in physical and social infrastructure, prior to reforms, also paid off handsomely. However, those factors in themselves were not adequate to dismiss the argument that Chinese reforms in particular–their contents and modes of implementation were very different from their Indian counterparts and that difference was the key to Chinese success during reforms period (Srinivasan, 2004).

Further, it is also assumed that greater cooperation with China could help India to understand its problems and seek better solutions. The future options may be different, both because of systematic differences and because the resource endowments of the two countries are now different. However, both countries face the same task of removing obstacles to growth, ensuring optimum deployment of resources and correcting the earlier misallocations (Purushottam, 1999). Consequently, both have a lot to learn from each other. Exchanges of ideas and comparisons of development experiences in different sectors have taken place, generating mutual goodwill. These are of immense mutual benefit and have implications for growing cooperation between the two Asian giants, and should be increased further. India can imbibe

Chinese pragmatism and dynamism in the process and Chinese can study India's institutional structure and reforms.

4.2 India, China and WTO

Since the last two decades, both India and China have emerged as star growth achievers in the world economy and strengthened their position in the world trade. However, one of the most significant recent developments in world trade has been the entry of China into the World Trade Organisation (WTO). China became one hundred and forty third member of WTO on December 11, 2001, after having the negotiation with the world community for fifteen years. On the other side, India was the founding member of General Agreement on Trade and Tariffs (GATT, predecessor of WTO). Given the size of the Chinese market, its accession to the WTO has been considered as a watershed event in the history of world trade. The world's reaction towards the China's entry into the WTO has been mixed.

While most countries welcome the opportunities for access to China's large domestic market, developed countries fear that inexpensive Chinese imports will flood their domestic markets, developing countries including India are concerned that China will undercut their export markets in the West and also shrink their receipts of foreign direct investment (Cerra, et al., 2005). China's accession to the WTO has, in fact, offered many opportunities and challenges for the Indian economy (Peiyong, 2004). This section of the chapter examines the background of China's protracted negotiations for accession to the WTO and its likely implications for the Indian economy.

4.2.1 Background of China's Accession to the WTO: December 11, 2001 marks a key date in the calendar of world trade. On that day, the sixth-largest economy in the world, representing a population of 1.3 billion people, and reflecting a unique political and economic system consisting of a hybridisation of Marxism and free-market principles, joined the rule-based international trading system, by acceding to the

World Trade Organisation (WTO). Though each accession to the WTO is a unique event, but few would argue with the proposition that China's accession is in a class of its own. After all, China was one of the twenty three original contracting parties of GATT in 1948 and her application for readmission to the multilateral trading system dates back fifteen years to July 1986, easily making it the longest and most arduous accession negotiation in the history of the GATT/WTO (Yongtu, 2007).

After China's revolution in 1949 and the split between Mao Zedong and Chiang Kai-Shek, the government in Taiwan announced in 1950 that China would leave the GATT. Although the government in Beijing never recognised this withdrawal decision, nearly forty years later, in 1986, China notified to GATT, its wish to resume its status as a GATT contracting party and its willingness to renegotiate the terms of its membership (Lanchovichina and Martin, 2001). From 1986, China sought, unsuccessfully, to revive its dormant position by becoming a founding member of the WTO.

China's lack of membership of the GATT did not preclude it from becoming an active member of the international trading community. Since the introduction of an open door policy in late 1970s and the appointment of Deng Xiaoping as paramount leader in 1986, China had pursued a vigorous trade policy. In the last twenty five years, it had undertaken a series of economic reforms aimed at freeing up of its imports and exports and encouraging of foreign investment (Bhalla and Qiu, 2004).

In short, China has undergone extensive political change, and has conducted major reforms in its legal system, both of which have contributed to increase its slice of the international trade pie. But China still remained outside the mainstream of international trading system.

In 1999, when the major bilateral negotiations were coming to close and the WTO working party on China's accession was moving towards its final stages, international events intruded. US forces accidentally bombed the Chinese Embassy in Belgrade. A Chinese national working in the US defence establishment was accused of spying.

The negotiations were briefly suspended. But, in November 1999 the US bilateral negotiations with China were finally concluded, with the European Union following soon afterwards in May 2000. By September 2001, the issues in dispute were reduced to a few narrow. However, after the attack on World Trade Centre in New York in 11 September, and a brief day adjournment of the working party, WTO announced that the conditions of membership were now satisfied (Lardy, 2002).

Finally, in November 2001, the stage was set for China's accession. After three days of discussion in Doha, a new series of trade liberalisation negotiations were launched and China's long awaited entry to the WTO was approved on 10 November, 2001. A day later China signalled that the Standing Committee of People's Congress had approved the terms of accession. Following GATT rules, thirty days later, on 11 December, 2001, China became the 143rd member of the WTO (Yongtu, 2007).

As a result of the negotiations, China agreed to undertake a series of important commitments to open and liberalise its regime in order to better integrate in the world economy and offer a more predictable environment for trade and foreign investment in accordance with WTO rules. The US and EU secured a large number of commitments and concessions from China. WTO (2001) mentioned few commitments to be undertaken by China, presented as follows:

- China will provide and accord the non-discriminatory treatment to all WTO members. All foreign individuals and enterprises, including those not invested or registered in China, will be accorded treatment no less favourable than that accorded to enterprises in China with respect to the right to trade.
- China will eliminate all dual pricing practices as well as

differences in treatment accorded to goods produced for sale in China in comparison to those produced for export.

- Price controls will not be used for purposes of according protection to domestic industries or services providers.
- The WTO Agreement will be implemented by China in an effective and uniform manner by revising its existing domestic laws and enacting new legislation fully in compliance with the WTO Agreement.
- Within three years of accession, all enterprises will have the right to import and export all goods and trade them throughout the customs territory with limited exceptions.
- China will not maintain or introduce any export subsidies on agricultural products.

Many of these conditions are not currently applicable to other WTO members, namely dual pricing practices, price controls and export subsidies on agricultural products. Further, implementation of China's commitments is time bound. However, this is not the case with other member countries of the WTO (Bhat, et al., 2006).

While, China will reserve the right of exclusive state trading for products such as cereals, tobacco, fuels and minerals and maintain some restrictions on transportation and distribution of goods inside the country, many of the restrictions that foreign companies have at present in China will be eliminated or considerably eased after a three year phase-out period.

Apart from providing market access, China will also remove restrictions on trade related activities. It will follow the main principles such as national treatment and non-discriminatory principles and will respect the Trade-Related Investment Measures (TRIMS) and Trade-Related Aspects of Intellectual Property Rights (TRIPS).

The compliance with such commitments is likely to have far reaching implications domestically, including encouraging greater internal integration of domestic markets. Moreover, the commitments to comply with the principles and rules of the international trading system will improve the transparency of the domestic policy environment (Rumbaugh and Blancher, 2004).

4.2.2 Implications for India: India and China are emerging as the two largest markets in the world today. Foreign trade has been one of the key factors fuelling high GDP growth rates in both these nations. In this context, the role of the WTO as a body, which regulates and promotes trade, assumes tremendous significance for these countries. India is a founder member of the WTO, while China has joined it in December 2001.

The entry of China had been held up because of disagreements on the removal of trade barriers, which protect the Chinese domestic industry from foreign competition.

However, all these disagreements have been resolved through mutual bilateral agreements under the rules of the WTO. China's entry opens up a host of opportunities and challenges for India. On one hand, it can lend strength to the lobby of developing nations within the WTO.

On the other hand, Chinese industry will be able to compete in the Indian market on favourable terms. This section of the chapter attempts to study the impact of China's accession to the WTO on Indian economy. China's entry into the WTO opened up a lot of opportunities for India, which are outlined below:

- The WTO as a body is presently sharply polarised between the developing and the developed nations. The bloc of developing nations led by India has been pressing for safeguards to domestic industries from international competition and gradual phasing out of trade restrictions by advanced countries. The developed nations on the other hand, want faster phasing out of restrictions by developing countries and more access of these markets for their vital industries. China's entry into WTO is in India's interest, as China shares India's point of view on various WTO issues. It has more diplomatic clout than India, and for the benefit of other third world countries, might be able to weak US and EU hegemony in the multilateral organisation. Thus, China's participation will increase the voice of the developing countries, so that the rules for the new game at WTO may become more balanced and more beneficial to the developing countries (Pappu and Kumar, 2002).

- Most of the commodities imported by China like machinery, mineral and mineral products, iron and steel, organic chemicals, medical and surgical equipments and agricultural products are principal commodities in the India's overall export basket (Agrawal and Sahoo, 2003). Given that China will have to lower tariffs on many of its imports and has also to phase out many subsidies, there would be availability of more market for the above mentioned Indian exports to China.

- India has strong comparative advantage in commercial and technical services, most notably in the areas of software. As per WTO provisions related to China's entry, China will open the services sector for foreign investment gradually. Further, China is also determined to be a major player in the coming revolution in Info-Tech services. Hence, in this area, India has a large opportunity to capitalise on its comparative advantage and increase service trade with China (Fude, 2004).

- China's entry into the WTO will force Indian industry to become more competitive and will pave the way for second generation market reforms in India, which will spur growth and competitiveness by cutting costs. China's huge market may become a potential market for Indian goods and increasing domestic competitiveness can be leveraged by pushing exports.

- With China's entry into the WTO, it will be easier for India to resolve disputes with China like dumping cases because China will be under the ambit of WTO Dispute Settlement Body (Peiyong, 2004). Though there is no clear cut data available regarding dumping, yet India has filed some cases against China for dumping of few goods such as dry cell batteries, sport shoes, porcelain tiles, toys, bias tyres, caustic soda, Compact Florescent Lamps (CFL), Ductile Iron (DI) pipes, raw silk, nylon filaments, steel wheels, potassium, magnesium, metallurgical coke, rubber chemicals, paracetamol, etc. India can better handle the problem of dumping from China by using the WTO platform. It is worth nothing here that Chinese dumping in India is just a recent phenomenon. This problem was not so serious during the period of the present study.

- Textiles and clothing represent the area in which India and China have predominantly revealed comparative advantages (Cerra, 2005). However, within this sector, there are areas of specialisation. India has relatively higher comparative advantage in basic materials while China has strong comparative advantage in produced articles of clothing using textiles. This pattern of specialisation in textile and clothing may provide an opportunity for India to expand its trade with China. Further, China has been a growing importer of high quality textiles. Hence, it is a great opportunity for India to export its textiles to China (Shafaeddin, 2004).

Hence, China's entry into the WTO will provide a lot of opportunities for the Indian economy in different ways. However, this is one side of the picture; the other side may be more serious. In other words, besides above mentioned opportunities, China's entry into the WTO will also offer a lot of challenges, which is a cause of concern for Indian policy makers. Some of such challenges are as follows:

- Since most of Indian export items such as textiles, garments, leather and leather products and light machinery, are also principle commodities in Chinese's overall export basket, further integration of Chinese economy with the world is likely to have a negative impact on India's exports (Agrawal and Saibaba, 2001). In fact, the Chinese corporations are financially stronger, have more efficient processes and turn out goods at extremely cheap prices. Armed with competitive advantage of low price, the Chinese are moving in new markets at a feverish pace and Indian exports will also come under serious challenge in third world markets with the entry of China into the WTO.

- United States is the largest export destination for both the countries, accounting for more than twenty percent of their exports at the time of Chinese accession. However, China's entry into the WTO has raised the fear that India may be one of the countries most likely to experience trade diversion to China (Cerra, et al., 2005).

- China has become one of the major destinations for FDI inflows. To fulfil the commitments made under WTO accession, China will further open more areas for FDI inflows which will negatively influence India's FDI inflows (Agrawal and Sahoo, 2003).

- China is one of the largest suppliers of cheap labour-intensive products (such as kitchen ware, textiles, electronic items, furniture, toys, cosmetics, footwear, bicycles, mobiles, watches etc.) in the world market. There are apprehensions that cheap Chinese goods may flood the Indian market and spell disaster for local manufactures (Pappu and Kumar, 2002).

Thus, China's entry into the WTO is viewed in India as a mixed blessing. On one hand, it helps India to voice for its concerns in the WTO on the issues of domestic interest, but there are also large downsides as our exports, especially labour-intensive manufactures, might become less competitive. There are also concerns that Chinese goods may flood into the Indian markets and spell doom for domestic producers.

However, the Chinese challenge can be overcome only if we further strengthen the competitiveness of our economy by undertaking additional reforms and improving infrastructure (Agrawal and Sahoo, 2003). Further, China's entry into the WTO also presents significant trade opportunities to India as it gains access to one of the largest markets in the world. Therefore, in order to maximise its gains, India must adopt a forward looking strategy aimed both at neutralising Chinese competition by making Indian goods more competitive as well as pushing Indian exports into China.

5

FDI, Services Trade and Mutual Exchange

Increasing globalisation of the world economy has stimulated the multinational enterprises to invest abroad on a large scale. At the same time, the host countries have created a favourable environment to attract more and more Foreign Direct Investment (FDI). In this regard, both India and China have drastically changed their economic policies. Each has moved from an economy with a pervasive government role to a more market-oriented one in terms of openness, deregulation and liberalisation. The policies of India and China regarding FDI have become significantly more liberal during the past few years. The domestic economic structure of China and India differs significantly, as industry dominates in the former and services in the later.

More specifically, industry contributes about a half to China's GDP, but less than one third to India's, wherein services represent around a half of the latter's GDP. Keeping this in view, this chapter has been divided into two parts. First part compares the success of the two countries in attracting FDI and indicates the reasons for the differences in inflows of FDI. Further, the mutual investment between these two neighbours has also been analysed. The second part of the chapter examines the global service trade of India and China in a comparative perspective. Further, the mutual trade in services between these two countries has also been examined under this section.

5.1 Foreign Direct Investment
Developing countries need huge amount of financial resources for promoting their economic development. But,

their domestic resources are not enough to meet their developmental requirements. Thus, the options left are: commercial and concessional loans, Official Development Assistance (ODA) and Foreign Direct Investment (FDI). Amongst these, FDI has gained a great importance during the last few years (Kumar and Singh, 2008). FDI is now widely treated as the most important resource for expediting the industrial development of developing countries in view of the fact that it flows as a bundle of capital, skill and sometimes even provide market access (Kumar, 2005a). Typically, FDI brings with it, apart from the investible resources, the technology, management and corporate governance that are superior to what are available in the domestic economy. It brings in newer and better products with gains for the domestic consumers.

FDI supplements the capital needed for investment in a country. It also benefits the ancillary industry and helps in the generation of direct employment in construction, transport, communication and indirect employment in several sectors. There are externalities associated with the FDI. Sometimes, technology may be purchased separately but it does not always come in the same fashion unless technology owners have a stake in the firm. There may be some costs of foreign investment in particular situations such as environmental consequences, loss of employment by wiping out some of the smaller enterprises, servicing of the equity which at times may be a strain on the balance of payments if the FDI does not help in export growth, directly or indirectly. But, it is held that, overall it is mutually beneficial, both for the parent and the host countries (Reddy, 2003).

Since the 1980s, a large number of countries have introduced globalisation and liberalisation to attract FDI. As most countries are adopting liberalisation policies, the multinationals have a greater choice in their locations and it becomes more difficult to attract FDI for the host countries as adequate core FDI policies are simply taken for granted.

Foreign investors assess a country's investment climate not only on the basis of FDI policies alone but also on the basis of overall nature of economic reforms (Bajpai and Dasgupta, 2004).

The driving force behind the exceptional growth performance of India and China has been the increasing openness of their economies, especially to trade and FDI. Interestingly, FDI has been a common pillar for policies of both the countries to increase their openness to the world economy. Consequently, both the countries have become the leading recipient of the FDI among the developing countries. For China, FDI flows have brought about an economic miracle and massive inflows of FDI have won worldwide acclaim. India, by contrast, has attracted a huge amount of FDI inflows, but still lags much behind than that of China. It needs to do a lot to catch up with the Chinese economy (Ghosh, 2005).

5.1.1 Foreign Direct Investment in India: Since 1948, particularly after the Industrial Policy of 1956, India emphasised the need for foreign capital in order to stimulate economic development of the country. Government of India allowed foreign capital in restricted manner in terms of its magnitude and in terms of areas of investment till 1990. Most of the developed countries had not positively responded to India's foreign investment policy, which was essentially against the interests of Multinational Corporations (MNCs) in general. Moreover, it is also held that whatsoever FDI accrued did not give the desired results to the economy (Goud, 2003).

However, the New Industrial Policy (NIP) announced on July 24, 1991 marked a major overhaul in India's policy towards FDI. Firstly, the industrial licensing (or approval) system in all industries was abolished except where it was required for strategic or environmental considerations. Automatic approval for foreign equity participation up to 50/51/74/100 percent was allowed depending on the type of industry. The cases other than those following the listed norms were subject to normal approval procedures. A new package for enterprises in Export Processing Zones (EPZs) and hundred percent Export-Oriented Units (EOUs) was announced, including automatic clearance for proposals fulfilling specified parameters on the capital goods imports, location and value addition, etc. The guidelines have been laid down for this approval process as well. The Foreign Exchange Regulation Act (FERA) of 1973 was amended in 1993 and restrictions placed on foreign companies were lifted by the adoption of Foreign Exchange Management Act (FEMA).

Like India's policies on inward investment, the policies governing Overseas Direct Investment (ODI) have also been liberalised since the early 1990s. The guidelines for Indian Joint Ventures (JV) and Wholly Owned Subsidiaries (WOS) for the automatic approval of outward FDI proposals up to a certain limit have been amended from time to time. It has been expanded progressively from US$ 2 million in 1992 to US$ 100 million in July 2002. In January 2004, the limit of US$ 100 million has also been removed and Indian enterprises are now permitted to invest abroad in JV/WOS up to hundred percent of their net worth on automatic basis. Major investment areas by Indian companies abroad are pharmaceuticals, metal products, auto components, edible oil processing, fertilisers and chemicals, oil exploration, software services, etc.

During the period under study, India's average inflows and outflows were US$ 3092 million and US$ 722 million respectively. But, during the last few years, the levels of both inflows and outflows have risen significantly. Similarly, India's average share in world's and developing countries' overall FDI inflows (i.e. 0.50 percent and 1.60 percent respectively) was higher than that of FDI outflows (i.e. 0.11 percent and 0.99 percent respectively). However, to look at the track-record of success of India's bold initiatives since 1991, FDI was to grow only at snail pace something that resembled China's case in 1980s. In fact, it is not up to the potential that exists in the country.

Cumulative amount of FDI equity inflows stood at ` 6,40,944 crore from August 1991 to March 2011. During the period from August 1991 to November 2004, total FDI approved in various sectors of the economy was ` 2,50,062 crore while the actual inflows were just ` 1,31,385 crore, i.e. 52.54 percent of the total FDI approved. The highest share of FDI inflows has gone to Electrical Equipments (including computer software and electronics) (i.e. 12.25 percent) followed by transportation industry; telecommunications; fuels (power and oil refinery); service sector; chemicals; food-processing industries; metallurgical industries; paper and pulp; and hotel and tourism. However, in all of these sectors, once again, there was a problem of big gap in FDI approved and actual inflows, except Electrical Equipments (including computer software and electronics) where actual inflows were nearly 85 percent of the total FDI approved.

Mauritius proved as a main source of FDI in India during August 1991 to November 2004. Since the mid-nineties, Mauritius emerged as the single largest source of FDI to India due to Avoidance of Double Taxation Agreement between the two countries and other tax concessions offered in that country.

5.1.2 Foreign Direct Investment in China: In the late seventies, China decided to open up its economy for FDI by creating Special Economic Zones (SEZs) in coastal provinces. The advantage of SEZs for foreign investors came from both its geographic proximity to Hong Kong and the lower labour costs compared to neighbouring Asian countries. Since then, China has gradually adopted a number of policies to improve its investment climate and its attractiveness to foreign investors. The competitiveness of domestic enterprises has been significantly upgraded through the decentralisation of economic decision-making and introduction and extension of the market mechanism (Guha and Ray, 2000).

China has continuously been improving its investment climate to attract FDI since 1980s. The government has formulated industrial and regional guidance for FDI. It provides preferential treatment towards FDI. All laws and regulations have been revised after China's WTO accession to meet the requirements of WTO rules and its commitments. These involved eliminating geographic and other restrictions in key sectors and increasing foreign ownership limits in various sectors. Similarly, regional guidance for FDI has also been in work ever since the beginning of China's opening up, which encourages FDI in various economic areas like Special Economic Zones (SEZs), Economic and Technological Development Zones (ETDZs), High-Tech Industries Development Zones (HIDZs), Export Processing Zones (EPZs), etc.

Like FDI inflows, Chinese government has gradually liberalised its policies on FDI outflows, since the later half of the nineties. In 2001, Chinese government proposed the 'going out' strategy and adopted encouraging measures on outflow investments. Afterwards, China has gradually adopted a series of measures to loosen the control and enhanced its guidance on enterprise outflow investment, for example, in deregulating the authority of the governments to examine and approve outflow investments and abolishing profit remittance deposit requirement.

China's average annual inflows and outflows, during the study period, were US$ 40921 million and US$ 3555 million respectively. As is clear, China's FDI inflows rose superbly and that's why its average share in world's and developing countries' FDI inflows was as high as 7.87 percent and 24.66 percent respectively. However, a part of China's success in attracting FDI may be exaggerated because of misreporting and round tripping. The later refers to capital originating in China that is sent to other economies and then returns as disguised FDI to take advantage of tax, tariff and other benefits accorded to foreign but not to domestic investment (Tseng and Zeberegs, 2003). On the other side, Chinese FDI outflows increased rapidly in the mid-nineties and reached to

US$ 2634 million in 1998. But afterwards, it fell suddenly and reached to US$ 916 million in 2000. However, afterwards, it rose significantly to US$ 12261 million in 2005. Similarly, its share in world's and developing countries' outflows also improved sharply, during the recent few years. However, Chinese performance in FDI outflows is nowhere near to its performance in attracting FDI inflows.

During the early reform period of 1979-86, FDI in China was highly concentrated in services, especially in real estate. The ratio of cumulative FDI in services, during this period, was nearly seventy percent. The ratio of FDI in real estate to total actual investment was 33.5 percent in 1984 and rapidly rose to 48.6 percent in 1986. After this, the share of industry gradually increased. During the period 1989 to 1990, the industry share was at the level of 80 percent all the time. However, the acceleration of growth in 1992 attracted a huge share of investment to real estate and its share increased to 39.3 percent in 1993.

By 2000, the share dropped to a low of 8.4 percent (Bhat, et al., 2006). But by 2004, its share increased to 9.81 percent. In the meantime, the industry's share declined to 46 percent in 1993 and then increased to 70.95 percent in 2004. The share of FDI in services is largely influenced by real estate. Initially, the FDI inflows in service sector such as banking, insurance, wholesaling and retailing etc. were severely restricted to specific geographical locations, business, etc. But, after China's accession to WTO in 2001, there is a substantial opening up of these sectors for FDI. Even then the contribution of real estate, in service sector, remained high than in the above mentioned sectors (Table 5.1).

Thus, it is clear that, during 1991-2005, Chinese FDI inflows were mainly concentrated in manufacturing industry. However, within the manufacturing sector, the distribution of FDI also witnessed some systematic changes since 1990s. During the eighties, the FDI was mainly concentrated on traditional   labour-intensive   manufacturing   industries, particularly textiles and garments. After 1992, FDI has gradually shifted to capital and technology-intensive sectors, especially chemicals, machinery, transport equipment, electronics and telecommunication. In the second half of nineties, while FDI in traditional labour-intensive manufacturing industries saw stagnation, the IT industry became a new focus for investment (Bhat, et al., 2006).

Table 5.1: Sector-Wise FDI Inflows into China:
2004 (US$ Million)

S.N	Sectors	FDI Inflows
1	Manufacturing	43017 (70.95)
2	Real estate management	5950 (9.81)
3	Leasing and business service	2824 (4.66)
4	Transport, warehousing, post & telecommunication	1273 (2.10)
5	Production, distribution of electricity	1136 (1.87)
6	Agriculture, forestry, animal husbandry & fisheries	1114 (1.84)
7	Information transmission, computer service and software	916 (1.51)
8	Hotels and restaurants	840 (1.39)
9	Construction	771 (1.27)
10	Wholesaling and Retail	740 (1.22)
11	Others	2049 (3.38)
	Total FDI Inflows	60630 (100.00)

Note: Figures in brackets show percentage share in total FDI inflows
Source: National Bureau of Statistics reproduced in "Investment Climate in China: 2005-06" of USA Consulate, Hong Kong.

Table 5.2 shows the source-wise destination of FDI inflows in China. It is clear that throughout the period 1979-2005, Hong Kong has been the most important source of FDI in China. It contributed 41.70 percent of the cumulative FDI inflows (1979-2005) and 29.75 percent share in total FDI inflows in 2005. During 1979-2005, other important sources of Chinese cumulative FDI inflows include US (8.21 percent); Japan (8.58 percent); Virgin Islands (7.38 percent); Taiwan

(6.71 percent); and Korea (5.00 percent). The dominant position of Hong Kong can be attributed to its geographical proximity.

Table 5.2: Source-Wise Distribution of FDI Inflows into China (US$ Million)

S. N	Countries	FDI Inflows in 2005	Cumulative FDI Inflows (1979-2005)
1	Hong Kong	17949 (29.75)	259523 (41.70)
2	Virgin Islands	9022 (14.96)	45917 (7.38)
3	Japan	6530 (10.82)	53376 (8.58)
4	Korea	5168 (8.57)	31103 (5.00)
5	United States	3061 (5.07)	51090 (8.21)
6	Singapore	2204 (3.65)	27743 (4.46)
7	Taiwan	2152 (3.57)	41756 (6.71)
8	Cayman Islands	1948 (3.23)	8660 (1.39)
9	Germany	1530 (2.54)	11439 (1.84)
10	Western Samoa	1352 (2.24)	5785 (0.93)
11	Others	9409 (15.60)	86034 (13.82)
Total FDI Inflows	60325 (100.00)	622426 (100.00)	

Note: Figures in brackets show percentage share in total FDI inflows
Source: National Bureau of Statistics reproduced in "Investment Climate in China: 2005-06" of USA Consulate, Hong Kong.

Hong Kong is geographically adjacent to Guangdong province where the first and most important SEZ Shenzhan is located. In the 1980s, the economy of Hong Kong developed to a level, which has made it possible to transfer the export-oriented labour intensive manufacturing industry to China, due to cheap labour prices (Bhat, et al., 2006). However, in the recent few years, there has been a continuous decline in the share of Hong Kong, which seems to indicate that the transfer of export oriented labour-intensive manufacturing industry from Hong Kong to China has entered a saturation stage.

5.1.3 A Comparison of FDI Inflows: In 1978, China was not evidently better placed to attract large amounts of FDI than India, which at that time shared a number of characteristics with China. Both countries have relatively closed economies, with low average incomes and a large share of their population dependent on agriculture. Neither China nor India was then receiving significant amounts of FDI. The picture changed dramatically and both emerged as the favoured destinations for the major part of world's FDI inflows.

There are significant differences in their FDI performance. According to World Investment Report (WIR, 2003), total FDI inflows to China grew from US$ 3.5 billion in 1990 to US$ 52.7 billion in 2002; if the round tripping is taken into account, then China's FDI inflows fell to US$ 40 billion and that of India rose from US$ 0.5 billion to US$ 5.5 during the same period. Another important refrain in this debate has been about Overseas Chinese (OCs) contribution. Beginning only from early 1990s while Non-Resident Indians (NRIs) do contribute very little to India's FDI inflows, OCs are known to present a unique example by whopping inflows of FDI into China (Chittle and Kim, 1999). Moreover, it is also believed that in comparison to China's statistics, the calculations on India's FDI appear to be under estimated. Many economists estimate India's real FDI to be at least double of India's current official figures. But hard facts still remain too stark to ignore and gap of India and China in this segment remains far too wide to be bridged by adopting different methods of calculations (Singh, 2005). This is well evident from UNCTAD's Inward FDI Performance Index which placed China on 62nd rank and India on 121st rank in 2005. Inward FDI Performance Index for the period 2005-2007 has placed China on 88th rank and India on 106th rank suggesting a marked improvement in India's tally.

The FDI has contributed to the rapid growth of China's merchandise exports which grew at an annual rate of fifteen percent between 1989 and 2001. In 1989, foreign affiliates accounted for less than nine percent of total Chinese exports;

by 2002 they provided half of the total exports. On the other side, in India, FDI has been much less important in driving India's export growth, except in information technology. FDI accounted for only three percent of India's exports in the early 1990s. And, even today, FDI is estimated to account for less than ten percent of India's manufacturing exports.

Going by the basic economic determinants of inward FDI, China does better than India. China's total and per-capita GDP are higher, making it more attractive for market-seeking FDI. Its higher literacy and education rates suggest that its labour is more skilled, making it more attractive to efficiency-seeking investors. China has also large resource endowments (World Bank, 2003). But, India may have an advantage in technical manpower, particularly in information technology. It also has better English language skills. But, its general situation related to education and health is not that sound. There are some other important determinants that explain why China does better in attracting FDI. Among them, first one is that China has more business-oriented and more FDI-friendly policies than India. Secondly, China's FDI procedures are easier and decisions can be taken quickly than India. Finally, China has more flexible labour laws, a better labour climate, and better entry and exit procedures for business. Even the Federation of Indian Chambers of Commerce and Industry (FICCI, 2003) admitted that China has a better FDI policy framework, market growth, consumer purchasing power, rate of returns, labour laws and tax regime than that of India.

China's accession to WTO in 2001 led to the introduction of more favourable FDI measures. With liberalisation in services sector, China's investment environment improved further. For instance, China allowed hundred percent foreign equity ownership in many industries such as leasing, storage and warehousing, whole sale and retail trade, advertising and multimodal transport services, etc. In India, government is planning to open some more industries for FDI and is in the process of relaxing the foreign equity ownership ceiling.

Following the Chinese model, in April 2000, the Government of India introduced a new SEZ scheme. The scheme allowed for converting some of the existing EPZs into SEZs to provide an internationally competitive and hassle free environment for export production and also to attract export oriented FDI. However, merely switching from EPZs to SEZs, without undertaking the required structural changes–can success of SEZs be guaranteed? EPZs and SEZs are different in size, while former is an industrial estate and later is an industrial township. In China, each SEZ is well over 1000 hectares, the minimum recommended area. In India, EPZs converted into SEZs are not even one third of the recommended size (Bhat, et al., 2006).

The prospects for FDI flows to India and China are promising, assuming that both countries want to accord FDI a key role in their development process. The large market size and potential, the skilled labour force, and low wage cost will remain key attractions (Tendulkar and Bhavani, 2007). China will continue to be a magnet of FDI flows and India's biggest competitor. But, FDI flows to India are set to rise-helped by vibrant domestic enterprise sector and if policy reforms continue and the government is committed to the objective of attracting FDI flows to the country.

5.1.4 Mutual Investment: Both, India and China have been ranked among the top FDI destinations in the world. In 2005, India and China hosted US$ 6676 million and US$ 72406 million FDI respectively. Outward FDI from these two countries has been increasing as well. However, the mutual investment between the two is quite small, which reflects a great potential for future cooperation. In fact, investment cooperation may prove an important field for the development of future bilateral economic relationship between the two. The presence of Indian companies in China has increased especially in sectors such as iron and steel, textiles, chemicals, automobile components and pharmaceuticals. Indian companies in China are also active in services sector like restaurants, entertainment, culture and banking.

According to the Ministry of Finance, Government of India, total Indian investments approved by the Government over 1996-2004 in China amounted to US$ 96.5 million. However, according to the Chinese Ministry of Commerce, India had invested in 101 projects in China by the end of 2003 and the amount of investment was US$ 79.1 million (GOI, 2005). However, Chinese economic reforms have created a small yet fast growing non-state sector that has provided Indian entrepreneurs with new opportunities and confidence to invest inside China. As a result, new business environment, beginning from Ranbaxy Laboratories in 1993, a large number of Indian companies have already established foothold in China (Singh, 2001). Among the Indian companies that have set up joint ventures or subsidiaries include pharmaceutical companies like Ranbaxy Laboratories, Aurobindo Pharmaceuticals, Dr. Reddy's Laboratories, and IT software companies like Aptech, NIIT, Tata Consultancy Services (TCS), Infosys, etc.

In manufacturing, Sundram Fasteners Ltd. for high tensile fasteners, Aditya Birla Group for carbon black production and Mahindra's for tractors have set up bases in China. Other companies present in China are Essel Group, Videocon and Asian Paints. Many others have opened trade/representative offices in China and might deepen their presence in future. A number of Indian companies are also planning investments in various fields in China in the coming years.

China is emerging as an important source of FDI in Asia as both state owned and private Chinese companies are starting to invest abroad. As stated earlier, Chinese FDI outflows rose significantly during the study period and reached US$ 12261 million in 2005. However, this is not true in case of Chinese investment in India, which not only continued to fluctuate heavily from time to time but also continued to suffer from a huge gap between contracted FDI and its actual absorption in projects on the ground. According to the Ministry of

Commerce and Industry, Government of India, during the period from January 1991 to March 2004, India approved Chinese FDI amounting to US$ 231.6 million.

However, the approved investments have been slow in materialising as actual inflow has been only to the order of US$ 0.63 million. According to the statistics of the Chinese Ministry of Commerce, total quantum of Chinese investments in India till 2003 was about US$ 20.6 million covering 97 Chinese proposals for foreign collaborations mainly in the area of telecom, metallurgy, transportation, electrical equipment and financial sectors. Chinese sources suggest that the official figures might under-estimate the actual investment, as some Chinese companies tend to invest before they declare their investment to the government. Obviously, there is need for reconciling the statistics of FDI inflows in India where Indian and Chinese sources diverge substantially. A part of the reason for discrepancy is the fact that some of the Chinese investments in India are routed through Hong Kong. Even after reconciliation of the figures, the existing bilateral investment flows between the two countries hardly represent the potential and synergies that exist between the two large and dynamic economies.

Thus, from above discussion, it is clear that the mutual investment between the two is the most neglected part of their economic interactions. Comparing the performance of their mutual investments with their overall performance in attracting FDI, both the countries have fared better which shows that the pace of their mutual investments still continues to be guided by their politico-strategic equations (Singh, 2001).

Though, in the recent years, the number of Indian companies in China has increased significantly, but it is not true for Chinese companies in India. According to many Chinese companies, it is very hard to find profits in India. Tax barriers everywhere are eroding cost advantages. Corruption is rampant, adding another layer of difficulty. Further, the Chinese goods have a low-quality image that is very hard to shake. Chinese companies, whose success so far has been largely built on their home-court advantage and low costs, are not well prepared to tackle those issues immediately. Winning over Indian consumers is much harder than wooing the Americans or Europeans, who treat televisions or DVD players almost as disposable items. Indians want to make sure that their hard-earned savings go to products that will last long. Branding and marketing are important strategies in India, but these are Chinese companies' weak points.

Though the mutual investment between the two countries is still low, yet there exists a vast potential for further cooperation. Chinese enterprises may find fruitful opportunities for investment in India among other sectors like power generation projects, infrastructure sectors, manufacture of electronic hardware, food processing, etc., for which there is growing market in India. Aiming to develop bilateral economic and trade relations, Chinese government is encouraging their enterprises to invest in India in fields such as crop planting, coal, iron ore, manufacturing of apparatus, meters and office equipment, electric power machines, high-press and low-press switch and dynamotor, mechanical manufacturing of refrigeration equipment and air conditioners, etc., electric equipment such as TV sets, plastic products, pharmacy, trade, software, construction, transportation, tourism, infrastructure, and generation and supply of electricity, etc. Indian enterprises, on the other side, may also find attractive investment opportunities in China in the areas of pharmaceuticals, auto components, light engineering goods, automotives, financial services besides IT software and training (GOI, 2005).

For the promotion of bilateral investment, the two countries have already signed an Agreement on the Avoidance of Double Taxation in July 1994. Moreover, India also signed Bilateral Investment Promotion and Protection Agreement (BIPA) with China on 21st November, 2006, but it is not yet in force. The major features of BIPA are national treatment for foreign investment, MFN treatment for foreign investment, free transfer of returns on investment, recourse to domestic dispute resolution and international arbitration for investor-state and state-state disputes, nationalisation/expropriation only in public interest on a non-discriminatory basis and against compensation etc.

5.2 Service Trade

During the 1950s and 1960s, many researchers suggested that development would be associated with a sharp decline in proportion of GDP generated by the primary sector, counter balanced by a significant increase in industry and a modest increase in the service sector. However, Kongsamut, et al. (2001) conducted a study on one hundred twenty three countries and showed that the sectoral share given up by agriculture, as the economy matures, goes more to the service sector and less to the industry. Furthermore, the modern view also suggests that the share of agriculture declines as the economy grows with an increase in the service sector, and the share of industry first increases and then stabilises or declines. India's growth trajectory fits in this pattern. In the four decades period 1950-1990, agriculture's share in GDP declined by 25 percent while industry and services, both gained equally.

The share of industry has stabilised since 1990 and the entire subsequent decline in agriculture has been picked up by the service sector. According to Kowalski (2008), since the nineties, in both India and China the declining share of agriculture in GDP has been taken primarily by manufacturing in China and by services in India. As a result, in 2005, services accounted for 54 percent of India's GDP as compared to 40 percent in China. This is also reflected in the recent trade developments. India quite clearly has not been able to match China's conquest of the world's goods markets, even though recently more dynamism has been observed in certain segments of the Indian manufacturing sector (Lehman

Brothers, 2007). Yet, for some time now, the developments in India's services sector have generated trade flows that are more comparable to those of China in absolute terms. Evidences are also mounting that the product composition of these two economies' trade is quite different and that, for the moment, the two enormous economies are not competing directly in the world markets (Dimaranan, et al., 2007).

Thus, the importance of service sector in Indian economy has increased more rapidly than that in China's economy. This is evident from Table 5.3, which shows that between 1991 and 2005, the average contribution of services in India's GDP was 48.72 percent while that of in China's GDP it was 37.02 percent. The share of services in India's GDP increased from 44.59 percent in 1991 to 54.06 percent in 2005, while that of in China's GDP it increased from 33.93 percent in 1991 to 39.94 percent in 2005. During the recent few years, the share of services in China's GDP has declined continuously, while it has shown a continuous rise in the case of India.

Table 5.3: Percentage Share of Service Sector in GDP: India and China

Years	India	China
1991	44.59	33.93
1996	45.61	32.95
2001	51.50	40.70
2002	52.71	41.72
2003	52.95	41.46
2004	53.75	40.67
2005	54.06	39.94
Average Share (1991-2005)	48.72	37.02

Source: ADB: Key Indicators, 2007.

Like the share of India's service sector in its GDP, the share of service trade in India's overall trade (i.e. goods and services trade) also increased significantly (Table 5.4). In

1991, the share of India's service trade in its overall trade was 21.72 percent which rose steadily to 30.47 percent in 2005. Similar trends were also observed in case of service exports and imports. On the Chinese side, during the study period, share of service trade in its overall trade declined rapidly. Though it increased from 9.23 percent in 1991 to 13.26 percent in 1996, however, after that, it declined continuously and reached to 10.21 percent in 2005. The similar trends are observed in case of China's service exports and imports. During 1991-2005, the average share of services in India's overall trade (i.e. 24.31 percent) was almost double that of China (i.e. 12.57 percent). Thus, it can be said that India's specialisation in services vis-à-vis China has been actually rising sharply over the time.

Table 5.4: Percentage Share of Service Trade in Total Trade of India and China

Years	India			China		
	Exports	Imports	Total Trade	Exports	Imports	Total Trade
1991	21.40	21.99	21.72	10.59	12.21	9.23
1996	17.67	20.33	19.19	12.00	13.54	13.26
2001	27.90	28.18	28.05	11.13	12.56	12.72
2002	27.58	27.78	27.68	10.88	12.37	12.44
2003	28.19	26.76	27.44	9.64	10.61	10.93
2004	32.94	27.17	29.88	9.52	10.46	10.66
2005	35.33	26.27	30.47	8.89	10.59	10.21
Average Share (1991-2005)	24.57	24.05	24.31	11.36	12.85	12.57

Source: Balance of Payment Statistics Yearbook, IMF, (Various Issues).

Though the relative share of service trade in India's overall trade is higher than that of China's, yet, in absolute terms, China's exports and imports of services have exceeded that of India's and is increasing rapidly. Like China's role in goods trade, its role in service trade has also remained more important than that of India's, although the later is growing rapidly but only in deregulated sectors such as IT and IT-enabled services (Bussiere and Mehl, 2008). During the study period, the service exports of both India and China increased quite rapidly from US$ 4.9 million and US$ 7 million in 1991 to US$ 55.8 million and US$ 74.4 million in 2005 respectively. Thus, China's global exports of services rose more rapidly than that of India. The share of both India and China in world exports of services has also increased considerably, from 0.55 percent and 0.78 percent in 1991, to 2.24 percent and 2.98 percent in 2005 respectively (Table 5.5).

Table 5.5: Service Exports to World: India and China
(US$ Million)

Years	India	China
1991	4.9 (0.55)	7.0 (0.78)
1996	7.2 (0.55)	20.6 (1.56)
2001	17.3 (1.14)	33.3 (2.18)
2002	19.5 (1.19)	39.7 (2.42)
2003	23.9 (1.27)	46.7 (2.48)
2004	38.3 (1.69)	62.4 (2.76)
2005	55.8 (2.24)	74.4 (2.98)

Note: Figures in parentheses show percentage share in world exports of services

Source: Balance of Payment Statistics Yearbook, IMF, (Various Issues).

Like the service exports, service imports of both the countries also showed sharp rise during the study period. Due to the substantial opening up of China's service sector, since the WTO accession in 2001, the imports in this sector rose quite sharply. Imports of both, India and China, from the world were just US$ 5.9 million and US$ 4.1 million in 1991, which rose rapidly to US$ 48 million and US$ 83.8 million in 2005 respectively. Similarly, the share of both the countries in world imports of services also increased sharply. In 1991, India's share in world imports of services was little higher (i.e. 0.63 percent) as compared to China's share (i.e. 0.44 percent). But, after that China's share in world imports of services rose significantly to 3.42 percent in 2005, well above that of India's share, i.e. 1.96 percent (Table 5.6).

Table 5.6: Service Imports from World: India and China
(US$ Million)

Years	India	China
1991	5.9 (0.63)	4.1 (0.44)
1996	11.2 (0.83)	22.6 (1.69)
2001	20.1 (1.29)	39.3 (2.52)
2002	21.0 (1.27)	46.5 (2.80)
2003	24.9 (1.32)	55.3 (2.92)
2004	35.6 (1.59)	72.1 (3.22)
2005	48.0 (1.96)	83.8 (3.42)

Note: Figures in parentheses show percentage share in world imports of services
Source: Balance of Payment Statistics Yearbook, IMF, (Various Issues).

However, since 2001, in the composition of service exports, there have been some drastic changes in case of India and little changes in case of China. The share of transportation and travel services declined continuously and reached to their minimum points in 2005, i.e. 10.24 percent and 13.42 percent respectively. The share of 'other business services' also declined substantially to 9.33 percent in 2003, but after that it revived rapidly to 26.21 percent in 2005. The most spectacular evolution was recorded by computer and information services whose share in India's overall service exports almost doubled between 2000 and 2003 and reached to almost half of India's total service exports. Their share in 2000 was nearly 28 percent which rose significantly to nearly 50 percent in 2003.

However, after that, the share of this category of services fell down suddenly to 39.41 percent in 2005. But, even then, it contributed the biggest share in India's service exports. Notwithstanding, India's performance in other types of services remained at lower level. To a great extent, this reflects the fact that a large share of India's services is still in the informal sector, which is often not open to competition (both in terms of market entry and labour regulation) and, thereby, scarcely productive (Bussiere and Mehl, 2008).

On the other hand, in China a large variety of service exports has experienced strong growth during the last few years. China is more strong in travel services, whose share in 2001 rose to more than half of total service exports of China (i.e. 53.37 percent), however, since then its share declined considerably to 39.37 percent in 2005. On the other side, the share of transportation services increased significantly from 13.90 percent in 2001 to 20.73 percent in 2005. Though the share of 'other business services' declined in the recent few years, yet its contribution in China's total service exports was quite high (i.e. 31.29 percent in 2005). Thus, transportation, travel and 'other business services' accounted for nearly 91 percent of all services export by China in 2005. China is also getting strong in exports of construction and computer and information services and emerging as a potential rival to India.

Like the service exports, in service imports three types of services namely transportation, travel and 'other business services', played a dominant role both in India and China. In case of India, the combined share of these three services was more than 90 percent in 1990 which slightly declined to 84 percent in 2005. During 2001-05, the share of transportation and travel services showed a declining trend while the share of 'other business services' showed a rising trend. During the same period, the share of financial and computer and information services also declined substantially from 8.86 percent and 4.53 percent in 2001 to 2.38 percent and 2.93 percent in 2005 respectively.

While the share of all the 'other services' in India's service imports remained fluctuating. In China, by contrast, the share of transportation services in total service imports declined sharply from 60.86 percent in 1991 to 28.84 percent in 2001; however, it revived somehow to 33.95 percent in 2005. On the

India and China

other side, the share of travel services improved from 12.40 percent in 1991 to 35.42 percent in 2001 and then declined to 25.97 percent in 2005. Similarly, the share of 'other business services' improved from 16.72 percent in 1991 to 31.95 percent in 1996 and then continuously declined to 19.44 percent in 2005. Except the above mentioned three services, the share of insurance and royalties and licensing fees also showed a rising trend during 2001-05. All the other remaining services have a very small and fluctuating share in China's total imports of services.

In order to understand the comparative advantage in the area of service-trade, the Revealed Comparative Advantage (RCA) index has been calculated. The RCA indices of the two countries in three broad service sectors-transportation, travel and 'other services' are reported in Table 5.7. The RCA indices show that India has comparative advantage in 'other services', including the exports of software and IT-enabled services. On the other side, India has comparative disadvantage in transportation and travel services. China, in contrast, has comparative advantage in travel services and comparative disadvantage in transportation and 'other services'. Thus, this analysis reflects that there is a vast potential for trade in services between India and China.

Table 5.7: Index of Revealed Comparative Advantage in Services Export: India and China

Years	India			China		
	Transport	Travel	Other Services	Transport	Travel	Other Services
1991	0.78	1.23	0.96	1.14	1.11	0.85
1996	1.17	1.22	0.75	0.64	1.55	0.80
2001	0.53	0.62	1.45	0.62	1.79	0.68
2002	0.59	0.55	1.45	0.67	1.76	0.70
2003	0.59	0.66	1.36	0.79	1.32	0.91
2004	0.51	0.58	1.45	0.87	1.48	0.79
2005	0.46	0.49	1.52	0.92	1.45	0.79

Source: Calculated from Balance of Payment Statistics Yearbook, IMF (Various Issues).

Thus, it is clear that India's service trade is mainly dependent on deregulated sectors, chiefly IT and IT-enabled services. By contrast, China's trade of services is more broad-based and somehow complementary to its manufacturing exports, thereby reflecting its importance in global trade in goods. Importantly, China is strong in (maritime) transportation and travel services, which is seemingly linked to its increasingly large role as a manufacturing hub in Asia.

5.2.1 Mutual Trade in Services: The share of India and China in world trade in services has been increasing continuously, which not only indicates that India and China have bilateral trade potential in services but also that enhanced bilateral trade would be mutually beneficial. There is a growing trade in services between India and China representing their complementary strengths in the sector. According to GOI (2005), in the year 2003, the total trade in services between the two countries amounted to US$ 75 million, representing the growth rate of 125.5 percent, higher than the overall growth rate of trade in services of either China or India. To strengthen their mutual economic relations the two countries have signed a number of cooperation agreements related to the services sector.

The major areas covered are: education, human resources, auditing, consultancy, tourism, marine transportation, environment and technology. However, at present, the scale of their mutual investments in service sector is not very large. The number of Indian investment projects in China has exceeded that of China in India. India's investment in Chinese services sector is focused on IT training, software solutions and higher education, pharmacy, banking and trade, etc. For example, APTECH and NIIT, two IT training and education enterprises of India, have set up over 250 franchises in China. State Bank of India, Bank of India, Punjab National Bank, Bank of Baroda and ICICI Bank have set up their representative offices in China. The top software producers and exporters of India including Infosys Technologies and

Tata Consultancy Services have also set up their offices and R&D centres in China.

On the other side, Chinese investments in Indian services sector are mainly in trade and IT related R&D. For example, China National Machinery and Equipment Import and Export Corporation, and China Metallurgical Import and Export Corporation have set up their representative offices in India; Huawei Technologies has also established its software R&D centre in India.

Though the mutual investments of the two nations in each other's service sectors are increasing, yet there exists a vast potential for further cooperation in this sector. It is expected that China's demand of services in the fields of software, consultancy, financial services, i.e. auditing and accountancy, legal services, environment, education and health will generate significant business opportunities for international and Indian service providers. India has competitive advantage in these fields and could increase its exports and investments. Similarly, India has recognised the importance of investment in its infrastructure. The demand for increased investment in infrastructure will provide many business and contractual opportunities for international construction and engineering firms. Chinese construction enterprises have experience in acquiring contracts for overseas projects in areas like electric power, telecommunications and highways, and might become strong bidders for Indian projects.

Thus, the comprehensive economic cooperation will increase the international competitiveness of the two countries in services sector. Chinese and Indian economies are complementary not only in the goods sector but also in the services sector. Through cooperation between industries and enterprises, it is possible to benefit from this complementarity. For example, while China has comparative advantage in manufacturing the hardware of computers and electronics and telecommunications equipment, India has comparative advantage in software development and R&D. Combining these advantages will greatly improve the international competitiveness of the two countries in this sector. Therefore, the rapid economic development of the two countries will generate opportunities for the development of bilateral trade in services and this, in turn, will contribute to the development of rapid and sustainable economic growth in the two countries.

6

Growth, Direction and Composition of Merchandise Trade

All countries of the world differ in their wants. They also differ in terms of natural resource endowments, technological possibilities, and a host of other variables. The differences among the countries in production possibilities, income levels, and taste preferences cause differences in the prices of commodities which becomes the basis for trade among the countries. A country gains when its total output increases as a result of division of labour and specialisation, the scope for which is enhanced by trade. International trade mitigates the disadvantages of disproportionate geographical distribution of productive resources (Ohlin, 1952). International trade decidedly increases the exchangeable value of possessions, means of enjoyment and wealth of the countries concerned (Krueger, 1980).

The success of high performing Asian Economies has proved it quite efficiently. These economies have consistently outperformed other developing regions and have become the new growth pole of the world economy. This is also going to be the case with both India and China, which are emerging as economic powerhouses in Asia. With their high growth rates and huge markets, these two Asian giants have attracted the attention of international business managers to take a fresh look at the rapidly emerging opportunities in the two countries (Javalgi, et al., 1997). The importance of India and China in international business is becoming apparent with each passing day. Their bilateral relations are today conspicuous by the fast rise of their mutual trade, which has already crossed US$ 42 billion in 2009-2010. Thus, India-China trade is extremely important as both the countries are close neighbours and enjoy unbounded cultural affinity.

However, in the past, their trade relations were negatively affected by their political hangover. After the Border War in 1962, their trade ties were cut down for fourteen years. This, further, attributed to the continuation of strain in their political relations. And, they followed the restrictive trade practices towards each other. As a result of this syndrome, trade advantages emanating from geographical proximity and ethnic similarity always remained elusive. However, the economic relations between India and China were re-established in the late seventies. In 1984, both the countries offered Most Favoured Nation (MFN) status to each other, which opened up the boundaries of the two for their economic interactions. After that, the high level officials' visits put a positive impact on their trade relations. However, their trade relations got a big momentum since 1990, when India started its liberalisation process.

This chapter deals with the growth, direction, and composition of India-China trade, which experienced various changes during the period from 1990-91 to 2004-05. An attempt has been made to present a complete picture of India's foreign trade with China. The analysis made is comparative in nature in the sense that the trade with the China has been examined and compared vis-à-vis the overall foreign trade of India. The data have been collected mainly from Monthly Statistics for Foreign Trade of India and Statistics of Foreign Trade of India by Countries, Directorate General for Commercial Intelligence and Statistics (DGCI&S); and Direction of Trade Statistics Yearbook, International Monetary Fund (IMF). The chapter is divided into four parts. The first part deals with the growth of the merchandise trade. Second part includes the direction of trade. Third part deals with composition of their merchandise trade. And, fourth part consists some vital ratios and indices of India-China trade.

6.1 Growth of Merchandise Trade
During the period from 1990-91 to 2004-05, the growth of

India's merchandise trade as well as China's merchandise trade was quite tremendous. Growth of their overall trade is analysed as under.

6.1.1 India's Overall Merchandise Trade: For about 40 years (1950-90), foreign trade of India suffered from strict bureaucratic and discretionary controls. During that period, India essentially followed inward-looking development policy with strong emphasis on import substitution, high degree of protection to domestic industry, strong role of public sector, more capital controls, restrictive entry of foreign technology and state involvement in foreign trade particularly in imports. Similarly, the government and the Reserve Bank of India tightly controlled foreign exchange transactions. There were greater controls of foreign exchange market with rigorous rationing of foreign exchange for domestic users. The national capital market was closely guarded and companies were put under strong regulations. In fact, the national capital market remained isolated from the global capital market.

The tariff rates were very high and non-tariff barriers were erected through quantitative restrictions and quota systems. The country's overall approach was that of highly cautious towards foreign trade and some sort of export pessimism was prevailing. It was felt that foreign trade's role at best could be that of a residual and not as the leading sector of growth. Moreover, it was thought that it is very difficult to diversify the export basket in favour of non-traditional goods, and primary products have their own sort of problems emanating from domestic supply, world demand and international prices fluctuations.

However, with the beginning of nineties, the government of India introduced a series of reforms to liberalise and globalise the Indian economy. The process of reforms started with the devaluation of the rupee during 1991. The subsequent years witnessed complete paradigm shift related to economic policy. The country adopted the market-based reforms in all spheres of economic life. The promotion of foreign trade emerged as the main plank of new economic dispensation. The import substitution got replaced with import liberalisation. The tariffs were streamlined and reduced considerably under the auspices of WTO.

The quantitative restrictions were eliminated over the short period. The country geared up all its energy for the enhancement of the level of foreign trade and foreign investment. Reforms in the external sector of India were introduced to integrate the Indian economy with the world economy. India followed a very systematic and comprehensive approach to economic reforms. It is held that India's approach to openness has been cautious, contingent on achieving certain preconditions to ensure an orderly process of liberalisation and ensuring macroeconomic stability (Mathur, 2006). India's foreign trade witnessed very significant changes during the period of economic reforms.

During the study period, both exports and imports increased steadily and their successive yearly values turned out to be higher than that of proceeding years. India's exports increased from ₹ 32,557.63 crore in 1990-91 to ₹ 37,5339.51 crore in 2004-05, while in the same period India's imports increased from ₹ 43,192.86 crore to ₹ 50,1064.59 crore, and thereby the total trade increased from ₹ 75,750.49 crore in 1990-91 to ₹ 87,6404.09 crore in 2004-05. The growth of India's trade remained impressive during all the years except 2001-02 when India's overall merchandise trade showed subdued growth rate, i.e. 4.55 percent. This subdued growth rate, during the year, was primarily on account of sharp decline in India's exports to and imports from major trading partners such as Belgium, USA, UK, France, Germany, Japan, Hong Kong, etc.

The most disturbing feature of India's merchandise trade was the continuous prevalence of unfavourable balance of trade. Though it varied frequently during the study period, but, in 2004-05, it reached its highest spot (i.e. ₹ 1,25,725.08 crore). The major reason for this was the steep rise in the prices of petroleum and fertilizers. Another reason was that Indian exports still consisted of many traditional items, raw materials and semi-manufactured products, with low income and price elasticities. On the other side, Indian imports constituted hi-tech capital intensive machinery and manufactured items. Though, in the recent years, India gave more attention to its manufactured exports, yet it is far behind the target.

6.1.2 China's Overall Merchandise Trade: China's integration with the global economy is reflected in its rapidly growing role in international trade. China's exports and imports have grown faster than world trade for more than 20 years (Rumbaugh, et al., 2004). As China's trade with world has deepened, the composition and geographical pattern of its trade has also shifted. China has also become increasingly important within the Asian regional economy. Vertical specialisation of production within Asia has led to an increasing share of China's imports coming from within the region. This, together with increasing imports for domestic consumption, has made China among the most important export destinations for other Asian countries.

China's international trade has expanded steadily since the opening of the economy in 1979. This process began relatively slowly in the 1980s after the relaxation of pervasive and complex import and export controls, but accelerated in the 1990s with broader trade reforms, including significant tariff reductions. Both exports and imports have increased rapidly, and China's share in world trade has grown steadily.

The value of China's exports, imports and total trade has increased substantially. China's total trade increased quite rapidly from US$ 135795 million in 1991 to US$ 1422555 million in 2005. However, it declined in 1998, by 0.29 percent (i.e. from US$ 325080 million in 1997 to US$ 324129 million in 1998). Like China's total trade, its exports and imports also increased rapidly. Both exports and imports increased more than tenfold (i.e. from US$ 71940 million and US$ 63855 million in 1990 to US$ 762337 million and US$ 660218 million in 2005 respectively).

However, the most peculiar feature of Chinese merchandise trade was its favourable balance of trade situation during 1991-2005, except the year 1993. In 1993, Chinese economy experienced unfavourable balance of trade by US$ 11941 million. But, except this year, China enjoyed favourable balance of trade during the whole study period. In fact, the Chinese government provided the favourable environment for its manufactured exports, which positively influenced its balance of trade situation.

6.1.3 Comparative Position of India and China in World Trade: For a comparative picture of India and China in the world trade, it is important to know that where the two economies stand in the world exports and imports? This has been revealed with the help of Table 6.1 and Table 6.2. As is clear, India's share in world exports did not rise more than 0.95 percent during 1991-2005. Though it increased from 0.51 percent in 1991 to 0.95 percent in 2005, yet it was very low. On the other side, India's share in world imports improved from 0.54 percent in 1991 to 1.26 percent in 2005. As is clear, India's share in world imports remained more than that of its share in world exports. The share of India's total trade in world's total trade also remained very low. Though it increased from 0.53 percent in 1991 to 1.10 percent in 2005, yet it was very low.

On the other side, China's share in world exports and imports increased quite tremendously (Table 6.2). The share of China in world exports increased from 2.06 percent in 1991 to 7.38 percent in 2005. As is clear, it increased throughout the study period, except the year 1996. In 1996, it decreased to 2.86 percent from 2.94 percent in 1995.

On the other side, China's share in the world imports increased from 1.77 percent in 1991 to 6.16 percent in 2005. Similarly, China's share in world's total trade also increased rapidly from 1.92 percent in 1991 to 6.76 percent in 2005.

Thus, as is clear, China's share in world exports and imports remained much higher than that of India's share. This is because China initiated its economic reforms process well before India's liberalisation process and thus outperformed India in world trade. It may also be noted that the share of China in world exports and imports increased quite rapidly since the year 2001. The reason for this was that China joined WTO w.e.f. December 11, 2001 and opened up for international markets.

Table 6.1: India's Percentage Share in World Exports, Imports and Total Trade

Years	Exports	Imports	Total Trade
1991	0.51	0.54	0.53
1992	0.50	0.60	0.55
1993	0.55	0.56	0.55
1994	0.57	0.59	0.58
1995	0.60	0.67	0.64
1996	0.61	0.67	0.64
1997	0.60	0.70	0.65
1998	0.67	0.76	0.72
1999	0.68	0.77	0.73
2000	0.67	0.76	0.72
2001	0.74	0.92	0.83
2002	0.79	0.89	0.84
2003	0.81	0.95	0.89
2004	0.83	1.05	0.94
2005	0.95	1.26	1.10

Source: Direction of Trade Statistics Yearbook, IMF, Washington D.C. (Various Issues).

6.1.4 Value of India-China Merchandise Trade: India and China are the two largest countries in the world in terms of their population. Both together are home to the world's largest pool of skilled human resources and there is a general consensus that these two countries will continue to be the engines of global economic growth in 21st Century (GOI,

2005). It is held that with the rapid growth of India and China, Asia is expected to regain its place as a centre of gravity of the world economy (Kumar, 2005b). The mutual relations between these two countries are today conspicuous by the fast rise of their trade, which reached to US$ 40 billion in 2008 and is hoped to cross US$ 60 billion by 2010 (The Tribune, 2008).

Table 6.2: China's Percentage Share in World Exports, Imports and Total Trade

Years	Exports	Imports	Total Trade
1991	2.06	1.77	1.92
1992	2.29	2.13	2.21
1993	2.47	2.75	2.61
1994	2.84	2.68	2.76
1995	2.94	2.57	2.75
1996	2.86	2.58	2.72
1997	3.32	2.54	2.93
1998	3.40	2.54	2.97
1999	3.44	2.85	3.14
2000	3.90	3.42	3.66
2001	4.34	3.81	4.07
2002	5.07	4.45	4.75
2003	5.85	5.32	5.58
2004	6.51	5.93	6.21
2005	7.38	6.16	6.76

Source: Direction of Trade Statistics Yearbook, IMF, Washington D.C. (Various Issues).

Though the growth of India-China trade was quite phenomenal, yet one major problem remaining from the Indian perspective was its growing trade deficit. During the study period, balance of trade remained in China's favour, except for the years 1991-92 and 1992-93, when India enjoyed favourable balance of trade with China by ₹ 67.35 crore and ₹ 44.22 crore respectively. But, except these two years, India suffered adverse balance of trade all the years and it increased year by year. India's trade deficit with China oscillated between ₹ 31.06 crore in 1990-91 to ₹ 6659.30 crore in 2004-05. The trade deficit with China accounted for 0.29 percent of India's overall trade deficit in 1990-91 and rose to 5.30 percent in 2004-05. However, it fluctuated rapidly during the study period. In the year 1994-95, it reached to 21.80 percent, due to a sharp rise in India's imports from China of commodities like organic chemicals, mineral fuels, silk and edible vegetables.

Thus, for most of the years, India experienced adverse balance of trade with China. The most important reason behind this was that a major part of India's exports to China constitutes raw material or semi-manufactured products such as iron ore and cotton yarn, etc. On the other side, Indian imports from China had a much broader base and were dominated by value added items.

6.1.5 Growth of India-China Trade: In absolute terms, India-China trade grew at a phenomenal rate. However, it did not reveal the true picture of the growth of India-China trade. For this, it becomes necessary to change these nominal prices into real prices (current values deflated by unit value indices), which is done in Table 6.3.

Table 6.3: Real Growth Rate of India's Exports and Imports: China and Overall (At Constant Prices of 1993-94)

Years	Overall		China	
	Exports	Imports	Exports	Imports
1990-91 to 1994-95	10.78	15.59	103.33	164.40
1995-96 to 1999-00	3.44	8.99	6.75	15.67
2000-01 to 2004-05	12.30	12.17	56.52	34.19
1990-91 to 2004-05	11.32	11.38	37.41	40.66

Note: Figures show the annual average trend growth rates.
Source: Calculated from Monthly Statistics of Foreign Trade of India, DGCI&S; Kolkata, (Various Issues).

During 1990-91 to 2004-05, India's overall exports and imports, at real prices, grew almost at the same pace, i.e. 11.32 percent and 11.38 percent respectively. In the sub-periods, from 1990-91 to 1994-95 and from 1995-96 to 1999-00, growth rate of India's overall imports (i.e. 15.59 percent and 8.99 percent respectively) was higher than that of overall exports (i.e. 10.78 percent and 3.44 percent respectively). However, during the sub-period 2000-01 to 2004-05, the growth rate of India's overall exports was marginally higher than that of its overall imports, i.e. 12.30 percent and 12.17 percent respectively.

In the case of China, during 1990-91 to 2004-05, growth rate of imports was higher than that of exports, i.e. 40.66 percent and 37.41 percent respectively. As is clear, the growth rates of exports and imports were much higher in case of India's trade with China than that of India's overall exports and imports. The similar trend could also be seen in the different sub-periods. During the first sub-period (from 1990-91 to 1994-95), Indian exports to and imports from China grew at a fabulous rate, i.e. 103.33 percent and 164.40 percent respectively. There were mainly two reasons behind this phenomenal growth rate. First, India initiated its liberalisation process during this phase. Secondly, the political relations between these two nations turned better which positively affected their trade relations.

However, during the second sub-period, i.e. from 1995-96 to 1999-00, their political relations again became snappy, due to the nuclear considerations, which negatively affected the growth of their trade. Thus, during this period, the growth rate of India's exports to and imports from China fell down substantially to 6.75 percent and 15.67 percent respectively. In third sub-period, i.e. from 2000-01 to 2004-05, the trade relations between the two countries improved once again. However, one thing worth nothing here that in this sub-period the growth of India's exports to China was much higher than that of its imports from China, i.e. 56.52 percent and 34.19 percent respectively. The main reason behind this was that during this sub-period, China joined WTO and opened up its market very wide for the outside world. India also utilised this opportunity.

6.1.6 Role of India and China in Each Other's Global Trade: There is no doubt, the presence of India and China in each other's international trade is growing day by day. Therefore, it is very important to know that where the two economies stand in each others' trade? The relative importance of India as China's trade partner and that of China as India's trade partner is depicted in Table 6.4 and Table 6.5 respectively. It is clear from the Table 6.4 that India is not a major trading partner of China.

Table 6.4: India's Percentage Share in China's Exports, Imports and Total Trade

Years	Exports	Imports	Total Trade
1991	0.20	0.19	0.19
1992	0.18	0.22	0.20
1993	0.28	0.40	0.34
1994	0.47	0.28	0.38
1995	0.51	0.30	0.41
1996	0.46	0.52	0.49
1997	0.51	0.63	0.56
1998	0.55	0.65	0.59
1999	0.60	0.50	0.55
2000	0.63	0.60	0.61
2001	0.71	0.70	0.71
2002	0.82	0.77	0.80
2003	0.76	1.03	0.89
2004	1.00	1.37	1.18
2005	1.17	1.48	1.32

Source: Direction of Trade Statistics Yearbook, IMF, Washington D.C. (Various Issues).

During the study period, India's share in China's total trade increased from 0.19 percent in 1991 to 1.32 percent in 2005, except the year 1999, when it dropped to 0.55 percent from 0.59 percent of the previous year. Similarly, India's share in China's exports increased from 0.20 percent in 1991 to 1.17

percent in 2005, while that of its imports increased from 0.19 percent in 1991 to 1.48 percent in 2005. As is clear, India's share in China's exports did not cross even one percent mark up to 2003, while India's share in China's imports crossed one percent mark only after 2002.

Table 6.5 depicts China's position in India's international trade. China's share in India's total trade increased from 0.13 percent in 1990-91 to 6.52 percent in 2004-05. However, it dropped twice in 1995-96 and 1998-99 to 1.67 percent and 2.02 percent from 1.85 percent and 2.40 percent of the previous years respectively. China's share in India's exports and imports also increased from 0.10 percent and 0.15 percent in 1990-91 to 6.72 percent and 6.36 percent in 2004-05 respectively.

Table 6.5: China's Percentage Share in India's Exports, Imports and Total Trade

Years	Exports	Imports	Total Trade
1990-91	0.10	0.15	0.13
1991-92	0.27	0.11	0.19
1992-93	0.76	0.58	0.66
1993-94	1.25	1.30	1.28
1994-95	0.97	2.66	1.85
1995-96	1.05	2.22	1.67
1996-97	1.84	1.93	1.89
1997-98	2.06	2.68	2.40
1998-99	1.29	2.59	2.02
1999-00	1.46	2.58	2.10
2000-01	1.87	2.97	2.45
2001-02	2.17	3.96	3.14
2002-03	3.75	4.55	4.18
2003-04	4.63	5.19	4.94
2004-05	6.72	6.36	6.52

Source: Monthly Statistics of Foreign Trade of India, DGCI&S; Kolkata, (Various Issues).

Thus, as is clear from both the tables, the share of India

and China in each others' international trade increased continuously. But, it is to be noted that there is some sort of disproportionate dependence between the two so far the relative trade shares are concerned. For example, India accounted for only 1.32 percent of China's foreign trade in 2005 and in sharp contrast China accounted for 6.52 percent of India's foreign trade during 2004-05. However, one interesting point worth nothing here is that after the China's entry into WTO, in 2001, the percentage share of both the countries in each other's exports and imports increased considerably, than in the previous years. This shows that WTO had offered newer opportunities to India and China for enhancing their trade relations.

6.1.7 Border Trade between India and China: The boundary question remains one of the most decisive factors in defining the nature of India-China mutual trade. Lack of the clearly defined boundaries has been a main challenge to their cross border trade and commerce. As regards India's border trade with China, it was pursuant of their Memorandum of Understanding (MoU) on Resumption of Border Trade signed on 13 December, 1991. India and China had opened their first two border trade routes through the mountain passes of Lepulekh (in Uttrakhand) and Shipki La (in Himachal Pradesh) passes during 1992-93. After the opening up of these two border routes, it took more than a decade to open third border route, i.e. Nathu La Pass, which adjoins the border trade markets of Changgu (in India's Sikkim) and Renqinggang (China-Tibet). This border route was reopened on 6 July 2006, forty four years after a frontier War.

Nathu La Pass is part of the historic Silk Road, a network of trails that connected ancient India with China, Western Asia and Europe. The pass used to be an important trade passage between India and China. It is held that the reopening of the pass will give a major boost to bilateral trade between the world's two most populous countries. Moreover, the potential of India-China border trade will be enhanced and will pioneer a new channel for the upcoming India-China trade relations. It is believed that with the passing of time, the Nathu La border trade markets will grow and boost India-China friendship bond, thereby increasing cooperation and common prosperity (Economic Times, 2006).

Nathu La followed the same procedures that were evolved in case of their earlier two border trade routes through Lipulekh and Shipki La. Also, the same 29 items of trade, that were permitted for duty free exchange across their earlier border trade routes, were included in the list of items for trade through Nathu La. Amongst those, the items that were exported from India generally includes agricultural inputs, tobacco, gur, mishri, fafer (a local wheat variety), blankets, tea, coffee, clothes, watches, shoes, canned food, rice, dry fruit, match-boxes and other such consumer items. Whereas, the items of import from China include goat skin, sheep skin, sheep wool, raw silk, yak tail, butter, borax, China clay, raw silk, goat wool or pashmina, other clothes and so on (Singh, 2005).

Since the inception of the new Century, India-China economic and political relations have improved significantly. This improvement in their mutual relations will further improve the position of India-China border trade. However, the fact worth nothing is that the earlier two routes had been opened primarily for enabling pilgrims to reach Kailash and Mansarovar and these routes had little significance so far as trade and commerce is concerned. As a result, the infrastructural developments on these border trade routes remain negligible.

However, Nathu La is expected to completely transform the future profile of their border trade and strengthen its role in building mutual confidence between India and China. In fact, in the recent years, two sides have begun to visualise their border trade as a possible tool for resolving their boundary question. Any assessment of India and China exploiting their earlier two border routes leaves so much to be desired, even at the level of logistics that remain within the ambit of local administration. This must provide caution to the designing of respective national expectations from the opening up of Nathu La as their third border trade route. Both the sides must emphasise on the unique role of border trade as the strongest and most agreeable instrument for socio-economic development that will go a long way in building mutual confidence for resolving the boundary question.

6.2 Direction of Trade: India and China

The direction of foreign trade refers to the spatial distribution of traded goods of a country. A country's indigenous goods meant for exports flow to different parts of the world and, similarly, foreign goods are imported from different countries. The countries to which the exports are made may or may not be identical with countries from which imports are obtained. Hence, it may happen that exports of a country flow towards a particular direction altogether. Even among exportables, it may happen that a country's markets for primary goods are different from that of the manufactured ones. Again, a developing country's developmental imports may come from countries which are more developed and other imports may flow from other countries, both developed and developing.

6.2.1 Direction of India's Trade: In the pre-Independence period, the direction of India's foreign trade was determined not according to comparative cost advantages but by the colonial relations between India and Britain. A major part of India's foreign trade was either directly with Britain or its colonies or allies. This pattern continued for some years even after Independence as well, since India had not till then explored the possibilities of developing trade relations with other countries of the world. However, as political and diplomatic contacts developed with other countries, economic relations also made headway. New vistas for trade relations with other countries opened up. The situation has changed very much since and now after sixty years of Independence, the trade relations exhibit a marked change.

During 1991-2005, the average annual percentage share of industrial countries in India's exports and imports remained dominating, i.e. 53.57 percent and 44.92 percent respectively. However, their share during different sub-periods, declined continuously for both exports and imports due to the sharp decline in India's exports to and imports from major industrial countries such as USA, Japan, Belgium, UK and Germany. On the other side, the share of developing countries in India's exports and imports remained quite impressive. Their share in India's exports increased from 38.80 percent during the first sub-period to 51.62 percent during the last sub-period. The rise in share was mainly because of the increase in India's exports to Asia, Middle East and African countries. On the other side, the share of developing countries in India's imports improved from 44.18 percent during first sub-period to 48.58 percent during the second sub-period, however, it declined sharply during the last sub-period to 36.82 percent because of the declining share of Middle East and African countries.

However, the share of Asian countries in Indian imports remained impressive and increased continuously. One interesting thing worth nothing here is that in the last sub-period, India's imports from 'Other Countries' increased remarkably and their share rose from 3.50 percent during second sub-period to 27.22 percent during the last sub-period. It happened mainly because of India's heavy imports (i.e. military trade, heavy transactions in free zones and import of aircraft or ships etc.) under the category called 'other countries'. Thus, during the study period, India's dependency on industrial countries declined considerably, while its trade relations with developing countries (especially Asian countries like China and UAE) strengthened substantially.

The country-wise direction of India's trade shows that during the period 1991-2005, there have been a lot of changes in the list of India's major trading partners. India's dependence on some markets declined substantially while some other new markets came up.

The total share of selected ten countries in Indian exports declined continuously from 67.32 percent in 1990-91 to 53.25 percent in 2004-05. During the study period, USA remained number one destination for Indian exports. Its share rose from 14.73 percent in 1990-91 to 22.80 percent in 1999-00. However, afterwards it declined sharply to 16.48 percent in 2004-05. The share of China and UAE increased quite rapidly, i.e. respectively from 0.10 percent and 2.42 percent in 1990-91 to 6.72 percent and 8.80 percent in 2004-05. These two countries emerged as major destinations for Indian exports. On the other hand, the share of many other countries like Russia, Japan, Germany and UK in Indian exports showed a declining trend. The share of the remaining countries was very small or negligible.

The total share of selected countries in Indian imports declined considerably from 56.36 percent in 1990-91 to 39.49 percent in 2004-05. Like Indian exports, here once again USA dominated in Indian imports. However, its share in Indian imports declined substantially from 12.14 percent in 1990-91 to 6.28 percent in 2004-05. On the other side, China emerged as the major source for Indian imports and, in 2004-05, it became number one source for Indian imports. China's percentage share in Indian imports rose significantly from 0.15 percent in 1990-91 to 6.36 percent in 2004-05. The share of Switzerland in Indian imports also improved rapidly from 1.11 percent in 1990-91 to 5.33 percent in 2004-05. While all other remaining countries showed a declining trend in their share in Indian imports. Thus, it is clear from the above that during 1990 to 2005, the supremacy of USA in Indian trade declined considerably, while trade relations with developing countries, especially China, deepened substantially.

6.2.2 Direction of China's Trade: China's transformation into a dynamic private sector based economy and its integration into the global economy have been among the most dramatic economic developments of recent decades. Indeed, China's growth performance over the last two decades has been spectacular, with GDP growth averaging almost eight percent or more. The expansion of its international trade has been a noteworthy aspect of China's rising prominence in the world economy. China's exports and imports have grown at an average rate of fifteen percent each year since 1979, compared with a seven percent annual expansion of world trade over the same period.

Like India, during 1991-2005, the average annual percentage share of industrial countries in Chinese exports and imports remained dominant, i.e. 51.41 percent and 48.58 percent respectively. The share of industrial countries in Chinese exports improved from 44.94 percent during first sub-period to 54.48 percent during the last sub-period, while their share in Chinese imports declined continuously from 51.90 percent during first sub-period to 43.14 percent during the last sub-period. The share of developing countries in Chinese exports declined considerably from 54.18 percent during first sub-period to 45.26 percent during the last sub-period. On the other side, share of developing countries in Chinese imports increased continuously from 46.40 percent during first sub-period to 50.74 percent during the last sub-period. Among the developing countries, the share of Asian countries declined sharply from 45.86 percent during first sub-period to 33.24 percent during the last sub-period. While their share in Chinese imports remained almost consistent around 37 percent during all the sub-periods. The share of all other regions in China's exports and imports remained small and negligible.

During 1991-2005, country-wise direction of Chinese exports and imports showed some major changes. The total share of these ten countries in Chinese exports fluctuated rapidly. In 1991, the total share of the selected countries in China's exports was 79.33 percent which rose to 81.11 percent in the very next year. However, it declined to 71.90 percent in 2002 and once again shot up to 94.72 percent in 2003. After that, it again went down to 68.65 percent in 2005. Thus, the total share of selected countries in Chinese exports fluctuated very sharply.

During the study period, Chinese exports were mainly dominated by three countries, namely USA, Japan and Hong Kong. The share of USA in Chinese exports increased continuously from 8.62 percent in 1991 to 28.44 percent 2003; however, it declined to 21.43 percent in 2005. The share of Japan in Chinese exports fluctuated sharply and oscillated between 11.03 percent and 20.43 percent. The share of Hong Kong went down drastically from 44.67 percent in 1991 to 16.33 percent in 2005. The share of all the other countries in Chinese exports remained very small. India's share in Chinese exports improved during the study period (i.e. from 0.20 percent in 1991 to 1.17 percent in 2005), but still it was at the lower side.

The total share fluctuated strongly, however in general it showed a declining trend. It declined from 71.90 percent in 1991 to 60.16 percent in 2005. The share of USA and Hong Kong declined very quickly, i.e. from 12.54 percent and 27.47 percent in 1991 to 7.42 percent and 1.85 percent in 2005 respectively. On the other side, the share of Korea and Taiwan in Chinese imports showed substantial improvement, i.e. from 1.67 percent and 5.70 percent in 1991 to 11.64 percent and 11.31 percent in 2005. While the share of Japan in Chinese imports fluctuated rapidly and oscillated between 15.22 percent and 22.75 percent. The share of other economies remained very small or negligible. India's share in Chinese exports remained very small. Though it improved from 0.19 percent in 1991 to 1.48 percent in 2005, yet it was very small.

Thus, it is clear that China's international trade was mainly dominated by USA, Japan, Hong Kong, Korea and Taiwan. The Indian presence in Chinese international trade remained unimposing. India's share in Chinese exports and imports remained low. India is actually in the overall sense, particularly from Chinese context, as yet may be described as a small trading partner of China.

6.3 Composition of India-China Merchandise Trade

The usefulness of foreign trade depends upon the structure and pattern of trade that is determined by the composition of the commodities exported and imported by a country. The colonial pattern of trade that consisted of exports of raw material and other primary commodities and imports of manufactured consumer goods resulted in unequal level of specialisation (Brar, 1996). However, this pattern and structure of India's foreign trade changed considerably since Independence. Many traditional items of India's exports and imports have been replaced by new products, which have become responsive to ever-changing international situation. The composition of India-China trade also exhibited some changes over the period of time, which is analysed as follows.

6.3.1 Composition of India's Exports to China: The total value of selected fifteen export commodities increased tremendously from ₹ 27.11 crore in 1990-91 to ₹ 23618.51 crore in 2004-05. However, it dropped twice in 1994-95 and 1998-99. Some commodities like ores, slag and ash; iron and steel; organic chemicals; and plastic played a crucial role in India's exports to China. The value of these commodities regularly increased during the study period. The value of one commodity namely ores, slag and ash increased from ₹ 6.11 crore in 1990-91 to ₹ 13155.09 crore in 2004-05. Some commodities such as residues and waste from the food industries; ores, slag and ash; iron and steel; cotton; organic chemicals; salt, sulphur, earths and stone; inorganic chemicals; pharmaceutical products; nuclear reactors and boilers, etc., showed a regular presence throughout the study period, while some other commodities namely fish and crustaceans; animals or vegetable fats and oils; plastic; prepared feathers and down; optical, photographic cinematographic measuring; and copper figured and got pace in the middle of the nineties.

In 2004-05, more than half of India's total exports to

China were constituted by ores, slag and ash. Thus, this commodity remained the dominating commodity in India's exports to China. The share of some other commodities such as iron and steel; cotton; organic chemicals; and plastic improved sharply. However, some other commodities such as residues and waste from food industries; inorganic chemicals; and pharmaceutical products lost their relative importance.

Here, once again ores, slag and ash dominated total exports by India to China standing at 78.31 percent during 2004-05. In case of the export of some other commodities such as iron and steel; organic chemicals; salt, sulphur, earths and stone; animal or vegetable fats and oils; inorganic chemicals; plastic; and prepared feathers and down, China's share improved with rapid pace. However, in case of commodities such as residues and waste from the food industries; iron and steel; animal or vegetable fats and oils; and copper, China's share varied from year to year.

Thus, the above discussion shows that Indian exports to China were mainly dominated by ores, slag and ash and it is not wrong to say that Indian exports to China were single commodity driven.

6.3.2 Composition of India's Imports from China: The total value of selected fifteen imports was just ₹ 49.56 crore in 1990-91, which went up to ₹ 26,061.57 crore in 2004-05. It dropped only once in the year 1991-92 to ₹ 40.83 crore from ₹ 49.56 crore of the previous year. As is clear, Indian import of electrical machinery and equipment increased amazingly. Due to the increasing popularity of Chinese electrical machinery and equipment, its imports from China increased from ₹ 1.04 crore in 1990-91 to ₹ 7987.20 crore in 2004-05. The value of four other import commodities namely organic chemicals; mineral fuels and oils; silk; and nuclear reactors and boilers, also increased quickly. Some other commodities namely inorganic chemicals; articles of iron and steel; natural or cultured pearls, precious or semi-precious stones; optical photographic cinematographic measuring; manmade filaments;

and impregnated, coated, covered or laminated textile fabrics also increased rapidly.

The total share of selected commodities, in India's overall imports from China, increased from 77.91 percent in 1990-91 to 81.72 percent in 2004-05. Their share remained above 75 percent during the study period, except for the year 1994-95, when it went down to 59.42 percent. The share of organic chemicals; electrical machinery and equipment; and nuclear reactors, boilers, machinery and mechanical appliances, in India's overall imports from China, increased rapidly during the course of time. However, some commodities such as mineral fuels and oils; silk; salt, sulphur, earths and stone; and edible vegetables, lost their relevance during the study period. Besides, the above mentioned commodities, the share of all the other commodities remained very low. It should be noted here that, like India's exports to China, India's imports from China were not single commodity driven. There was no commodity that constituted more than 30 percent share in India's total imports from China.

India's dependence on China for the import of silk increased tremendously. China's share in Indian imports of some other commodities, i.e. organic chemicals; electrical machinery and equipments; nuclear reactors, boilers, machinery and mechanical appliances; inorganic chemicals; articles of iron and steel; salt, sulphur earths and stones; man-made filaments; and impregnated, coated, covered or laminated textile fabrics, also increased sharply.

6.3.3 How Diversified is the India-China Trade?: It is very important to know the extent of diversification of India's trade with China. It has been attempted through the number of commodities at different level of commodity classifications for both exports and imports. The number of items, for both exports and imports, in different commodity classifications, increased very rapidly during the study period. In 1990-91, India's export to China at 2-digit level were 34; at 4-digit level 62; at 6-digit level 72; and at 8-digit level 84, which rose to 96,

860, 2337 and 3923 respectively, in 2004-05. Similarly, the number of various items in India's imports from China, in 1990-91, at 2-digit level were 44; at 4-digit level 154; at 6-digit level 238; and at 8-digit level 270, which improved to 95, 1084, 3955 and 7173 respectively, in 2004-05.

The major change has been seen at the level of 8-digit level. The number of commodities at 8-digit level, for both exports and imports, increased at a rapid pace, except for the year 2004-05, when the number of commodities, for both exports and imports, fell suddenly. The export commodities fell due to the decline in exports of organic chemicals; cotton; pharmaceutical products; electrical machinery and equipments; fish and crustaceans, etc. On the other hand, import commodities fell due to the decline in imports of electrical machinery and equipments; nuclear reactors, boilers, machinery and mechanical appliances; inorganic chemicals; articles of iron and steel, etc.

One interesting point worth nothing here is that at every digit level and in each year, the number of India's imports from China was more than that of India's export to China, except for the year 2004-05, when at 2-digit level, the number of India's exports to China was more than that of India's imports from China. This clearly shows that India's exports to China were comparatively less diversified than Chinese exports to India.

6.3.4 India's Exports of Ores, Slag and Ash to China: As is clear, India's exports to China, during the study period, were dominated by the single commodity group namely ores, slag and ash. The share of this commodity group in India's total exports to China increased dramatically from 18.78 percent in 1990-91 to 52.13 percent in 2004-05. Thus, in 2004-05 more than a half of Indian exports to China were constituted by ores, slag and Ash. It would be interesting to see the various aspects of this commodity group to China. It is done at the most disaggregate level (i.e. 6-digit HS classification).

Sub-commodity group namely iron ores and concentrates (non-agglomerated) played a drastic role in the enhancement of India's overall exports of ores, slag and ash to China. In 1990-91, its value was mere ₹ 2.10 crore which rose quite surprisingly to ₹ 10,707.04 crore in 2004-05. Consequently, its share increased from 34.38 percent in 1990-91 to 81.39 percent in 2004-05.

Two more commodities namely iron ore and concentrate (agglomerated); and chromium ore and concentrates played important role in India's overall exports of ores, slag and ash to China. The share of iron ores and concentrates (agglomerated) remained very fluctuating and oscillated between 5.05 percent and 28.35 percent. On the other side, the chromium ores and concentrates lost their relevance in India's overall exports of ores, slag and ash to China. Its share declined viciously from 65.62 percent in 1990-91 to 5.40 percent in 2004-05. The remaining commodities played a very small or negligible role in India's exports of ores, slag and ash to China.

Since Indian exports to China are found to be heavily dependent on ores, slag and ash, it is important to examine the unit values realised for this commodity from China. For this purpose, the unit values realised by India from both China and Rest of the World (RoW) have been compared. Here, RoW refers to the whole world excluding China. Some trends are discernible in some cases. For instance, the unit values for exports of iron ore and concentrates (non-agglomerated) were higher in case of China during most of the years.

In case of other commodities, the unit values showed mixed scenario. The noticeable point is that in this commodity group as a whole, the average unit values realised from China were higher than the rest of the markets. In 2004-05, average unit value for ores, slag and ash from China (i.e. ₹ 0.021 lakh per ton) was nearly double than that of from RoW (i.e. ₹ 0.011 lakh per ton). Moreover, for the largest commodity sub-group, i.e. iron ore and concentrates (non-agglomerated), China had provided better unit values.

6.4 India-China Trade: Some Vital Ratios and Indices

The various aspects of India-China mutual trade have been examined by using the various ratios and indices. These ratios and indices help in understanding and explaining the trade in more elaborated and different perspectives.

6.4.1 Export-Import Ratio: The imports by a country must be managed in such a way that the overall import spending is within the safe limits set by the export earnings in order to avoid undesirable external borrowings (Brar, 1996). But, in the case of India, mismatch between exports and imports has always been there. Table 6.6 presents the Triennium Averages (TAs) of ratios of India's exports to her imports for China and the world.

Table 6.6: Ratio of India's Exports to her Imports:
China v/s Overall (Triennium Averages)

Triennium Averages	China	Overall
1990-91 to 1992-93	131.42	84.05
1993-94 to 1995-96	55.58	91.36
1996-97 to 1998-99	61.58	82.58
1999-00 to 2001-02	48.04	82.48
2002-03 to 2004-05	74.26	80.82
Average Ratio (1990-91 to 2004-05)	74.18	84.26

Note: The values are in percentages.
Source: Calculated from Monthly Statistics of Foreign Trade of India, DGCI&S; Kolkata, (Various Issues)

As is clear, during the study period, India's export-import ratio for China fluctuated rapidly than that of her overall export-import ratio. In case of China, the export-import ratio declined from 131.42 percent during TA (1990-91 to 1992-93) to 74.26 percent during TA (2002-03 to 2004-05). Similarly, India's overall export-import ratio declined from 84.05 percent during TA (1990-91 to 1992-93) to 80.82 percent during TA

(2002-03 to 2004-05). It is noteworthy that except TA (1990-91 to 1992-93), India's export-import ratio during all the TAs is higher for world than that of China. During the period 1990-91 to 2004-05, on an average, India was in position to meet her 84.26 percent bill of overall imports through the earning from overall exports, while in case of China its exports were able to pay only 74.18 percent bill of imports.

For a comparative analysis between India and China, it is important to know that up to what extent the Chinese exports are able to bear the cost of its imports. Table 6.7 presents the Triennium Averages (TAs) of ratios of China's exports to her imports for India and for world. China's export-import ratio for India increased rapidly from 89.53 percent during TA (1991 to 1993) to 155.83 percent during TA (1994 to 1996), but after that it declined sharply to 82.41 percent during TA (2003-2005). Similarly, China's overall export-import ratio improved significantly from 101.86 percent during TA (1991 to 1993) to 125.73 percent during TA (1997-1999), and then declined to 109.11 percent during last TA (2003-2005).

Table 6.7: Ratio of China's Exports to her Imports: India v/s Overall (Triennium Averages)

Triennium Averages	India	Overall
1991 to 1993	89.53	101.86
1994 to 1996	155.83	108.65
1997 to 1999	119.05	125.73
2000 to 2002	115.04	110.14
2003 to 2005	82.41	109.11
Average Ratio (1991-2005)	112.37	111.10

Note: The values are in percentages.
Source: Calculated from Monthly Statistics of Foreign Trade of India, DGCI&S; Kolkata, (Various Issues).

During 1991-2005, on an average, China was in position to meet the extent of her 111.10 percent bill of overall imports though the earnings from overall exports, while in case of

India, its exports were able to pay 112.37 percent bill of imports.

6.4.2 Intensity and Integrity Indices: During the last few years, India's trade relations with China have been strengthened deeply. Therefore, it is interesting to view the growing orientation and integration between the two countries in terms of their mutual trade. This is done with the help of intensity indices (Kojima, 1964) and integrity indices (Wei, 2004) of India's export-trade and import-trade with China. The Export-Intensity Index (x_{ij}), Import-Intensity Index (m_{ij}) and Trade Integrity Index (I_{ij}) are defined as follows:

$$\text{Export-Intensity Index } (x_{ij}) = \frac{X_{ij} / X_i}{M_j / (M_w - M_i)} \times 100$$

$$\text{Import-Intensity Index } (m_{ij}) = \frac{M_{ij} / M_i}{X_j / (X_w - X_i)} \times 100$$

$$\text{Trade Integrity Index } (I_{ij}) = \frac{X_{ij} / X_i}{M_j / M_w}$$

Where

x_{ij} = Export intensity index of country i with country j
X_{ij} = Exports of country i to trading partner j
X_i = Total exports of country i
M_j = Total imports of country j
M_w = Total world imports
M_i = Total imports of country i
m_{ij} = Import intensity index of country i with country j
M_{ij} = Imports of country i to trading partner j
X_j = Total exports of country j
X_w = Total world exports
I_{ij} = Trade integrity index of country i with country j

An Export Intensity Index value of more (or less) than 100 indicates that 'i[th]' country is exporting more (or less) to 'j[th]' country than might be expected from that country's share in total world trade. The same argument holds true in the case of imports also. On the other side, Trade Integrity Index varies between 0 and 1. Increase in the value of Trade Integrity Index reflects that the 'i[th]' country is integrating more with 'j[th]' country through trade and vice-versa.

Table 6.8 presents India's Export-Intensity Index, Import-Intensity Index and Trade Integrity Index with China. As is clear from the table that in 1991 the values of Export-Intensity Index and Import-Intensity Index were very low (i.e. 15.05 percent and 5.19 percent respectively). But, after that these values rose tremendously and reached new heights in 2005 (i.e. 105.52 percent and 97.99 percent respectively). It is also important to mention that since China's accession to the WTO in 2001, the rise in values of these indices was sharper. However, almost all the years, these values remained below hundred which reflects insignificance of India-China trade. In other words, during the study period, India's trade with China remained below the desired level.

Table 6.8: India's Export Intensity Index, Import Intensity Index and Trade Integrity Index with China

Years	Export Intensity Index (Percent))	Import Intensity Index (Percent)	Trade Integrity Index (I_{ij})
1991	15.05	5.19	0.37
1992	23.75	17.56	0.31
1993	51.01	49.19	0.49
1994	36.03	85.30	0.80
1995	35.78	79.58	0.77
1996	64.53	67.75	0.69
1997	75.77	81.56	0.73
1998	91.99	82.52	0.72
1999	46.17	79.48	0.77
2000	51.65	73.28	0.82
2001	88.81	81.07	0.77
2002	75.88	86.51	0.92
2003	82.59	85.71	0.80
2004	92.48	92.69	0.95
2005	105.52	97.99	0.93

Source: Calculated from Direction of Trade Statistics Yearbook, IMF, Washington D.C. (Various Issues).

The Trade Integrity Index reflects almost the same results as shown by intensity indices. In 1991, the value of Trade Integrity Index was very lower than unity (i.e. 0.37) but after that it rose tremendously and reached near to unity in 2005 (i.e. 0.93). However, like the intensity indices, during the study period, the integrity indices also remained below the desired level. In other words, values of the index remained below unity. Thus, it can be concluded that though during recent few years the value of intensity indices and integrity indices increased sharply but still are below the desired level.

6.4.3 Export Concentration Index or Hirschman Concentration Index: The Export Concentration Index or Hirschman Concentration Index (HCI) is being used to measure the commodity concentration in export-trade of a country (World Bank, 2008). The index is calculated by using the following formula:

$$HCI = \text{sqrt} \left[\text{sum} \, (X_i/X_t)^2 \right]$$

Where X_i is country j's exports of product i; X_t is country j's total exports; and sqrt stands for square root. Highest value for this index is unity which occurs when exports consist of only one good. The lower value of concentration index shows that the exports are more evenly distributed over the various possible categories. The commodity-concentration has been examined at 2-digit HS classifications, from 1996 to 2005.

Table 6.9 presents the HCI of India's exports to China and that of China's exports to India. The value of HCI of India's exports to China was 0.38 in 1996, which declined to 0.31 in 2000. However, after that it rose sharply to 0.55 in 2004 and then slightly declined to 0.53 in 2005. On the other side, the value of HCI of China's exports to India declined from 0.35 in 1996 to 0.32 in 2005. One thing worth nothing here is that during 1996-2005 the value of HCI of China's exports to India remained below than that of India's exports to China, except the year 2000.

Thus, this shows that during the study period Chinese exports to India remained more diversified vis-à-vis Indian export to China.

Table 6.9: Hirschman Concentration Index (HCI):
India and China

Years	HCI of India's Exports to China	HCI of China's Exports to India
1996	0.38	0.35
1997	0.38	0.34
1998	0.34	0.31
1999	0.33	0.31
2000	0.31	0.32
2001	0.35	0.31
2002	0.38	0.33
2003	0.38	0.31
2004	0.55	0.33
2005	0.53	0.32

Source: Calculated from UN Commodity Trade Statistics, United Nations.

6.4.4 Economic Distance Index: The different nature of India's and China's competition in the goods markets is illustrated by the measurement of economic distance between countries in terms of export composition (Bussiere and Mehl, 2008). To this end, the following Economic Distance Index (δ_{ij}) between the two countries has been calculated:

$$\delta_{ij} = \text{sqrt} \left[\sum_{k=1}^{N} (\sigma^k_i - \sigma^k_j)^2 \right]$$

Where σ^k_i represents the share of sector/commodity k in country i's total exports and σ^k_j represents the share of sector/commodity k in country j's total exports and sqrt stands for square root.

The Economic Distance Index between the two countries has been computed at 2-digit HS classification for the period 1996-2005. The lower this index, more similar the two economies are to each other and the more they may compete

with each other for export markets. The results from Table
6.10 indicate that the value of the Economic Distance Index
(δ_{ij}) increased continuously from 0.21 in 1996 to 0.32 in 2005
(except the year 2000). Thus, this suggests that the economic
distance between India and China is yet low but increasing,
which will further lead to a decrease in competition level
between these two countries in the goods markets.

**Table 6.10: Index of Economic Distance between
India and China**

Years	Economic Distance Index
1996	0.21
1997	0.22
1998	0.24
1999	0.27
2000	0.25
2001	0.26
2002	0.28
2003	0.30
2004	0.32
2005	0.32

Source: Calculated from UN Commodity Trade Statistics, United
Nations.

6.4.5 Grubel-Lloyd Intra-Industry Trade Index:
Ricardian trade theory predicts that countries would trade on
the basis of their comparative advantage in different products.
Thus, trade would be inter-industry. However, much actual
trade between countries consists of differentiated goods within
the same industry. This pattern is consistent with new trade
theory involving product differentiation (Cerra, et al., 2005).
So, in this context, it becomes important to compute the
Grubel-Lloyd Intra-Industry Trade index which measures the
proportion of total trade comprised by intra-industry trade
(World Bank, 2008). The Index is measured as follows:

$$IIT_i = \frac{\Sigma_i (X_i + M_i) - \Sigma_i |X_i - M_i|}{\Sigma_i (X_i + M_i)} \times 100$$

Where X_i and M_i are the values of exports to China and Imports from China by India in product group i. For higher degree of intra-industry trade, the value of this index will be closer to 100. With the help of data at 2-digit HS classification, the index has been computed for the period 1996-2005.

Table 6.11 shows that during 1996-2000 the Aggregate Intra-Industry Trade (AIIT) between India and China varied between 17 percent and 29 percent. The AIIT index increased from 17.18 percent in 1996 to 28.63 percent in 2000. But after that it declined continuously to 22.31 percent in 2005 (except year 2003). Therefore, the AIIT index confirms that intra-industry trade played a very little and declining role in India-China bilateral trade.

Table 6.11: Aggregate Intra-Industry Trade (AIIT) Index between India and China

Years	Aggregate Intra-Industry Trade Index (Percent)
1996	17.18
1997	18.11
1998	20.83
1999	23.28
2000	28.63
2001	25.23
2002	24.14
2003	27.49
2004	22.44
2005	22.31

Source: Calculated from UN Commodity Trade Statistics, United Nations.

The index has been calculated for six broad categories of 2-digit HS classification for the period 1996-2005. The table depicts that during the period 1996-2005, out of six sectors, three sectors namely mineral and mineral fuels; chemicals and plastics; and resource based manufactures showed high values of intra-industry trade between India and China. The average values of SIIT index for these three sectors remained at 70.61, 65.95 and 70.30 percent respectively. On the other side, another three sectors namely agricultural and allied products; machinery and equipments; and miscellaneous manufactures showed relatively low level of intra-industry trade, as the average values of SIIT index for these three sectors remained at 40.75, 11.89 and 23.20 percent respectively.

6.4.6 Export Specialisation Index: The Export Specialisation (ES) index is a slightly modified form of RCA index, in which the denominator is usually measured by specific markets or partners (World Bank, 2008). It provides product information on revealed specialisation in the export sector of a country and is calculated as the ratio of the share of a product in a country's total exports to the share of this product in imports to specific markets or partners rather than its share in world exports:

$$ES = \frac{(x_{ij}/X_{it})}{(m_{kj}/M_{kt})}$$

Where x_{ij} - exports of country i of product j, X_{it} - total exports of country i, m_{kj} – imports of country k of product j, and M_{kt} - total imports of country k.

The ES is similar to the RCA in the sense that the value of the index less than unity indicates a comparative disadvantage and a value above unity represents specialisation in this market. The index has been computed for six broad categories of 2-digit HS classification for the period 1996-2005.

6.4.7 Trade Complementarity Index: Through Trade Complementarity Index (TCI), it is measured that how well the export profile of one country matches with the import profile of another country (World Bank, 2008). In other words, it gives the measurement of the scope for trade co-operation through inter-industry trade. Furthermore, changes in the index over time can help to determine whether trade profiles are becoming more or less compatible. TCI is measured as follows:

$$TCI_{ij} = 100 - \Sigma \left(|m_{ik} - x_{ij}| / 2 \right)$$

Where m_{ik}–share of good i in the imports of country k, x_{ij}–share of good i in the exports of country j. The value of the index ranges between 0 and 100. It takes the value 0 when there is no compatibility between exports of country j and imports of country k. On the other side, the index takes the value 100 when exports of country j and imports of country k match perfectly with each other. The index has been computed for the period 1996-2005, by using the data at 2-digit HS classification.

Table 6.12 shows that the TCI_{ij} declined continuously from 38.47 percent in 1996 to 34.01 percent in 1998. However, after that it rose sharply to 48.60 percent in 2005. Thus, these increasingly high values show that there has a wide scope of having trade co-operation between the two countries through complementarities in terms of inter-industry trade.

Table 6.12: Trade Complementarity Index (TCI) between India and China

Years	Trade Complementarity Index (Percent)
1996	38.47
1997	38.31
1998	34.01
1999	34.28
2000	40.53
2001	42.04
2002	43.06
2003	45.05
2004	48.23
2005	48.60

Source: Calculated from UN Commodity Trade Statistics, United Nations.

6.4.8 Trade Overlap Index: No doubt, intra-industry

trade has become an important component of world trade. However, in India-China bilateral trade, intra-industry trade seems to play a minor role. The importance of intra-industry trade as compared to inter-industry trade can also be measured by Trade Overlap Index (Bhat, et al., 2006). The index is measured as follows:

$$TOI = 2 [\Sigma \min (X_i, M_i) / \Sigma (X_i + M_i)]$$

Where, X_i and M_i are exports to China and imports from China of product i by India. The value of index ranges between 0 and 1. The closer it comes to 1, more is the intra-industry specialisation. Alternatively, if the index is closer to 0, it signifies the dominant role of inter-industry specialisation. The index has been computed for the period 1996-2005, by using the data at 2-digit HS classification. Table 6.13 shows that in 1996, the value of TOI was very low (i.e. 0.17), which suddenly rose to 0.58 in very next year.

Table 6.13: Trade Overlap Index (TOI) between India and China

Years	Trade Overlap Index
1996	0.17
1997	0.58
1998	0.42
1999	0.27
2000	0.30
2001	0.28
2002	0.25
2003	0.28
2004	0.23
2005	0.22

Source: Calculated from UN Commodity Trade Statistics, United Nations.

However, after that it started declining with lot of fluctuations and finally reached to 0.22 in 2005. Thus, the table reveals that during the recent years, the importance of intra-industry trade between India and China has declined considerably.

6.4.9 Trade Competition Index: To assess the trade challenges posed by India and China to each other as well as to the rest of the world, Qureshi and Wan (2008) constructed two well-known indices: the Coefficient of Specialisation (CS) and the Coefficient of Conformity (CC), defined as follows:

$$CS = 1 - \tfrac{1}{2} \Sigma_n |a_{ni} - a_{nj}|$$

$$CC = \frac{\Sigma_n (a_{ni} \cdot a_{nj})}{\text{sqrt} [\Sigma_n (a_{ni})^2 \, \Sigma_n (a_{nj})^2]}$$

Where a_{ni} and a_{nj} represent the share of good n in the total exports of countries i and j. Sqrt stands for square root. If both countries (i and j) have the same exporting structure, then the indices will be equal to 1, indicating intensive competition. However, when both countries have totally dissimilar exporting structures, then both the indices will be equal to 0, which indicates the absence of competition. To compute the index, the data have been collected at 2-digit HS classification and the period covered is 1996-2005.

Table 6.14 shows the Coefficient of Specialisation (CS) and the Coefficient of Conformity (CC) between India and China. The results for the two indices do not differ much. The values of both the indices were relatively higher in 1996 (i.e. 0.53 and 0.52 respectively) showing a high degree of competition between Indian and Chinese exports. However, during recent few years, both the indices weakened noticeably and, in 2005, they reached to 0.46 and 0.37 respectively. Hence, it can be concluded that the extent of competition between the exports of two countries seems to have weakened over time.

To sum up, the trade relations between India and China have been developing by good momentum and dynamism. There is a strong political impetus on both sides to advance their trade and economic ties further. During the recent visit of

Indian Prime Minister to China, both the countries have decided to move faster on the track of trade. Due to the tremendous growth of their mutual trade, the target has been revised to US$ 60 billion for 2010, rather than US$ 40 billion. The institutional framework of bilateral cooperation, including the Joint Economic Group, Joint Working Group and other sector-specific mechanisms, has been strengthened and expanded to cover new areas. Business exchanges and the flow of delegations between the two countries have been consistently increasing. Both the countries have also been making efforts to expand areas of economic linkages which could further boost and broaden bilateral trade ties.

Table 6.14: Coefficient of Specialisation (CS) and Coefficient of Conformity (CC) between India and China

Years	Coefficient of Specialisation	Coefficient of Conformity
1996	0.53	0.52
1997	0.52	0.51
1998	0.50	0.46
1999	0.49	0.41
2000	0.53	0.46
2001	0.52	0.44
2002	0.50	0.39
2003	0.49	0.40
2004	0.46	0.35
2005	0.46	0.37

Source: Calculated from UN Commodity Trade Statistics, United Nations.

However, during the study period, one major problem from the Indian perspective was its rising trade deficit with China. Most of the years, India experienced adverse balance of trade with China and the deficit of trade widened substantially due to the higher growth rate of imports from China.

The other major problem with India-China trade is the narrowness of trade basket. Indian exports were mainly dominated by exports of ores, slag and ash. Importantly, this commodity constituted about 52.13 percent of India's total exports to China in 2004-05. Moreover, during the same year, out of India's total world exports of ores, slag and ash, nearly 78.31 percent was exported to China alone. The rapid depletion of China's iron ore reserves, thereby, making its front-running steel industry dependent on imports from India to meet the growing demand for steel for its construction and defence industries. On the other side, India's imports from China were more diversified and balanced than Indian exports to China. Moreover, the bulk of the Indian imports from China constituted manufactured goods, with electronic machinery alone constituted about 25.04 percent of the total Indian imports from China in 2004-05. Thus, in the interests of continuing high growth rates of trade, the two countries have to ensure the diversification of trade basket and must create new mechanisms for developing cooperation in hitherto uncharted areas of economic cooperation.

Further, export-import ratio analysis showed that during the period 1990-91 to 2004-05, on an average, India was in position to meet 84.26 percent bill of her overall imports through the earnings from her overall exports. While in the case of China, on an average, her exports were able to pay just 74.18 percent of bill of her imports during the same period. In other words, it can be said that India's export earnings were not sufficient to cover the cost of imports. The analysis of intensity and integrity indices revealed that though during the last few years, the orientation and integration of trade between India and China grew rapidly, yet the values of these indices were below the desired level. Export Concentration Index showed that China's exports to India were more diversified vis-à-vis India's exports to China. Other indices like Intra-Industry Trade Index, Complementarity Index and Trade Overlap Index showed that during the last few years, in India-China bilateral trade, the inter-industry trade grew rapidly while the intra-industry trade played a minor role. Similarly, the indices namely Economic Distance Index, Coefficient of Specialisation and Coefficient of Conformity revealed that the extent of competition between the exports of the two countries had declined over time.

In a nutshell, India and China are only beginning to discover the full scope and opportunities for expanding trade and economic cooperation at the regional and international levels. If coordinated well, the combined market size of the two can provide significant leverages to both countries in regional and global trade across a range of product categories. The complementarities inherent in the economies of the two countries could be harnessed to propel trade and economic cooperation between India and China to greater heights.

7

Terms of Trade and Unit Value Analysis

The distribution of gains for trade between trading partners has remained an important concern in international trade theory. The concept of terms of trade has been developed to measure the distribution of gains from trade (Chishti, 2002). Terms of trade are considered to be an appropriate instrument to see whether trade has been beneficial or not to a particular country. The benefits of trade may not, however, be equally distributed among trading partners. Nevertheless, there is a likelihood of equal distribution of gains from trade when it is among equals because in that case there is relatively little scope for unequal exchange of value (Ghuman, 1986).

During the last twenty years, India and China have emerged as global economic powers. Their economic interaction, particularly merchandise trade, has increased quite tremendously. India's exports to China have also got more diversified since last few years. Many new items have also been included in India's export list. This chapter pertains to the mutual gains from trade between India and China. The chapter is divided into two parts. First part deals with India's terms of trade with China. Second part deals with the comparison of unit values realised by India for its export-trade and import-trade with China.

7.1 Terms of Trade: Concepts and Issues

The theory of gains from trade is at the core of the classical theory of international trade. According to Adam Smith, the gains from trade result from the division of labour and specialisation both at the national and international level. However, J.S. Mill analysed the gains from international trade by reciprocal demand which depends upon the terms of trade.

According to the modern analysis, gains from international trade accrue from the gains from exchange and gains from specialisation. Viner (1937) points out that the economists followed three different methods for measuring gains from trade: (i) difference in comparative costs, (ii) increase in level of national income and (iii) terms of trade. The terms of trade method has been in vogue to measure the gains from trade.

The terms of trade refer to the rate at which the goods of one country are exchanged for the goods of another country. If the export prices of a country rise relatively to its import prices, then its terms of trade are said to have improved. The country gains from trade because it can have a larger quantity of imports in exchange for a given quantity of exports. On the other hand, when its import prices rise relative to its export prices, its terms of trade are said to have worsened.

7.1.1 Terms of Trade: Theoretical Argument: It has been argued that gains accrue from international trade due to its potential, which as a result affects international division of labour and product specialisation. The gains are in the form of more production, economies of scale, greater magnitude of goods, and diversification of production. It increases the value of possessions, means of enjoyment, and wealth of the nations concerned (Khatkhate, 1991). The concept of terms of trade was first introduced by J.S. Mill for the analysis of gains from trade between the trading partners (Chishti, 1974).

The issue of terms of trade became serious with the publication of the paper by Prebisch (1950). He studied the Board of Trade's mean price indices for British imports and exports. Based on those data, he argued that from 1860s to the years leading up to the Second World War, the terms of trade had continually moved against primary commodity producers. Along the same lines, Singer (1950) claimed it was a historical fact that, since 1870, price trends had moved sharply against vendors of foodstuffs and raw materials and in favour of enterprises selling manufactures.

This view was also supported by Nurkse (1953) who

maintained that the markets of developed world would not be in position to absorb the goods produced by developing countries on account of low elasticity of demand for their product. Thus, it was contended that there was a secular tendency for the terms of trade of the developing countries to move unfavourably, implying a bias in the distribution of the gains from trade.

The gains from increased productivity, even in the production of the primary commodities, were distributed in the rich countries in the form of higher wages and profits, because of the strong trade union activities, and thus, prices did not decline, whereas, lack of organisation among the workers employed in the primary product producing countries prevented them from obtaining wages increases when productivity increased (Spraos, 1980).

According to Prebisch-Singer thesis, the productivity growth in the manufactures was not permitted to be reflected in falling prices of manufactured exports from the developed countries. On the contrary, the developing countries had to pay huge price. They argued that stickiness of factor income of the centre, through trade union movement in the centre, transferred the higher productivity to higher wages. Corporations also exert pressure towards increase of profits. In developing countries, on the other hand, productivity was reflected in lower prices as there was no trade union movement and also, as some economists have argued, the owners of the primary production in the developing countries were mainly corporations from the developed countries. Thus, developing countries suffered as suppliers as well as consumers (United Nations, 1950).

The long term deterioration of net barter terms of trade as well as the consequent unequal distribution of income was generally accepted in the fifties. Even some authoritative economists with dominating thinking like Kindleberger (1956) also accepted the "fact that the terms of trade favour developed and run counter to underdeveloped countries".

The negative long-run trend of primary commodity prices has been well documented in the literature (Grilli and Yang, 1988; Reinhart and Wickham, 1994). Lutz (1999), for instance, lends support to the fact that there is a negative long-run trend in the relative prices of primary products, using a general time series framework that encompasses uni-variate and bi-variate models. León and Soto (1995), by using non-parametric measures such as variance ratios, show that for 19 commodities out of the 24 commodities the prices remain persistently at lower level than previous estimates over the 1900-1992 horizon. Cashin and McDermott (2002) focus on volatility trends and acknowledge the downward trend in real prices of primary products.

Regarding the terms of trade between primary and manufactured products, Ardeni and Wright (1992) find a robust secular deterioration of terms of trade. More recently, Zanias (2005) employs the extended Grilli and Yang (1988) terms of trade series and finds declining trend of terms of trade for the period 1900 to 1998.

Most of the studies done in the 1980s tended to corroborate the Prebisch-Singer hypothesis (Spraos, 1980 and 1983; Sapsford, 1985; Sarkar, 1986; Evans, 1987; and Scandizzo and Diakosavvas, 1987). Although the trend could not be confirmed for certain sub-periods and products, the evidence indicated that, on an average, the real prices of raw materials had trended downward throughout the Twentieth Century. This trend was also found to exist for raw materials (other than petroleum) as a group and for most products in the years after the Second World War (Ocampo, 1993).

The hypothesis developed by Prebisch and Singer marked a historic turning point in the analysis of the trend in the commodity terms of trade and gave rise to a wide array of empirical studies which did not, however, reach a consensus on the matter. Of the seventy analyses after 1949 that were summarised in Scandizzo and Diakosavvas (1987), nearly half support the Prebisch-Singer hypothesis and about forty percent fail to detect empirically convincing or analytically justifiable trends and the remainder find the trend to be positive.

John Spraos thoroughly examined the issues related to Prebisch-Singer thesis by taking into account three more series published by the United Nations, League of Nations and Lewis. He concluded that there could be some controversy about the 'extent of deterioration', but beyond doubt a deteriorating trend was detectable in the data over the period from 1870 to 1938 (Spraos, 1983). The original terms of trade model of Prebisch of primary versus manufactures ultimately developed into a general model of terms of trade of developing countries vis-à-vis the developed countries. Even Kindleberger in the early fifties stressed that the tendency of deterioration should not be viewed in the context of primary commodities versus the manufactures, but within the framework of overall backwardness of a country. He, further, argued that it is not bad terms of trade that led to poverty, but poverty led to bad terms of trade (Tandon, 1985).

The fact that the industrialised countries do not export only manufactures was addressed early by Meier and Baldwin (1957), who pointed out that many primary commodities like wheat, beef, wool, cotton and sugar, are heavily exported by industrialised countries. Indeed, Scandizzo and Diakosavvas (1987) noted that the developing countries' share in agricultural primary commodities was only thirty percent in 1983, down from forty percent in 1955. Yet Spraos (1980) argues that this fact is immaterial, because the same trends that are observed in the broad index of primary commodity prices are found in a narrower index that includes only developing-country products.

Several studies have taken a more rigorous approach in measuring the importance of commodity prices for the terms of trade of developing countries. Bleaney and Greenaway (1993), for example, estimate a co-integrating regression for non-oil developing countries for period 1955-89, in which terms of trade of the developing countries is expressed as a log-linear function of an index of commodity prices and real oil prices. The results show that the series are co-integrated and that for every one percent decline in the relative price of commodities there is a 0.3 percent decline in the terms of trade of non-oil developing countries. These results are similar to those of Grilli and Yang (1988) and Powell (1991).

The development of unit root tests have become the basis for most of the recent terms of trade studies (e.g. Cuddington and Urzua 1989; Deaton and Laroque 1992; Bleany and Greenway 1993; Powell 1991; Ardeni and Wright 1992). These have offered far more sophisticated treatment of the time series, but have excluded economic variables that might help explain relative price behaviour and its impact. Cuddington (1992), for example, applies modern time series techniques to the twenty six individual commodity prices contained in Grilli-Yang index of non-fuel commodity prices, allowing for the possibility of structural breaks and the pressure of unit roots. The study covers the period 1900-1983 and concludes that the majority (sixteen) are best characterised as trend less. Of the remainder, five had negative and five had positive trends. Thus, these findings suggest that a secular deterioration in primary commodity prices should certainly not be considered a universal "stylised fact" of the full Twentieth Century.

It is important to understand the terms of trade of developing countries than to understand commodity prices. This is the approach taken by Hadass and Williamson (2001). They bypass the question of the relationship between the terms of trade and commodity prices altogether and simply re-examined the evidence on the Prebisch-Singer hypothesis, by using country-specific terms of trade data, instead of commodity price data. They constructed the estimates of the terms of trade for nineteen countries, developing and industrialised, and clubbed these into four regions: land-scarce Europe, land-scarce Third World, land-abundant New World and land-abundant Third World. Simply by comparing averages, they find that the terms of trade improved for all regions except the land-scarce Third World. They argue that this is due in part to rapidly declining transport costs during the sample period, which is consistent with Ellsworth's (1956) criticism of Prebisch and Singer thesis.

7.1.2 Studies on India's Terms of Trade: There is some literature available on India's terms of trade based on different time series data. The first systematic analysis of India's terms of trade over a very long period of time, i.e. from 1930-31 to 1967-68, was made by Chishti (1974). Author divided the above mentioned time period into five different sub-periods. The study shows that from 1930-31 to 1938-39, India's NBTT remained unfavourable. It remained highly favourable from 1939-40 to 1948-49, except one year, i.e. 1941-42. However, it remained unfavourable from 1949-50 to 1953-54. In the subsequent years they remained favourable from 1954-55 to 1959-60. But remained highly favourable in all the eight years from 1960-61 to 1967-68.

The study by the Eastern Economist (1974), from 1960-61 to 1969-70, shows that India's overall terms of trade remained unfavourable during the first half of 1960's, but remained highly favourable during the second half of the 1960's. The study by Thiruvenkatachari (1976) concluded that the index of NBTT increased from 100 in 1960-61 (base year) to 104.1 in 1964-65 and subsequently remained below 100 up to the year 1968-69. Mukherjee and Mukherjee (1980) calculated India's terms of trade from 1952 to 1978. According to the study, India's terms of trade improved from 84.09 in 1952 to 110.9 in 1972. But in the subsequent years, i.e. from 1973 to 1978, it remained unfavourable. Da Costa (1983) examined India's terms of trade from 1968-69 to 1979-80. It remained favourable from 1968-69 to 1972-73 and declined afterwards and remained unfavourable continuously up to 1979-80.

According to Tandon and Hatti (1987), the NBTT of India remained favourable continuously over the period from 1960 to 1970. The index of terms of trade improved from 111 in

1960 to 113.7 in 1966 and 116 in 1970. The study is based upon 84 percent of imports and 92 percent of exports of India. Tandon (1978) stated that India's NBTT (base year=1958-59) remained highly favourable in all the years from 1958-59 to 1968-69. The index of terms of trade increased rapidly from 100 in 1958-59 to 119.7 in 1963-64 and then reached to 128.4 in 1968-69. Thus, India experienced favourable terms of trade in sixties. Leonard (1993) computed India's overall terms of trade from 1977-78 to 1984-85.

According to the author, excluding the base year 1980-81, India enjoyed favourable terms of trade, except the years 1977-78 and 1979-80. Similarly, Brar (1996) reported in his study that during 1978-80 to 1988-89, India's overall terms of trade remained highly favourable, except the year 1980-81. In 1980-81, it went below hundred, i.e. 87.4. However, after that, it remained favourable continuously for eight years from 1981-82 to 1988-89. Economic Survey (2006-07) shows that India's NBTT remained unfavourable during 1978-79 to 1982-83 (base year = 1978-79). However, after 1982-83, it remained favourable during the whole period from 1983-84 to 2004-05. During the nineties it remained highly favourable. Devi (2006) examined India's terms of trade during the period 1980-81 to 2002-03.

It is found that the general index of Net Barter Terms of Trade was unfavourable to India in the early few years of the study period, however, since 1983-84, it reveals a favourable trend. The author points out that the mean values of NBTT for the commodity groups like food and food articles, beverages and tobacco, animal and vegetable oil, fats and waxes, manufactured goods classified chiefly by material deteriorated in the post-liberalisation period compared to pre-liberalisation period. On the contrary, some commodity groups like crude materials except fuels; mineral fuels, lubricants, etc; chemicals and related products; machinery and transport equipment; and miscellaneous manufactured articles, indicated an improvement since the pre-liberalisation period in terms of the mean values of NBTT.

There is some literature available on India's terms of trade with different countries. Mathur (1973) examined India's terms of trade with US from 1951-52 to 1968-69. He concluded that India's terms of trade with US remained favourable during the First Plan and unfavourable during the Second and Third Plans. The study of Roy (1986) shows that India's NBTT with US remained favourable from 1960-61 to 1965-66 (base year=1958). But remained unfavourable from 1970-71 to 1975-76 continuously in all the years (base year= 1968-69).

Tandon (1978) examined India's terms of trade with the former West Germany from 1951-52 to 1968-69. He concluded that by and large NBTT with this country remained unfavourable during 1950s and favourable in 1960s. Thiruvenkatachari (1976) examined India's NBTT with the formerly USSR from 1960-61 to 1969-70 and concluded that India experienced favourable terms of trade during the sixties with formerly USSR. Chishti (1973) calculated India's terms of trade, with the formerly East European countries from 1960-61 to 1969-70 and her results show that during sixties, terms of trade remained favourable to India for all the years, except 1961-62 and 1969-70. The study conducted by Gill (1983) shows that India's terms of trade with formerly USSR remained favourable from 1969-70 to 1975-76 in all the years, except 1974-75 and 1975-76.

Leonard (1993) analysed India's NBTT with Japan from 1977-78 to 1984-85 (base year=1980-81). During the study period, India's NBTT index with Japan remained highly favourable except the year 1979-80, when the index went below hundred, i.e. 93.49. Brar (1996) examined India's NBTT with European Union and its four member countries, i.e. Belgium, France, former West Germany and UK from 1979-80 to 1988-89. India's NBTT with European Union remained favourable for four years, i.e. 1983-84, 1985-86, 1987-88 and 1988-89, while remained unfavourable for five years, i.e. 1980-81, 1981-82, 1982-83, 1984-85 and 1986-87. On the other side, within the European Union, India's NBTT with UK, France and former West Germany remained adverse, while with Belgium it remained favourable for majority of the years. Similarly, Madaan (1998) calculated India's NBTT with Bangladesh from 1980-81 to 1993-94 (base year=1986-87). It covered selected commodities comprising more than fifty percent of India's trade with Bangladesh. India enjoyed favourable terms of trade with Bangladesh during the study period, except during the years 1981-82 and 1985-86.

Thus, from the above studies, it becomes clear that the movement of overall terms of trade of a country did not reflect the behaviour of terms of trade with any individual country or group of countries. It is not necessary that a favourable movement of India's overall terms of trade was shared by each and every country.

7.1.3 India's Terms of Trade with China: Meier (1963) has classified the various concepts of terms of trade into three categories: first, the ratio of exchange, i.e. net, gross and income terms of trade; second, the exchange of productive resources, i.e. single and double factoral terms of trade; and third, in terms of utility, i.e. real cost and utility terms of trade. All these concepts have their respective merits and demerits. But, the empirical verification of all of these concepts is not possible or extremely difficult. Among the various concepts of terms of trade, the Net Barter Terms of Trade (NBTT) developed by Taussing is widely prevalent and largely accepted. The nature of the available data permitted us the use of this concept only. It is also preferred because the traditional terms of trade controversy centred on this concept. The economic wisdom also suggests that the price of exports should be measured in terms of imports. Hence, the concept fulfils that objective too. Therefore, it is decided to use this concept of simple commodity terms of trade, which is defined as below:

$$NBTT = \frac{\text{Index of Unit Value of Exports}}{\text{Index of Unit Value of Imports}} \times 100$$

The rise in the index of NBTT over the period indicates that comparatively a large volume of imports could be received on the basis of price relations only in exchange for the given volume of exports. Export unit value index and import unit value index have been calculated with the help of Passche indices based on current quantities. India's terms of trade with China have been computed for two different time periods, i.e. (i) from 1992-93 to 2004-05; and (ii) from 2000-01 to 2004-05.

However, before examining India's terms of trade with China, it is necessary to view India's overall terms of trade. Table 7.1 shows India's overall terms of trade from 1992-93 to 2004-05, with base year 1993-94. It shows that out of thirteen years, the overall terms of trade remained favourable only thrice: 1994-95, 1997-98 and 1998-99, with index value at 105.16, 100.64 and 103.52 respectively. The unfavourable movement of overall terms of trade resulted from the slow increase in the price of overall exports as compared to relatively high increase in the prices of overall imports. It is noteworthy that since 1999-00, India's overall terms of trade index deteriorated sharply and reached to its minimum (i.e. 73.75 in 2004-05).

The major cause of this deterioration of NBTT index is the sharp rise of unit value index of imports, which further, increased due to sharp rise in the prices of crude petroleum and other metals.

(i) India's Terms of Trade with China from 1992-93 to 2004-05: The measurement of terms of trade with China involves some specific problems and issues. The terms of trade with China have been measured during the period from 1992-93 to 2004-05 and not from 1990-91. The two initial years, i.e. 1990-91 and 1991-92 have been skipped, because of the irregularity of major commodities in India's exports to China. The measurement of terms of trade involves that the exportables and importables must have regular presence every year in the trade during the study period. However, this was not the case in trade with China. It is important to note that the fast growth in trade leads to major structural changes in the trade and commodities appear and disappear from trade basket quite frequently. It creates problems in constructing the long term time series. Therefore, the terms of trade with China have been calculated for two different periods; first, from 1992-93 to 2004-05; and second from 2000-01 to 2004-05. In fact, among the selected commodities, many commodities in both exports and imports did not exist during the initial two years. But, these commodities played a very dominating role during the subsequent years.

Table 7.1: India's Overall Terms of Trade (1992-93 to 2004-05)
(Base Year 1993-94)

Years	Export Unit Value Index	Import Unit Value Index	Net Barter Terms of Trade
1992-93	89	101	87.88
1993-94	100	100	100.00
1994-95	104	99	105.16
1995-96	102	107	95.21
1996-97	106	122	87.12
1997-98	124	124	100.64
1998-99	129	125	103.52
1999-00	127	138	92.63
2000-01	132	149	88.43
2001-02	130	151	86.51
2002-03	131	167	78.38
2003-04	142	167	85.10
2004-05	154	209	73.75

Note: figures are adjusted by changing the base from 1978-79 to 1993-94.

Source: Economic Survey (2005-06), Statistical Tables, Government of India, p. S-96.

Thus, it was not possible to integrate the first two years with the rest of the years for calculation of terms of trade. So, it was decided to drop the initial two years. For calculating NBTT index with China from 1992-93 to 2004-05, sixteen export commodities were selected. Their share in India's total exports to China oscillated between 31 percent and 66 percent. On the imports side, nineteen commodities were selected. Their share in India's total imports varied between 21 percent and 46 percent. The smaller percentage share of import commodities compared to those of export commodities was due to the non-availability or inappropriate quantum data for major commodities (e.g. projected goods, woven fabrics and tyre cord fabrics of nylon/other polyamides, etc.) Further, the more diversification of Chinese exports to India was also responsible for this smaller share.

Table 7.2 shows India's NBTT with China from 1992-93 to 2004-05 with base year 1993-94. India enjoyed favourable terms of trade with China for all the years during the study period, except 1992-93 and 1994-95, when India's NBTT index with China went below hundred, i.e. 73.85 and 93.29 respectively. However, India's NBTT index rose steadily from 107.28 in 1995-96 to 130.63 in 1997-98. But in 1998-99, it fell suddenly to 109.64. However, after that the NBTT index increased with tremendous pace, i.e. from 109.64 in 1998-99 to 172.81 in 2004-05. It is noteworthy that since 2001-02, the NBTT index increased quite sharply.

During 1992-93 to 2004-05, the unit values of both exports to and imports from China increased rapidly but with a lot of variations. As is clear from Table 7.2, the unit value of exports rose quite sharply from 90 in 1992-93 to 167 in 1996-97 and then declined continuously to 144 in 2002-03 except 2000-01 (when it rose to 151 from 149 in previous year). However, in the year 2003-04 and 2004-05, it increased tremendously and out-stepped the import unit value index with huge margin. It increased to 193 and 329 in 2003-04 and 2004-05 respectively. That's why India's NBTT index with China touched new heights in 2003-04 and 2004-05. On the other side, during the same time period, unit values of imports increased with moderate variations and did not show huge ups and downs except the year 2004-05, when it went up quickly to 191 from 131 of previous year.

Table 7.2: India's Terms of Trade with China (1992-93 to 2004-05) (Base Year 1993-94)

Year	Export Unit Value Index	Import Unit Value Index	Net Barter Terms Trade
1992-93	90	122	73.85
1993-94	100	100	100.00
1994-95	105	112	93.29
1995-96	134	125	107.28
1996-97	167	128	129.63
1997-98	161	123	130.63
1998-99	145	133	109.64
1999-00	142	127	112.31
2000-01	151	132	114.13
2001-02	149	128	117.14
2002-03	144	115	125.21
2003-04	193	131	146.54
2004-05	329	191	172.81

Source: Calculated from Statistics of Foreign Trade of India by Countries, DGCI&S; Kolkata, (Various Issues).

But, since 1994-95, the import unit value index remained well below the export unit value index and that's why India enjoyed favourable terms of trade with China during the corresponding period. In other words, it can be said that the sharp rise in the prices of exports to China as compared to relatively slow rise in the prices of imports from China was the major cause for India's favourable terms of trade with China.

(ii) India's Terms of Trade with China from 2000-01 to 2004-05: During the period 2000-01 to 2004-05, some drastic changes occurred in India-China mutual trade. This is the period when China entered into WTO, i.e. on 11 December

2001. With the Chinese accession to the WTO, many tariff and non-tariff barriers on India-China trade were removed. With this, not only the trade of existing commodities, but the number of India's exports to and imports from China also increased quite rapidly. Many new items were included in both exports and imports, which turned the picture of India's terms of trade with China. Therefore, it was decided to calculate India's terms of trade with China differently for the period from 2000-01 to 2004-05. For this purpose, forty three export commodities were selected, whose share in India's total exports to China varied between 56 percent and 74 percent. While, on the imports side 34 commodities were selected, whose share in India's total imports from China oscillated between 45 percent and 51 percent.

Table 7.3 shows India's NBTT index with China from 2000-01 to 2004-05, with base year 2000-01. As is clear, during the initial two years (i.e. 2001-02 and 2002-03), India's NBTT index with China deteriorated sharply (i.e. 89.67 and 86.97 respectively). However, during the last two years (i.e. 2003-04 and 2004-05), it improved considerably (i.e. 139.32 and 160.55 respectively).

Table 7.3: India's Terms of Trade with China
(2000-01 to 2004-05) (Base Year 2000-01)

Year	Export Unit Value Index	Import Unit Value Index	Net Barter Terms Trade
2000-01	100	100	100.00
2001-02	89	100	89.67
2002-03	85	98	86.97
2003-04	103	74	139.32
2004-05	162	101	160.55

Source: Calculated from Statistics of Foreign Trade of India by Countries, DGCI&S; Kolkata, (Various Issues).

On the other side, in 2001-02 and 2002-03, India's export unit value index with China also declined sharply to 89 and 85 respectively. That had happened due to the sharp decline in the prices of some commodities such as simply cut or sown granite; medicaments put for retail sale; fish fillets; chromium ores and concentrates; and aluminium oxide. However, in the next two years, i.e. 2003-04 and 2004-05, it increased substantially to 103 and 162 respectively.

Here, once again the major commodity was iron ore and concentrates (both agglomerated and non-agglomerated) which made the difference. China's increasing demand for this commodity, raised its unit value. On the imports side, the unit value index deteriorated sharply to 74 in 2003-04, due to the decreasing prices of coke and semi-coke of coal; magnesium; zink non alloyed; antibiotics; natural calcium phosphates; input or output units; and telephonic or telegraphic switching apparatus. However, in 2004-05, the prices of many commodities (like zink not allowed; machines and parts; cinnamon and tree flowers; and cotton) rose sharply which further pushed up the import unit value index to 101. Thus, it can be concluded that though in the initial years, i.e. 2001-02 and 2002-03, India's terms of trade deteriorated but in 2003-04 and 2004-05, it rose noticeably.

7.2 Gains from Trade: Unit Value Analysis

Gains from trade could also be measured in terms of unit values realised from exports and unit values paid for imports. In this section, an attempt has been made to examine the problem that whether it was beneficial for India to trade with China or with the Rest of the World (RoW-refers to whole world minus China). In other words, it has been examined that were the prices that India obtained from its exports to China superior, comparable or inferior to the prices that India obtained from identical exports to RoW? Conversely, were the prices that India paid for its imports from China higher, equal or lower than the prices that India has to pay for identical imports from RoW? This problem of India-China trade has been examined via Relative Terms of Trade Index (RTTI).

However, gains or losses from trade cannot strictly be determined solely in terms of higher/lower unit value obtained/paid. The comparison of unit values does not reflect the inherent and other deep rooted quality changes incurred over the period of time. It is to be noted that the process of price formation is a complex phenomena and depends upon large number of factors. The price differences may occur because of quality changes. Such qualitative differences across products could be reflected in price differences. Another problem relates to the financing arrangements of trade. That is, if imports are credit financed, it would be natural to find that per unit cost of such imports were higher than per unit cost of similar imports from alternative sources with the imports not being credit financed (Ambegaokar, 1974).

Despite these limitations and in the absence of a better alternative, some sort of exercise can be performed on the basis of unit values realised for exports and paid for imports. But the dimensions of the problem can be reduced by considering specific items within commodity categories rather than broad commodity groups such as bars, tubes or sheets instead of broad iron and steel group.

7.2.1 Unit Values Realised from Exports: For calculating the unit values realised from Indian exports to China and that of to RoW, thirty five commodities were selected on the basis of their share in India's total exports to China. The commodities were collected at 6-digit HS classification and the data was collected from Monthly Statistics for Foreign Trade of India and Statistics for Foreign Trade of India by Countries, Directorate General for Commercial Intelligence and Statistics, Kolkata. Further, the study period covered is 1990-91 to 2004-05.

However, before computing unit value realisation from exports, it is necessary to view the share of selected commodities in India's total exports to China. As is clear, the total share of the selected commodities to China fluctuated rapidly. There was a period when it touched the greatest point, i.e. 94.10 percent in 1991-92 and after two years in 1993-94, it touched the lowest point, i.e. 32.01 percent. And, that happened mainly due to India's exports of iron ores and concentrates (non-agglomerated) and chromium ores and concentrates. Therefore, it is difficult to draw a concrete result. However, since 1997-98, the total share of selected commodities somehow showed a declining trend.

The decline in aggregate share reflects the reduced importance of the items like frozen fish excluding livers and roes; castor oil and its fractions; granite crude or roughly trimmed; chromium ores and concentrates; single yarn, of both uncombed and combed fibres measuring 714.29 DCTX or more (not exceeding 14 metric number), etc., and is partly attributed to the increasing diversification of India's export basket to China. However, as is evident, Indian exports to China was mainly dominated by iron ore and concentrates (non-agglomerated). This was the only commodity, which made the difference in India's total exports to China. In 2004-05, this commodity alone constituted 42.43 percent share of India's total exports to China. Thus, it can be concluded that throughout the whole study period, Indian exports to China were mainly dominated by one or two commodities which further affected India's terms of trade with China.

It is difficult to conclude much from the disparate trends and the clear trends are discernible only in some cases. For instance, unit values were generally superior for export commodities namely granite merely cut, into blocks or slabs of a rectangular (including square) shape; antibiotics; organic compounds; and all types of medicaments. On the other side, unit values were generally inferior for exports of all type of sea foods like fish, shrimps, prawns etc.; sesamum seeds, whether or not broken; mucilages thickeners, whether or not modified, derived from locust beans, locust bean seeds or guar seeds; chromium ores and concentrates; polyethylene having a specific gravity >0.94; polypropylene; human hair, dressed, thinned, bleached or otherwise worked, wool or other animal hair or other textile; and simply cut or sawn granite with a flat or even surface etc. to China. For the rest of the commodities the unit values did not show any definite pattern.

It is difficult to draw a single conclusion. Therefore, it is useful to have a summary index that captures the individual results at the aggregate level. This is done in Table 7.4. The index is constructed as follows. For any particular year, the weights of the selected thirty five items in India's exports to China are used to compute (using unit values) what would have been the realisation had the same basket been exported to RoW. This is divided by the earnings from exports to China and multiplied by hundred. Naturally, the weights are different for individual years.

Table 7.4: Ratio of Export Unit Value Index for RoW and Export Unit Value Index for China

Years	Export Ratio
1990-91	56.43
1991-92	111.08
1992-93	67.23
1993-94	78.04
1994-95	89.69
1995-96	83.55
1996-97	59.40
1997-98	90.90
1998-99	52.43
1999-00	75.57
2000-01	72.03
2001-02	70.72
2002-03	84.61
2003-04	90.64
2004-05	115.18

Note: The values are in percentage.
Source: Calculated from Table 7.4 and Table 7.5.

The index is, therefore, a measure of the realisation differentials. An index below 100 reflects the desirability of exporting to China. An index in excess of 100 reflects the desirability of exporting to RoW.

The results of the table reveal that the unit values realised for selected Indian exports to China remained relatively favourable during the whole study period, except two years, i.e. 1991-92 and 2004-05, when the export ratio went above hundred. However, there is no clear temporal trend during the whole study period and the export ratio oscillated between 52.43 percent and 115.18 percent. Thus, it can be said that India's exports were earning higher unit values from China vis-à-vis RoW.

7.2.2 Unit Values Paid for Imports: Let us now turn to the import side of the picture. Here, once again, thirty five commodities were selected to calculate unit value paid for Indian imports to China and RoW. The period covered is from 1990-91 to 2004-05 and data are collected at 6-digit HS classification from DGCI&S sources.

During the study period, total share of these commodities fluctuated within the range from 34.01 percent to 58.17 percent. The smaller percentage share of import commodities to that of export commodities was due to the more diversification of Chinese exports to India. As is clear, like Indian exports to China, Indian imports from China did not show big ups and downs and also not driven by one or two commodities. This clearly shows that Chinese exports to India were more diversified than Indian exports to China. Many commodities like organic compounds; coal, whether or not pulverized, but not agglomerated; silk yarns (other than yarn spun from silk waste) not put up for retail sale; antibiotics, etc., had lost their comparative relevance during the study period. On the other side, some commodities like cotton, not carded or combed; input or output units, whether or not containing storage units in the same housing; portable digital automatic data processing machines, weighing <10 kg, consisting a central processing unit, a keyboard and a display; molybdenum ores and concentrates roasted etc., had improved their position during the same period.

Most of the times, during the study period, unit values paid for import commodities (like organic compounds; phosphorus; naphthols and their salts; magnesium; silicon; zinc not alloyed; parts and accessories of all type of machines; storage units; silver; aluminium etc.) from China were perceptibly lower. On the other side, for some commodities (like coke and semi-coke of coal/lignite/peat; raw silk not thrown; antibiotics; refined lead; natural calcium phosphates, aluminium, calcium, phosphates and phosphatic chalk etc.) unit values were higher for imports from China. However, it can be concluded that for most of the selected commodities, India paid lower unit values to China as compared to RoW.

Like exports, it is also important for imports to aggregate the individual item-wise results in a summary index. This is done in Table 7.5. The index is constructed as follows. For any particular year, the weights of the selected thirty five items in India's imports from China are used to compute (using unit values) what would have been the cost had the same basket been imported from RoW. The import cost from China is divided by the cost from RoW and multiplied by hundred to obtain the index. An index below 100 reflects the desirability of importing from China. An index in excess of 100 reflects the desirability of importing from RoW.

The results in the table are quite important and also in the expected lines. The results indicate that the imports from China cost less than imports from RoW, for the whole study period. The index oscillated within the range between 64.90 percent and 99.34 percent.

Thus, this shows that the prices paid for Indian imports from China were lower than that of RoW. But, here one thing which demands attention is that the trade statistics even among the extremely narrow range of commodities remained silent about the quality differences. Many Chinese exports to India were considered of low quality and that is why their unit values may be on the lower side than that of RoW.

**Table 7.5: Ratio of Import Unit Value Index for China and
Import Unit Value Index for RoW**

Years	Import Ratio
1990-91	94.81
1991-92	97.27
1992-93	81.02
1993-94	77.34
1994-95	99.34
1995-96	82.03
1996-97	76.45
1997-98	74.18
1998-99	64.90
1999-00	65.09
2000-01	73.70
2001-02	84.51
2002-03	84.99
2003-04	70.17
2004-05	68.01

Note: The values are in percentage.

Further, Chinese industry also gained such efficiency that can produce a similar type of product at lower price. The other reason may be the dumping of goods by China in other countries, including India, as there has been many trade related duties going on about such practices by China. The other factor could be the valuation of imports. The data sources provide the information of imports value on cost, insurance and freight (c.i.f) basis. The two components other than cost, i.e. insurance and freight may be responsible for lower values because the goods had to travel less from China in order to reach India. Thus, these be may some of the reasons responsible for low unit values of Indian imports from China than RoW.

7.2.3 Relative Terms of Trade Index: It is interesting to see the results of exports and imports together by splicing them into a single index. This is done with the help of Relative Terms of Trade Index (RTTI) (Debroy, 1990). It involves a straightforward multiplication of the export and import ratios, as follows:

$$RTTI = \frac{\text{Export Ratio} \times \text{Import Ratio}}{100}$$

A value below 100 indicates the superiority of India-China trade and a value in excess of 100 indicates the superiority of trading with RoW. Table 7.6 shows that India's relative terms of trade index with China remained favourable during the whole study period, except the year 1991-92 when it crossed hundred mark and reached at 108.05. Thus, it can be said that except the year 1991-92, India's trade with China remained more superior vis-à-vis RoW.

Table 7.6: India's Relative Terms of Trade Index:
China and RoW

Years	Relative Terms of Trade Index
1990-91	53.50
1991-92	108.05
1992-93	54.47
1993-94	60.36
1994-95	89.10
1995-96	68.54
1996-97	45.41
1997-98	67.42
1998-99	34.03
1999-00	49.19
2000-01	53.09
2001-02	59.77
2002-03	71.91
2003-04	63.60
2004-05	78.33

Note: The values are in percentage.
Source: Based on Table 7.6 and Table 7.9.

To sum up, the first section of the chapter concludes that India experienced favourable terms of trade with China as compared to its overall adverse terms of trade. The prices of

India's exports to China increased quite faster than the prices of India's overall exports. On the other side, during 1992-93 to 1998-99, the prices of India's overall imports remained below the prices of India's imports from China. However, since 1999-00, India's import unit value index with China remained well below India's overall import unit value index. That's why during that period, India's terms of trade with China improved significantly as compared to India's overall terms of trade. However, there are some more reasons which are responsible for the divergence between India's overall terms of trade and India's terms of trade with China.

The first reason may be that China is well known for its low or cheap price products, while on the other side, Indian exports to China are more costly. The second reason is that Indian exports to China were mainly dominated by ores, slag and ash whose prices to China went up sharply vis-à-vis RoW. On the other side, Indian imports from China were mainly dominated silk; machinery and parts; antibiotics; etc., whose prices remained stable and did not show big fluctuations like Indian exports to China. Third reason may be the low weightage of selected imports as compared to selected exports. Thus, these factors have played the role of maintaining the prices of Indian imports from China at the lower level.

Further, on export side, it has been found that iron ore and concentrates (non-agglomerated) is the only commodity which played the dominant role in India's terms of trade with China and its share reached nearly half of the total exports to China in 2004-05. In fact, Chinese construction industry has been growing rapidly which needs a great deal of iron ore. However, Chinese own sources of iron ore are depleting rapidly. Further, the Chinese iron ore is not of best quality. Therefore, China has to depend upon Indian iron ore which is cheap than Japanese or Korean iron ore (Bhat, et al., 2006). Thus, with the sharp rise in the demand, the unit value of this commodity went up sharply. This sudden rise in the unit value of this commodity made terms of trade index in India's favour.

On the import side, the unit value of Chinese products were lower not because of genuine price differences but because of low but acceptable quality of the products. This again made the terms of trade index to move in India's favour.

The second section concludes that export unit values realised from China were more favourable than the unit values realised from RoW. Similarly, imports from China cost less than the imports from RoW. In other words, on the basis of export ratio and import ratio, it can be concluded that India is gaining more if it exports to China rather than the RoW and its losses can be minimum if it imports from China rather than the RoW. The Relative Terms of Trade Index (RTTI) also reveals the same that during the study period, India's trade with China remained more superior as compared to its trade with the RoW. Hence, like the NBTT, the RTTI also reveals that during the period 1990-91 to 2004-05 India experienced favourable terms of trade with China.

8

Instability and Competitiveness of Exports

Exports have assumed a place of paramount importance in the development process of an economy and played a major role in generating investible surpluses and in financing of imports. Thus, any change in exports of a country brings a major change in the economy (Singla and Brar, 2008). For a better export performance, a country should concentrate on the stability and competitive factors of its exports. Since 2001, China has emerged as one of the leading destinations for Indian exports. Thus, it is of great importance to analyse the instability and competitiveness of Indian exports to China.

8.1 Instability of Exports

It is a fairly widespread view that underdeveloped countries typically suffer from wider fluctuations in their export earnings which produce short-term instability of domestic income and prices and also inhibit long-term growth (Macbean, 1966). Heavy and sudden fluctuations in exports may create serious problems in balance of payments (BoP), national income, investment and then may also create the severe adverse impact on overall growth of a country. Not only this, the export instability of a country may also create income instability in other countries because the world has been synchronising with the process of globalisation (Sinha, 1999).

The exports of a developing country are unstable in the sense that they show a succession of shortfalls and surpluses in relation to a trend. The fluctuations in export earnings influences the economy of a country through variations in exporters' income, which are transmitted through the multiplier effects to other sectors of the economy and ultimately in that process brings about changes in external purchasing power.

There has been a strong controversy in the literature about the exact causes and consequences of exports instability. The exports of both the developed as well as the developing countries fluctuate. But, many studies established that the developing countries have substantially higher degree of export earnings instability than that of developed countries (Macbean, 1966; Schiavo-Campo and Erb, 1969; Massell, 1970; Glezakos, 1973; Savvidos, 1984; and Lanceiri, 1987).

It is generally agreed that, excessive fluctuations in foreign trade originate from variations in supply or demand or other economic and non-economic factors. But, most of the studies based on statistical evidence conclude, though inconclusively, that instability index of exports are largely positively correlated with the degree of commodity concentration of exports and with the proportion of export receipts obtained from the sales of primary goods and negatively correlated with per capita income and with the concentration of exports by geographical area of destination (Knudsen, et al., 1975).

Conventionally, commodity and geographic concentrations were considered to be important factors contributing to such instability. With a high concentration, a country could not reduce the fluctuations in stability in other export goods (Macbean, 1966). In a similar way, Massell (1970) stated that a high geographic concentration would imply greater dependence on economic conditions in one or a few countries and that fluctuation in demand in any recipient country would have a more profound effect on receipts of the exporting country than if receipts were more diversified among recipients.

The studies of Coppock (1962), Massell (1964), Macbean (1966) and Kingston (1973) by and large establish very weak relationship between concentration of exports and exports instability. But, Massell (1970) found a significant relationship between commodity concentration and instability of exports as contrary to his previous study of weak relationship between the two. Love (1979) on the basis of sample of 52 developing countries, over the period from 1961 to 1974, concluded that there existed only casual relationship between export instability and commodity and geographical concentration of exports.

The earlier studies found that there exists no significant relationship between export earning instability and domestic economic development (Coppock, 1962; Macbean, 1966; and Kennen and Voivodas, 1972). But, these views have strongly been refuted by Maizels (1968), Schivo-Campo and Erb (1969), Glezakos (1973), Massell (1970) and Lanceiri (1987). They, in fact, challenged the very statistical soundness of these studies particularly of their limited sample size and cross-country approach of analysis.

It is argued that developing countries are more prone to export earnings instability than the developed ones. Michaely (1962) pointed out that the fluctuations of the terms of trade were larger among the developing countries than among the developed ones. These fluctuations automatically affected their national income. Myrdal (1956), Cairncross (1962) and Meier (1963) claimed that the economic growth of the developing countries suffered from the harmful effects of the export instability mainly because they were primary product exporters. Massell (1970) found that the instability of the merchandise exporters of 36 developing countries was 50 percent more than that of 19 developed countries during 1950-66.

Glezakos (1973) statistically established that the export instability was generally larger in the case of developing countries than that of the developed countries during 1953-66. And, the instability was found to be detrimental to the economic growth in the developing countries but not to that in the case of developed ones. Similarly, Love (1992) by using a sample of 20 developing countries by applying the reduced form approach concluded that export earnings instability significantly induces the short run macro-economic instability. Lanceiri (1987) by using a very large sample of 101 countries over the period from 1961 to 1972, by using the Spearman's Rank Correlation coefficient method, found that export instability significantly negatively affected the four variables, i.e. (i) size of exports (in value terms), (ii) economic size of countries (in terms of national income), (iii) per-capita income, and (iv) growth rate of national income. Askari and Weil (1974), by examining export earning instability for 70 developing countries over a time period from 1954 to 1968, rejected the traditional hypothesis that primary product exporters suffered from a larger degree of export instability. They held the view that the instability appeared to be a larger problem for exporters of manufactured, than for those of non-manufactured goods.

Schivo-Campo and Erb (1974) found that the export instability of both developed and developing countries were markedly lower in 1954-66 than in 1946-58. In both periods, they found that the export instability of developing countries was more than twice as high as that for developed countries. Kenen and Voivodas (1972) did not find a relationship between the rate of economic development and the degree of export instability.

Ozler and Harrigan (1988) studied relationship between GDP growth rate and export instability index by using the cross-section data. The study found a negative correlation between export instability and economic growth. Gyimah-Brempong (1991) used average data for 1960-86 for 34 sub-Saharan African countries. The study found that no matter how export instability was measured, export instability had a negative effect on economic growth. Moran (1983) used cross-section data for 30 countries (18 of them in Latin America) to study the relationship between export fluctuations and economic growth. Using several measures of export instability, he observed that the results were very sensitive to the period under consideration and no general conclusions can be reached.

Sinha (1999) used the time series data to study the relationship between export instability and economic growth for the following nine Asian countries: India, Japan, South Korea, Malaysia, Myanmar, Pakistan, Philippines, Sri Lanka and Thailand. The study brought about a variety of results between export instability and economic growth. For India, the results were mixed. For Japan, Malaysia, Philippines and Sri Lanka, the evidence suggested a negative relationship between export instability and economic growth. For Korea, Myanmar, Pakistan and Thailand, the results showed a positive relationship between export instability and economic growth. These results showed that cross-section studies which lump all countries together may lead to misleading conclusions because results differed among the countries.

Similarly, Sebastian (1988) argued that studies, which lump exports of all goods, are misleading because export instability of a given product is influenced by the characteristics of the individual product and the degree of development of the exporting country. Thus, export instability of a particular product will vary depending upon whether the country is a developed or a developing. The author confined the study to the exports of synthetic fiber (a growing product) and natural fiber (a mature product) and found that export instability of synthetic fiber was higher for the low developing countries than for the developed countries. However, there were no significant differences between the LDCs and DCs when it comes to the natural fiber.

Katrak (1973) and Love (1979) recommended diversification by exporting additional commodities that would differ in type from traditional exports, with the view to lessening instability. Massell (1964) regarded the case of diversification as being closely connected with the arguments for industrialisation. According to Soutar (1977), developing countries experienced export earnings instability mainly because their exports were doubly concentrated, first in primary products and second in few correlated commodities that constituted a large fraction of their exports.

The instability of India's exports and the relationship between instability and economic development have been examined by many researchers such as Chishti (1974), Shetty (1976), Agarwal (1982), Gill (1983), Sharan (1986), Singhal and Kaur (1986), Mukherjee (1987), Kaur and Singhal (1989), Das and Pant (1989), Kaur (1993), Leonard (1993), Brar (1996), etc.

On the basis of above studies, it can be said that there is lack of consensus among economists regarding the relationship between export instability and economic development of a country. According to some, the export earnings instability affected economic growth of developing countries more than that of developed countries, while others found that it affected developed countries more. Generally, it was considered that the export concentration especially in the primary products in developing countries caused the earnings to fluctuate. In all these exercises, there were problems concerning data deficiencies and limitations of statistical devices employed. With explicit recognition of these problems, in the present chapter, an attempt has been made to measure instability in India's exports to China and with its help to test whether India's export trade with China has stabilised India's overall export earnings.

8.1.1 Stabilisation Effect of China: Like most of the studies, the present study is based upon the Coppock's instability indices. These indices help us to ascertain the impact of a particular market on the particular exports of a country, whereas the other methods such as Macbean's moving averages, give the extent of fluctuations only.

The instability of India's fifteen major exports to China has been calculated in terms of value, volume and unit value. The data are collected from the various yearly March issues of Statistics of Foreign Trade of India by Countries and Monthly Statistics of Foreign Trade of India, published by Directorate

General of Commercial Intelligence and Statistics (DGCI&S), Kolkata. The analysis is made over the period 1992-93 to 2004-05. The average annual share of the selected fifteen commodities in India's total exports to China was 49 percent during the study period. Along with this, the indices of instability have also been constructed with reference to India's exports to the whole world and to the Rest of the World (RoW) for the various commodities involved. Here, RoW stands for India's exports to all countries minus China. The criterion applied is that if the overall instability index for the world is lower than that of the RoW, then the movement of exports to China has been compensatory.

(a) **Value Instability:** Instability indices pertaining to the value of India's major commodity groups exported to China, to the world, and to RoW, during the period from 1992-93 to 2004-05, were worked out and are presented in Table 8.1. As is clear from the table, all the export items do not exhibit a uniform pattern of instability. The extent of instability varied from commodity to commodity. With China, the magnitude of the instability was highest in the case of the commodity called cotton yarn containing 85 percent or more by weight (658.79) and lowest in the case of granite crude or roughly trimmed (35.62). China had a destabilising effect upon value of eight commodities, i.e. oil-cake and other solid residues, obtained from soya-bean oil; chromium ores and concentrates; iron ores and concentrates (non-agglomerated); granite crude or roughly trimmed; aluminium oxide; shrimps and prawns frozen; simply cut or sawn granite with a flat or even surface; and organic compounds, because for these eight commodities, the world instability indices (i.e. 24.12, 53.64, 33.95, 24.65, 45.63, 11.46, 14.10 and 14.49 respectively) were higher than those for RoW (i.e. 22.32, 26.75, 24.37, 23.84, 44.21, 11.43, 14.09 and 14.36 respectively). But, in the case of rest of the seven commodities, China had a stabilising effect.

(b) **Volume Instability:** Table 8.2 shows instability indices pertaining to volume of India's exports to China, to the world, and to RoW. The instability indices of the volume of exports to China for fifteen commodities varied between 21.70 and 894.19. The lowest degree of instability was marked in the case of iron ores and concentrates (agglomerated) at 21.70 and the highest was in the case of cotton yarn containing 85 percent or more by weight at 894.19.

Table 8.1: Instability Indices Pertaining to the Value of India's Major Exports to China, World and RoW (1992-93 to 2004-05)

Commodities	China	World	ROW
Oil-cake and other solid residues, obtained from soya-bean oil	175.74	24.12	22.32
Chromium ores and concentrates	79.58	53.64	26.75
Frozen fish excluding livers and rose	85.41	23.23	23.36
Iron ores and concentrates (non-agglomerated)	40.90	33.95	24.37
Iron ores and concentrates (agglomerated)	37.44	53.69	124.93
Granite crude or roughly trimmed	35.62	24.65	23.84
Aluminium oxide	87.73	45.63	44.21
Shrimps and prawns frozen	147.96	11.46	11.43
Simply cut or sawn granite with a flat or even surface	68.09	14.10	14.09
Phthalic anhydride	58.61	40.99	50.01
Organic compounds	116.89	14.49	14.36
Mucilages thickeners, whether or not modified	77.17	15.98	16.81
Cotton yarn containing 85 percent or more by weight	658.79	85.33	86.72
Granite merely cut, into blocks or slabs of a rectangular shape	47.56	23.01	27.41
Appliances of taps, cocks, valves	121.17	68.49	72.61

Note: Here RoW refers to Rest of the World (whole world minus China).

Source: Calculated from Statistics of Foreign Trade of India by Countries and Monthly Statistics of Foreign Trade of India, DGCI&S, Kolkata, (Various Issues).

Table 8.2: Instability Indices Pertaining to the Volume of India's Major Exports to China, World and RoW (1992-93 to 2004-05)

Commodities	China	World	ROW
Oil-cake and other solid residues, obtained from soya-bean oil	161.32	21.48	19.91
Chromium ores and concentrates	254.19	224.17	115.22
Frozen fish excluding livers and roes	68.02	25.03	27.88
Iron ores and concentrates (non-agglomerated)	30.74	26.61	30.09
Iron ores and concentrates (agglomerated)	21.70	30.59	122.52
Granite crude or roughly trimmed	37.10	24.76	22.60
Aluminium oxide	154.86	47.22	40.17
Shrimps and prawns frozen	119.74	5.99	5.91
Simply cut or sawn granite with a flat or even surface	77.62	12.44	12.22
Phthalic anhydride	51.83	37.52	44.63
Organic compounds	95.88	21.24	20.93
Mucilages thickeners, whether or not modified	83.55	4.95	5.49
Cotton yarn containing 85 percent or more by weight	894.19	90.68	91.86
Granite merely cut, into blocks or slabs of a rectangular shape	61.54	46.11	46.67
Appliances of taps, cocks, valves etc.	185.42	51.95	54.51

Note: Here RoW refers to Rest of the World (whole world minus China).

Source: Calculated from Statistics of Foreign Trade of India by Countries and Monthly Statistics of Foreign Trade of India, DGCI&S, Kolkata, (Various Issues).

Further, out of the fifteen commodities studied, in the case of seven commodities, i.e. oil-cake and other solid residues, obtained from soyabean oil; chromium ores and concentrates; granite crude or roughly trimmed; aluminium oxide; shrimps and prawns frozen; simply cut or sawn granite with a flat or even surface; and organic compounds, the world instability indices (i.e. 21.48, 224.17, 24.76, 47.22, 5.99, 12.44 and 21.24 respectively) were higher than those for the RoW (i.e. 19.91, 115.22, 22.60, 40.17, 5.91, 12.22 and 20.93 respectively). It indicates that, in volume terms, India's trade with China had a destabilising effect on her overall trade of these seven commodities. While for rest of the eight commodities, China had a stabilising effect.

(c) Unit Value Instability: Instability indices pertaining to unit value of India's exports to China, to the world, and to RoW have been presented in Table 8.3. In unit value terms, the extent of instability, with China, varied between 9.25 and 110.77. The lowest degree of instability was marked in case of the commodity namely granite crude or roughly trimmed at 9.25 and highest was in the case of chromium ores and concentrates at 110.77. China had destabilising effect upon eight commodities, i.e. oil-cake and other solid residues, obtained from soyabean oil; frozen fish excluding livers and roes; iron ores and concentrates (non-agglomerated); granite crude or roughly trimmed; aluminium oxide; phthalic anhydride; organic compounds; and mucilages thickeners, whether or not modified, because for these eight commodities, the world instability indices (i.e. 14.04, 5.38, 14.07, 3.55, 14.76, 21.04, 15.58 and 14.74 respectively) were higher than those for the RoW (i.e. 14.03, 5.04, 6.88, 3.48, 13.21, 20.22, 15.04 and 14.67 respectively). But for rest of the seven commodities, China had a stabilising effect.

Thus, to sum up, it can be said that out of fifteen commodities, China had stabilised the value and unit value of seven commodities and volume of eight commodities. In terms of value, the seven commodities for which China had a stabilising effect constituted 11.73 percent of the total value of India's exports to China and rest of the eight commodities for which China had a destabilising effect, constituted 37.06 percent of the total exports. Thus, China had more of destabilising effect on India's exports than the stabilising

India and China

effect.

Table 8.3: Instability Indices Pertaining to the Unit Value of India's Major Exports to China, World and RoW (1992-93 to 2004-05)

Commodities	China	World	ROW
Oil-cake and other solid residues, obtained from soya-bean oil	27.91	14.04	14.03
Chromium ores and concentrates	110.77	130.14	130.99
Frozen fish excluding livers and roes	12.16	5.38	5.04
Iron ores and concentrates (non-agglomerated)	18.04	14.07	6.88
Iron ores and concentrates (agglomerated)	19.76	17.49	18.09
Granite crude or roughly trimmed	9.25	3.55	3.48
Aluminium oxide	76.35	14.76	13.21
Shrimps and prawns frozen	21.72	7.84	8.38
Simply cut or sawn granite with a flat or even surface	27.38	2.63	2.99
Phthalic anhydride	29.85	21.04	20.22
Organic compounds	47.95	15.58	15.04
Mucilages thickeners, whether or not modified	13.13	14.74	14.67
Cotton yarn containing 85 percent or more by weight	55.36	6.91	6.92
Granite merely cut, into blocks or slabs of a rectangular shape	29.60	49.22	50.49
Appliances of taps, cocks, valves etc.	27.80	11.83	12.85

Note: Here RoW refers to Rest of the World (whole world minus China).
Source: Calculated from Statistics of Foreign Trade of India by Countries and Monthly Statistics of Foreign Trade of India, DGCI&S, Kolkata, (Various Issues).

Further, from the above tables, it can also be observed that the index of instability pertaining to volume was uniformly higher than that of unit value for all the fifteen major export commodities considered during the period from 1992-93 to 2004-05. This implied that the instability in value of exports was more due to the instability in volume of the commodities exported rather than due to the fluctuations in unit value obtained, because value of a commodity would be its volume multiplied by its unit value.

Hence, the analysis shows that India's export earnings from China were subject to strong variations. The export earnings were unstable both due to the instability of export prices and volume exported. So, the dual nature of the instability makes the task of stabilisation of export earnings very complicated. The instable export earnings from China were primarily due to the volume instability. Hence, there is a need to explore the relationship between three variables, i.e. value, volume and price, which would be helpful in understanding the movements of export earnings. Further, all the commodities and markets do not contribute equally to the export instability. Hence, there is a need of disaggregate studies, both commodity-wise and market-wise. The commodities and markets with higher instabilities must be identified. The over dependence on higher instable markets or commodities can prove very harmful. Attempts can also be made to explore the possibilities of shifting the exports from higher instable commodities and markets to lower ones. So, there is a need of commodity as well as market specific policies. The commodities with stable export proceeds with China must be encouraged in order to sustain the long run export earnings.

8.2 Competitiveness of Exports

One of the widely accepted paradigms in international trade is that potential benefits of open trade outweigh the costs. The unsustainable and often growth decelerating effects of inward looking development strategies glorified in sixties, have given way for recognising the positive link between openness and export, and export and growth. The classical and neo-classical economists' argument that international trade could be an engine of economic growth has come to the fore. As Krueger (1998) pointed out, trade policy is integrally tied up with overall development strategy. Therefore, promotion of foreign trade, particularly of exports has now become a leading effort of development of many developing countries like India (Hosamane, et al., 2006).

The export promotion of a country depends heavily on the international competitiveness of her exports. While the concept of international competitiveness can be said to consist of different factors, ultimately the litmus test of the competitive position of a country vis-à-vis other countries is in the relative market share of its exports in the world market (Marjit, et al., 1997).

The interest in analysis of competitiveness has grown rapidly because the economic progress of a country is critically linked with the behaviour of their exports. McGeehan (1968) reported that studies undertaken in several western countries have shown a clear association between price and export performance. Similar findings were reported about the export performance of some of the less developed countries also. Cohen (1964) concluded that the declining market share of India's exports in the fifties was associated with an increase in the price of her export products relative to competitors' prices. These studies do not by any means prove that non-price factors such as quality, marketing and service, are unimportant in determining competitiveness. Most of the available evidence, however, underscores the importance of price as a major determinant of competitiveness.

In spite of the dominant role of price competitiveness in export performance, there have not been any systematic attempts to investigate the factors causing price differences between competing countries. McGeehan (1968) reviewed a number of studies which had examined the impact of factors such as costs, productivity, size of plant and internal demand on export performance. The common feature of those studies was their partial approach to the problem. Their focus in every case was on explaining competitiveness by reference to one or the other of the foregoing factors. What appears to have been overlooked was the fact that most of these factors had a joint effect on competitiveness, price being an index of the net effect of their interaction. Balassa (1962) showed that how closely prices tend to move with costs, export prices being no exception. On the other hand, even if costs remain unchanged, it is possible for prices to rise in response to the growing pressure of internal demand. Ball, et al. (1966) and Singh (1964) also examined this possibility with reference to British and Indian exports respectively.

The competitiveness of exports is a multi-dimensional phenomenon, which depends upon a lot of price and non-price factors. In general, it is the outcome of domestic resource endowment, production structure, development stage, development strategy and other economic policies. However, a country cannot maintain her share in world trade, though her exports are competitive, but if they are facing declining world demand or concentrated on stagnating markets. Tiwari (1986) argued that exports from a country depend upon the absorption capacity, i.e. purchasing power of the importers of her exports. Thus, the competitiveness can be viewed as the capacity, in terms of price and non-price factors, of exporting country to improve the exportability of a commodity in foreign markets.

Price is frequently regarded as the most important factor which influence the competitiveness of exports because changes in export prices directly affect the export performance. As a general rule, if the price of a country's product is lower, the higher the export demand and so greater the level of its competitiveness and vice-versa. A change in relative prices, thus, affects competitiveness of exports (Paul and Mote, 1970). However, price is by no means the sole determinant of export competitiveness. In fact, the term also connotes many other factors, which can be explained as follows.

Like all prices, export prices are closely related to costs. It follows that India's competitiveness in the world market would have been partially influenced by changes in the cost structure of her export industries. The main determinants of costs are factor productivity and factor prices (Nayyar, 1976). Therefore, at a given point of time, the difference in costs of production (hence export prices) as between competing countries can be explained almost entirely in terms of differences in factor prices. The pressure of domestic demand is likely to affect the price competitiveness of exports. If the domestic markets are more profitable, then the exporters would like to sell in the home market. Apart from the costs of production and the pressure of domestic demand, supply constraints in export industries also influence the price competitiveness and physical availability of exports. The share of a country in world trade can also decline due to the lack of export surpluses, though exports might be competitive.

Trade policies followed by a country significantly affect the competitiveness of exports. Exchange rate variations are important instruments of trade policy available to governments for the purpose of attaining external balance. Such changes in exchange rate directly affect the returns of exporters and consequently influence competitiveness. The undervalued exchange rate and the subsidisation of exports positively affect the competitiveness of exports. Similarly, the export competitiveness of a country can also be affected by the trade policies, particularly tariff and non-tariff barriers, adopted by the importing country. The prevalent of quantitative restrictions in the developed country markets significantly hit the exports of developing countries. Exports from some countries enjoyed the duty free or reduced duty entry into some markets. The exports from such countries are clearly at an edge than the other countries. Some countries even started following the strategic trade policies, i.e. selection of few commodities, facilitating their entry into particular markets by all out efforts and then defending their share in the market.

In addition to relative prices and trade policies, export competitiveness is also dependent upon factors which are not reflected in prices. In fact, non-price factors such as designing, quality, marketing strategies such as network marketing, direct marketing, relationship marketing, etc., efficiency, credit, delivery dates, after sales services, reliability, good will visit, attractiveness of the particular brand names and overall get up of the service centres, etc., have an important bearing on a country's ability to export and its potential for expanding exports.

So, two types of competitiveness gained grounds, i.e. price competitiveness and non-price competitiveness. Thus, in order to increase the exports, a country will have to fight on the above two fronts. The significance of each of these factors cannot be ignored in any way. Hence, the competitiveness of exports is a multi-dimensional phenomenon, embracing the impact of so many factors.

Since the inception of liberalisation policy in 1991, India's export trade rose substantially. Though its share in world exports is low, yet it has been increasing continuously. In 1991, India's share in world exports was 0.51 percent which rose to 0.95 percent in 2005. During the period 1991-2005, the direction of India's exports also changed sharply and China emerged as one of the leading destination for Indian exports. China's share in India's overall exports increased rapidly from 0.27 percent in 1991 to 6.58 percent in 2005. Thus, it becomes a really important exercise to identify the different factors responsible for this sharp rise in India's exports to China. However, here the major consideration of the study is to access the competitive factor. But, before starting this exercise, it is necessary to view some important studies regarding India's export competitiveness.

8.2.1 Studies on India's Export Competitiveness: There are a lot of studies available in the literature, which thoroughly examined competitiveness of India's overall exports by taking different time series data sets. A few studies have been reviewed here to place the present study in the proper perspective. Bhagwati and Srinivasan (1976) assessed India's export performance over the period from 1951 to 1960. They analysed the loss of export earnings that followed from the failure to maintain export shares. They held the domestic policies responsible for this. Bhagwati (1970) examined the competitiveness of India's exports from 1959-68. The analysis showed that the currency over-valuation had put a negative impact on export competitiveness while the attenuation of over-valuation through export subsidies had influenced export competitiveness positively. The analysis was not an argument for such subsidies but for the avoidance of currency over-valuation and other similar measures that impede the growth of exports from many low-income countries.

Tiwari (1986) analysed India's export competitiveness over the period from 1970 to 1977. The study concluded that during this period, the exports of India exhibited positive competitiveness effects. Study held that the domestic improved supply position responsible for this. Kapur (1991) examined the export performance of India over the period 1962 to 1984. He concluded that India's exports were competitive in the markets of Italy, Belgium, Netherlands and former West Germany and they were non-competitive in the markets of USA, UK, France and Japan. Further, he concluded that the non-traditional exports exhibited more competitiveness than the traditional exports, because the domestic export promotion policies favoured the former type of exports.

Marjit, et al. (1997) examined export competitiveness from 1971 to 1990. The study concluded that price factors did not explain changes in aggregate competitiveness in a significant way. However, this conclusion modifies slightly in case of India's manufacturing exports. On the other hand, costs are seen not to affect the competitiveness of the manufacturing sector at all. There are many non-price factors which influence the export competitiveness greatly. The study suggested that government policies must be sufficiently tuned to influence the non-price factors.

Tiwari (1998-99) examined the state of competitiveness in newly industrialised countries (NICs) in terms of price and non-price factors emanating from external demand and to that of internal supply. The study concluded that in case of India both price competitiveness and non-price competitiveness fall during 1983-1995. The inefficient marketing network was held responsible for unfavourable competitiveness in certain non-traditional goods. Tariff and non-tariff barriers were seen largely responsible for the fall in competitiveness of various products under traditional and non-traditional sectors.

Hosamane, et al. (2006) made an attempt to examine the export behaviour of India during the post-reform period. The study revealed that openness leads to economic growth and increased the volume of country's trade with the world trade in developing and transitional economies. It is observed that as the economy opens up, the export of manufactured goods also increases. The study revealed that during the liberalisation period the incremental export of 53.5 percent was due to competitiveness of products in the world market. The globalisation helped Indian economy to increase the competitiveness of its products in the world market.

Kumar and Joseph (2007) analysed the international competitiveness of India's exports through an empirical analysis covering a sample of more than four thousand enterprises. A detailed study of five key knowledge-based industries, i.e. electronics, pharmaceuticals, chemical, automotive and non-electrical machinery provides an in-depth coverage of the issue. The study advocates a strategic approach to enhance the export competitiveness of enterprises in India and outlines policy lessons for the government, industry bodies and enterprises.

Veeramani (2007) investigated the sources of India's export growth during the pre and post-reform periods. The pace of India's export growth had not been distinctly high in most part of the post-reform period (1993-2005), though it had accelerated since. 2002. In contrast to the pre-reform period, however, India's exports grew faster than the rate of growth of world exports during the post-reform period. However, decomposition of export growth showed that the actual export growth of India had been far below the potential offered by the growth of world trade in most part of the pre-reform period. The negative competitiveness effect and negative commodity composition effect had been the major retarding factors of export growth in the pre-reform period. In contrast, the actual growth of India's merchandise and services exports had been above the potential throughout the post-reform period. Further, the author suggested that export policy should focus on other measures that could improve the competitiveness of Indian exports on sustained basis.

Thus, all the studies have measured the competitiveness of India's overall exports by taking different time series data sets. Most of the studies have used the Constant Market Share (CMS) model to assess the competitiveness of India's exports. However, this method is difficult to apply on the present study because it is difficult to measure the market distribution effect between the two countries. Therefore, the present study has used an empirical procedure (used by Bhat, et al., 2006) to assess the competitiveness factor of India's exports to China. Further, the market shares and unit values have also been computed to analyse the competitiveness of India's exports to China at individual commodity level. However, this is the limitation of the study that it is only concerned with the price competitiveness of India's exports to China, while all other variable are assumed to be constant.

8.2.2 Competitiveness of India's Exports to China: To measure the competitiveness of India's exports to China, two different approaches have been adopted which are based on aggregated and disaggregated data sets of commodities. In the first approach, which is based on aggregated data set, the total change in the value of India's exports to China is decomposed into three different effects, i.e. demand effect, competitiveness effect and diversification effect. On the other side, the second approach is based on market shares and unit values of individual commodities at disaggregate level. The first approach is an empirical procedure which is followed to isolate the effects of demand, competitiveness and diversification of India's exports to China. To avoid the complexity of the analysis, a sample of those commodities has been taken whose share is more than 0.50 percent in India's total exports to China. Further, the analysis is made for two different sub-periods, i.e. I sub-period (1996 to 2000) and II sub-period (2001 to 2005). The data was collected at 6-digit HS-96 level of classification, provided by UN Commodity Trade Statistics. The data was collected in c.i.f. form. The empirical procedure to isolate the effects of demand, competitiveness and diversification changes of India's exports to China can be explained as follows.

(i) Demand Effect: The influence of demand for a specific product of a country can be measured by the change in the total (global) value of imports of that product. Suppose D_{oj} and D_{tj} represent China's total imports of product j at period 'o' and 't' respectively. The change in export of the product 'j' by India to China attributed solely to demand effect (ΔE_{dj}) is:

$$\Delta E_{dj} = S_{oj} \times (D_{tj} - D_{oj})$$

Where S_{oj} is the share of country i, say India, in global Chinese imports of product 'j' in period 'o'. So, for all the products (n) exported by India to China, the change in export due to change in demand can be measured by taking the sum total of all the products exported by India to China.

$$\Delta E_{dn} = \Sigma\, S_{oj} \times (D_{tj} - D_{oj}) \sum_{j=1}^{n}$$

(ii) Competitiveness Effect: The competitiveness effect (ΔE_{cj}) of India in exporting product 'j' into China can be measured as follows:

$$\Delta E_{cj} = D_{tj} \times (S_{tj} - S_{oj})$$

Where S_{oj} and S_{tj} are the share of India in total Chinese imports of the product 'j' in period 'o' and 't' respectively and D_{tj} represents China's total import of product 'j' at period 't'.

To get the increase of India's exports of all products (n) to China due to increase in competitiveness can be measured by taking summation of all the products exported by India to China.

$$\Delta E_{cn} = \Sigma\, D_{tj} \times (S_{tj} - S_{oj}) \sum_{j=1}^{n}$$

(iii) Diversification Effect: Now a country's total export to another country can be increased because of another factor that is increase in product diversification. Any difference between changes in a country's total exports and sum of above two effects, i.e. demand effect and competitiveness effect, is due to product diversification effect.

$$\Delta E_{rn} = \Delta E_{Tn} - (\Delta E_{dn} + \Delta E_{cn})$$

Where ΔE_{rn} is diversification effect of n commodities, ΔE_{Tn} is total change in the value of n products exported by India to China, ΔE_{dn} is demand effect of n commodities and ΔE_{cn} is competitiveness of n commodities.

As stated earlier, the study is limited to the products that have more than 0.50 percent share in the total Indian exports to China (Table 8.4). The number of such products in 1996 was 30. In the year 2000, it increased to 39. And, there are 14 products that India exported to China in the year 1996 as well as in the year 2000. Therefore, product diversification has taken place. Sixteen products, which appeared in 1996 list, disappeared in 2000 list and twenty five new products, which did not appear in year 1996 list, were added in the 2000 list. Indian exports to China went up in 2000 as compared to 1996 by US\$ 495.18 million. In this export increase, US\$ 60.86 million were due to increase in the Chinese demand of these products.

It constituted 12.29 percent of total export increase. Due to increase in competitiveness, the increase in export was US\$

237.67 million. It constituted 48 percent of total export increase.

Table 8.4: Different Factors behind the Increase in Indian Exports to China

Period	Initial Year (1996) and Present Year (2000)	Initial Year (2001) and Present Year (2005)
Number of commodities in the initial year	30	32
Number of commodities in the present year	39	24
Number of commodities existed in both the years	14	13
Total exports of listed commodities in initial year (in US$ million)	599.21	1319.98
Total exports of listed commodities in present year (in US$ million)	1094.39	8164.56
Change in export value between initial and present year (in US$ million)	495.18 (100.00)	6844.57 (100.00)
Change in Indian exports due to change in demand (in US$ million)	60.86 (12.29)	3964.61 (57.92)
Change in Indian exports due to change in competitiveness (in US$ million)	237.67 (48.00)	2043.03 (29.85)
Change in Indian exports due to change in product diversification (in US$ million)	196.65 (39.71)	836.93 (12.23)

Note: 1. Here only those commodities have been considered whose share is more than 0.50 percent in India's total exports to China; 2. Figures in parentheses show the percentage share in total change in the export value between the present year and the initial year.
Source: Calculated from UN Commodity Trade Statistics.

Moreover, due to product diversification the increase in export was US$ 196.65 million. It accounted for the remaining 39.71 percent of total export increase.

Thus, during 1996-2000, all three effects remained positive. However, during this period, competitiveness effect played a leading role in augmenting Indian exports to China. The role of diversification factor was also an important one, while the increase in Chinese import demand played a least role in augmenting Indian exports to China during this period.

During the second sub-period, i.e. 2001-2005, the number of commodities declined from 32 in 2001 to 24 in 2005. In addition, the number of common products that India exported to China in the year 2001 and 2005 became 13. Nineteen products, which appeared in 2001 list, disappeared in the year 2005, while only eleven new products got into the product list of the year 2005. It shows the low degree of product diversification. Indian exports to China went up during 2005 as compared to 2001 by US$ 6844.57 million. In this export increase, US$ 3964.61 million were due to increase in Chinese demand of these products. It constituted 57.92 percent of the total export increase. Due to increase in competitiveness, the increase in exports was US$ 2043.03 million.

It constituted 29.85 percent of total export increase. In addition, due to product-diversification, the increase in exports was US$ 836.93 million. It accounted for the remaining 12.23 percent of export increase. Thus, once again, during 2001-05, all three effects remained positive. However, during this period, Indian exports to China rose mainly due to increase in Chinese global import demand. Further, these results were also supported by the study of Veeramani (2007), in which the author had concluded that the rapid growth of India's overall merchandise exports, since 2002, has been mainly driven by a buoyant world economy, and the competitiveness effect, though positive, has not been the major contributing factor in the acceleration of the growth of merchandise exports.

Hence, in both the periods, all the three factors had a

positive influence on the increase in Indian exports to China. However, the influence of competitiveness effect and diversification effect went down in the second sub-period as compared to the first sub-period. The most important factor behind the increase in export growth, during 2001-05, was the massive increase in Chinese import demand. During this period, increase in Chinese import demand was the most important factor behind the increase of Indian exports to China, while the increase in competitiveness was the second important factor. Increase in product diversification had the least impact on overall export increase.

8.2.3 Competitiveness: Commodity-Specific: After analysing the competitiveness of India's exports to China at aggregate level, it is important to view the competitiveness of India's exports to China at the level of individual commodities. This exercise has been done by using market shares and unit values. In fact, competitiveness in trade is broadly defined as the capacity of a country to increase its share in international markets at the expenses of its rivals. The Competitiveness Index is an indirect measure of international market power, evaluated through a country's share of world markets in selected export categories.

The Competitiveness Index is the share of total export of a given product (say i) from a country under study (say j) in the global imports of partner country (say k) of the same product. In mathematical terms:

$$\text{Competitiveness Index} = \frac{X_{ijk}}{M_{ikw}}$$

Where,

X_{ijk} - represents exports of product i by country j to country k.

M_{ikw} - represents country k's global (w) imports of product i.

The analysis of market shares and unit values of India's exports to China has been limited to the period from 2001 to 2005. This is the period when China joined the WTO. During this period, growth of India's exports to China remained quite high, i.e. 56.52 percent per annum. The data was collected from UN Commodity Trade Statistics at 6-digit HS-96 level. The analysis has been made by taking into account the China's imports which are reported as c.i.f. values for better comparison of unit values instead of exports data which is f.o.b.

To compute the market shares and unit values of India's exports to China, fifteen commodities were selected whose share remained more than sixty percent during 2001-05. These are actually items of India's export-interest in case of China. The total share of the selected commodities was 60.04 percent in 2001, which increased continuously and reached to 75.98 percent in 2005. The share of single commodity namely iron ore, concentrates, not iron pyrites, unagglomerated, increased quiet surprisingly and it constituted nearly half of the total Indian exports to China in 2005 (i.e. 49.31 percent). This sharp rise in the share of this commodity was mainly due to the quick rise of Chinese demand for this product for its construction and manufacturing industries. The share of some other commodities like aluminium oxide, except artificial corundum; and cotton, not carded or combed also rose during 2001-05.

On the other hand, the share of granite, crude or roughly trimmed; chromium ores and concentrates; polypropylene in primary forms; cotton yarn >85 percent single combed 714-232 dtex, not retail; diamonds (jewellery) worked but not mounted or set; fish nes, frozen, whole; and polyethylene-specific gravity <0.94 in primary forms declined rapidly during the same period. The share of remaining commodities witnessed sharp fluctuations.

As is clear, the market share of hot rolled stainless steel coil, w >600mm, t <3mm increased sharply from 8.90 percent in 2001 to 30.90 percent in 2005. It is also interesting to note that even with the continuous rise in the unit value, the market share of this commodity rose continuously. Similarly, the market share of iron ore, concentrate, not iron pyrites, unagglomerated; aluminium oxide, except artificial corundum; polyethylene-specific gravity >0.94 in primary forms; and cotton, not carded or combed also increased rapidly. In fact, the unit values and market shares of these commodities rose simultaneously.

The market share of the commodity namely chromium ores and concentrates declined substantially from 73.01 percent in 2001 to 39.29 percent in 2005. The unit value of this commodity rose from US$ 0.07 per kg in 2001 to US$ 0.24 per kg. in 2005. Similarly, the market share of four other commodities namely iron ore, concentrate, not iron pyrites, agglomerated; cotton yarn >85 percent single combed 714-232 dtex, not retail; fish nes, frozen, whole; and polyethylene-specific gravity <0.94 in primary forms also declined considerably. The market share and unit value of granite, crude or roughly trimmed remained quite consistent during the study period. The remaining commodities showed sharp fluctuations.

8.2.4 Market Shares and Unit Values: The Relative Level: The analysis becomes more interesting when the market share and unit values of India's selected exports to China are compared with the market share and unit values of India's major competitors in the Chinese market. For this purpose, the top two suppliers of the same selected fifteen commodities to Chinese market have been identified and their market share and unit values have been compared with that of India's market share and unit values of the same commodities from 2001 to 2005.

There were four products in which India enjoyed the largest market share in China. These products were granite, crude or roughly trimmed; chromium ores and concentrates; diamonds (jewellery) worked but not mounted or set; and fish nes, frozen, whole. In another two products namely iron ore, concentrate, not iron pyrites, agglomerated; and cotton yarn >85 percent single combed 714-232 dtex, not retail, India enjoyed second largest market share. In the remaining nine products, in terms of market share India was nowhere. However, the unit values of four products, in which India enjoyed the largest market share, were either lower or equal to the country with second largest market share. India was in competitive position in these four products in terms of unit values. However, there were four products in which India had lower unit values than those of the countries which occupy the largest market shares. Thus, even though India has lower unit values of these commodities but still had very low market share. It may be due to the inferiority in quality of Indian products.

India got the largest market share in case of three products namely granite, crude or roughly trimmed; chromium ores and concentrates; and diamonds (jewellery) worked but not mounted or set. In two products, namely iron ore, concentrate, not iron pyrites, agglomerated; and aluminium oxide, except artificial corundum, India got the second largest market share. In the remaining ten products, in terms of market share, India stood nowhere. On the other side, the unit values of two products, in which India enjoyed the largest market share, were lower than the country with second largest market share. Thus, in 2002, India was in a competitive position in these two products on the basis of lower unit values. However, for nine products, India obtained lower unit value from China in comparison to the country with the largest market share even then India got very low market.

Like the year 2002, India again got the largest market share in the same products during 2003 and similarly the unit values of granite, crude or roughly trimmed; and chromium ores and concentrates were lower than the country with second largest market share. Due to the improved market share of iron ore, concentrate, not iron pyrites, unagglomerated; flat rolled i/nas, coated with zinc, width >600mm, nes; and hot rolled stainless steel coil, w >600mm, t <3mm, over the previous year, India got the second largest market share in case of five products during 2003. In the remaining seven products, in terms of market share, India was nowhere in the Chinese global imports. On the other hand, there were seven products for which India obtained lower unit value vis-à-vis the country with largest market share. Even then India got a very small market share.

In the year 2004, India got the largest market share in case of five products namely granite, crude or roughly trimmed; iron ore, concentrate, not iron pyrites, unagglomerated; chromium ores and concentrates; diamonds (jewellery) worked but not mounted or set; and hot rolled stainless steel coil, w >600mm, t <3mm. However, in case of iron ore, concentrate, not iron pyrites, unagglomerated; and chromium ores and concentrates, the unit values obtained by India were higher than the unit values obtained from the country with the second largest market share. Thus, these products showed a high degree of price-competitiveness in Chinese market. On the other hand, in case of two products namely iron ore, concentrate, not iron pyrites, agglomerated; and polyethylene-specific gravity >0.94 in primary forms, India stood second in terms of market share. In the remaining eight products, India was nowhere in Chinese global imports. However, in seven products, like previous year, India obtained lower unit value from China than the country with largest market share and even then, India's market share in case of these commodities was lower.

In year 2005, India's share was the largest in case of four products namely granite, crude or roughly trimmed; chromium ores and concentrates; diamonds (jewellery) worked but not mounted or set; and fish nes, frozen, whole. In another four commodities, India's share was the second largest. These were iron ore, concentrate, not iron pyrites, unagglomerated; iron ore, concentrate, not iron pyrites, agglomerated; aluminium oxide, except artificial corundum; and hot rolled stainless steel coil, w >600mm, t <3mm. In the remaining seven products, in terms of market share, India was nowhere. In case of chromium ores and concentrates; and fish nes, frozen, whole,

India obtained higher unit values than the country with second largest market share, and moreover India got the biggest share in Chinese market. In six products, India obtained lower unit values than the country with largest market share, but even then India's market share remained low in these commodities.

The limited exercise related to market shares and unit values indicate that the market share and unit values do not show any unique or one to one relationship. The market share and unit values exhibit extremely divergent scenarios. Actually, it seems that the market share is not the function of unit values alone. There is plethora of factors that influence the market share which ranges from supply side to the demand side and are based on price and non-price factors. But, the analysis throws much light on the range of price differences among the important suppliers. Moreover, the commodity specific important suppliers are being identified. Further, it is important to know that in many commodities the important suppliers were the countries located at considerable difference from China such as Brazil, Australia, Norway, South Africa, etc. These countries suffer from the locational disadvantage as compared to India in China's market. The opening up of the trade under the WTO may change the situation in the coming years. There is a need to examine the reasons for the decline in the market share of particular commodities by focusing upon both the supply side and demand side.

9

Revealed Comparative Advantage

Prior to the reforms, both India and China followed a relatively autarkic trade policy accompanied by a battery of trade and exchange controls, cutting the link between domestic and world relative prices (Lal, 1995). China had a non-market command economy while India always had a large private sector and functioning markets (though subjected to state controls). Exchange rate was over-valued in both the countries, creating a bias against exports. In China, foreign trade activities were monopolised by a handful of centrally controlled foreign trade corporations. In India, since foreign trade was largely in the hands of the private sector, an elaborate system of exchange controls and allocation was instituted to ensure that the foreign exchange earned by exporters was used to import only those commodities that conformed to the priorities set in the various five year plans (Srinivasan, 1990).

However, China started its trade liberalisation process in 1978, while India undertook a series of economic reforms towards opening up of the economy in the decade of the nineties. Notable among these had been the extensive effort to liberalise its international trade. It is, further, expected that trade liberalisation in India and China would have led to changes in the composition of exports so as to reflect their comparative advantage in the global economy. The rationale behind trade liberalisation suggests that greater competition would induce the production units to improve productivity, which is instrumental in accelerating the overall economic growth.

Similarly, reduction of trade barriers would create competitive pressures and the potential for technology transfer so as to lead to productivity gains and restructuring of an economy toward its comparative advantage. Since firms respond to the world market signals, the commodity structure of the country's trade would undergo changes in accordance with the changing patterns of specialisation. The conventional wisdom, based on the Heckscher-Ohlin-Samuelson (H-O-S) model, also suggests the same that trade liberalisation would induce reallocation of productive resources from the import-competing industries to those industries where the country has comparative advantages (Veeramani, 2008).

It is well known that the export performance of China since the beginning of 1980s has been spectacular and that India's performance, in comparison, leaves much to be desired. Between 1980 and 2004, China's share in the world exports steadily increased from less than one percent to more than six percent, while India's share increased from 0.4 percent to only 0.8 percent (Srinivasan, 2006). China's recent move towards export-oriented development strategy may have altered the picture of comparative advantage for labour intensive manufactures in the world market. Across developing countries, there is an ongoing debate and emerging concern about the threat and opportunity in relation to the rise of China and the consequent intensification of competition in labour-intensive manufactures.

The debate is even more pertinent in case of India, as China and India are not just similar in size but also with respect to factor endowments (Batra and Khan, 2005). It is important, therefore, to explore the structure of comparative advantage of India and China and the extent to which the two economies compete with each other in the global market for a range of product categories. This chapter is an attempt to develop some insights on the subject.

9.1 Global and Indian Reviews of Comparative Advantage

The concept of 'revealed' comparative advantage, was introduced by Liesner (1958) but refined and popularised by

Balassa (1965) with his Concomitant Index. Balassa (1979) investigated the changing pattern of comparative advantage in the process of the accumulation of physical and human capital that characterises economic development. In another study, Balassa (1986) showed that the differences in physical and human capital endowments explain a substantial part of inter-country differences in the pattern of trade in manufactured goods. It was further shown that the pattern of specialisation was also affected by the extent of trade orientation, the concentration of the export structure, and foreign direct investment.

Leu (1998) analysed if there was any systematic shift of comparative advantage in East Asian economies. For this purpose, the author calculated the revealed comparative advantage indices of ten selected East Asian economies in the US market. The results showed that significant changes in comparative advantage occurred in case of East Asian Economies since 1980s. In particular, Korea, Taiwan and Singapore took over some of Japan's export shares in the US market while Singapore and Hong Kong faced stronger competition from Malaysia and Indonesia respectively.

Richardsan and Zhang (1999) used Balassa's index of revealed comparative advantage for the US to analyse pattern of variation across time, sectors and regions. The study found that there were different patterns for different time periods, for different parts of the world, and also for different levels of aggregation of the export data. These differences were accounted for by factors like geographical proximity of trading partners and per capita income with the extent of influence of these factors varying over time and across sectors/sub sectors.

Bender and Li (2002) examined the performance of manufactured exports in a number of Asian and Latin American economies over the period 1981-1997 and computed revealed comparative advantage indices between economies in East Asia, Southeast Asia and Latin America. The evidence strongly suggested that despite the strong export performance experienced by East Asian economies, they were losing their comparative advantage to the lower-tier economies in Southeast Asia and Latin America.

Fertő and Hubbard (2002) investigated the competitiveness of Hungarian agriculture in relation to that of the EU employing four indices of revealed comparative advantage, for the period 1992 to 1998. The results suggested that despite significant changes in Hungarian agriculture during the 1990s, the pattern of revealed comparative advantage remained fairly stable. RCA indices, despite their limitations, provided a useful guide to underlying comparative advantage and offered a further insight into the competitiveness of Hungarian agri-food sectors and the implications for trade when membership of the EU would become a reality.

Biandara and Smith (2002) analysed trade flows between Australia and SAARC countries by using trade intensity index and revealed comparative advantage index. The study suggested that it was necessary for Australian exporters to increase their exports to the South Asian region within those commodity groups in which they had a comparative advantage before other countries (such as the US and EU) increased their penetration levels in this market.

Lee (2003) examined the competitiveness of Canada in the United States vis-à-vis thirty one other major exporters to the US based on revealed comparative advantage measure for the period 1985 to 1999. Canada was shown to have comparative advantage in a range of food and live animals, crude materials and mineral fuels. Canada had comparative disadvantage in manufactured goods. The pattern of Canada revealed that comparative advantage remained fairly stable with a few exceptions.

Utkulu and Seymen (2004) analysed the competitiveness and pattern of trade flow/trade specialisation from Turkey to EU on sectrol levels. The study calculated seven indices of revealed comparative advantage for the period 1990 to 2003.

All the tests showed that Turkey had revealed comparative advantages for seven out of the sixty-three product groups: clothing and clothing accessories; vegetables and fruit; sugar, sugar preparations, honey; tobacco; oil seeds and oleaginous fruits; rubber manufactures; textile yarn, fabrics and related products.

Kilduff and Chi (2006) employed revealed comparative advantage index to evaluate international competitiveness for thirty nations over a forty-two years period. ANOVA-model was used to determine the significance of the observed patterns across five income-defined groups of nations. The study found that higher income nations generally remained stronger in more capital-intensive sectors, and the lower income countries emerged to dominate in labour-intensive sectors. However, inclusion of a more complex array of variables was necessary to obtain a fuller understanding of international competitiveness.

There are also a lot of studies available which analysed the revealed comparative advantage for India and China, separately, jointly or in comparative framework. Some important studies are reviewed herein.

Cerra, et al. (2005) compared the revealed comparative advantage index of India and China by using broad industry group to look for areas of common specialisation. Study showed that India had comparative advantage in agriculture products and metals, and China had comparative advantage in manufacturing of instruments, arms, toys and other products. Textiles and clothing represented the area in which India and China had the predominant revealed comparative advantage. Exports from this sector had averaged about thirty percent of total exports for the both countries over the period 1992-2001. Even within this sector, there were areas of specialisation. India had relatively higher comparative advantage in basic materials, while China had stronger comparative advantage in manufactured articles of clothing.

The same pattern was noted by Shafaeddin (2004), who

pointed out that India and China compete in textiles and clothing, but only in limited items. India concentrated on exporting undergarments and miscellaneous textile items and China in outer-garments. India gained comparative advantage in textiles and non-knitted undergarments, while China was strong in headgear and knitted undergarments. The study, further, revealed that China had been a growing importer of high-quality textiles, mainly from Japan and the newly industrialised economies, for the sale of clothing items in foreign markets. However, India had not been able to take the comparative advantage of this opportunity, in part because India's textile industry operated under a variety of government-imposed restrictions such as export quotas on cotton and cotton yarn, and restrictions on firm size, labour utilisation, and importation of production materials (Elbehri, et al., 2003).

Batra and Khan (2005) analysed the pattern of revealed comparative advantage by using the Balassa index for export data. The index was calculated at the sector and commodity level based on the Harmonised System (HS) of classification. The study also analysed revealed comparative advantage according to factor intensity. The analysis showed broad similarities in the structure of revealed comparative advantage for India and China. Both, the countries enjoyed revealed comparative advantage for labour and resource-intensive sectors in the global market.

Dash (2006) evaluated the changes occurring in revealed comparative advantage in service sectors of India and US. Traditionally, the Heckscher-Ohlin model characterised that US was rich in human capital which gave it a comparative advantage in services. India had also developed a comparative advantage in services' outsourcing. As a result, it appeared that in the future both India and US might actually be competitors in the services sector.

Chadha (2006) computed Balassa's Revealed Comparative Advantage (BRCA) index and Vollrath's Revealed

Comparative   Advantage   (VRCA)   index   for   Indian
pharmaceutical exports and found that both the indices were
quite high and being greater than unity for all the years. Thus,
India had a comparative advantage in pharmaceutical exports
due to its known ability for low-cost reverse-engineering of
branded drugs to produce generic drugs. However, despite this
proven comparative advantage, Indian pharmaceutical exports
contributed negligible share to world pharmaceutical exports,
and hovered around one percent of world pharmaceutical
exports.

Rodrick (2006) and Schott (2008), by using revealed
comparative advantage indices, concluded that China's export
basket had switched towards high-tech exports and that the
share of high-tech goods in China's exports was now
significantly higher than what was expected. Schott also
noticed that Chinese exports to the United States had lower
prices than exports from OECD countries, which suggested
that OECD exporters would attempt to react to the competition
from Chinese products by producing goods with a higher
technological content.

Batra (2007) investigated the extent of competition
between India and China in the world and ASEAN markets by
using the concepts of revealed comparative advantage, relative
market shares, long-term trend analysis and statistical tests of
convergence. The study suggested that threat perceptions at the
product level currently prevail for both economies from each
other across all sectors, even though the intensity of the
competitive threat varies across products. However, long-term
trend   analysis   showed   that   the   patterns   of   revealed
comparative advantage of India and China were evolving
along divergent paths and, therefore, competition between the
two economies might not be a major issue.

Shen and Gu (2007) used 4-digit SITC data to identify
groups of manufactured goods exported from China to the
USA that had strong or rising comparative advantages. The
study found that most of the trade was inter-industry, with only

a small portion being vertical intra-industry trade. Results of
the study confirmed that Sino-US trade was complementary.

Loke (2007) provided a simple exercise to examine and
compare Malaysia's comparative advantages in selected goods
with China during the period 2001-04. The study as a whole
showed that China does better than Malaysia in many of the
labour-intensive manufactures and Malaysia's comparative
advantages in labour-intensive manufactures declined over the
years since the 1990s. This was not a surprise in view of the
structural change that the Malaysian economy had undergone
in the past two decades during which labour shortage,
especially in the unskilled group, became a constraint to the
economy.

Sharma and Dietrich (2007) analysed structural changes in
India's exporting industries at 3-digit SITC level for the period
1980-2000. Trade indices such as Balassa's revealed
comparative advantage indices and variants were used. The
results of the study pointed towards substantial industrial
restructuring in manufactured exports and found evidence of
de-specialisation within India's manufactured exports for the
time period under study, which was consistent with increasing
specialisation in a subset of manufactured exports.

Bussiere and Mehl (2008) compared some of the most
relevant aspects of China's and India's roles in global trade
and finance using, in particular, estimates from a gravity
model to gauge the overall degree of their trade-intensity and
the depth of their bilateral relations, as well as measures of
revealed comparative advantages and economic distance. The
study concluded that China's revealed comparative advantage
was clearly in the high-tech sector like a mature economy
while India's comparative advantage remained in low-tech
sector.

To explore the dynamism of specialisation in India and
China, Qureshi and Wan (2008) calculated the Balassa's index
of revealed comparative advantage for ten industrial clusters
over the period from 1995-2005. China posed a tough

challenge to India in low-technology industries, and to the EU, US and East Asia in medium and high-technology industries. China's competition with Latin American countries was moderate with the notable exception of Mexico, which had comparative advantage in product groups similar to China. African countries were little affected by China's trade expansion. On the other side, India specialised in low-technology products and was a strong competitor for its neighbouring South Asian countries, who had a less diversified export base and enjoyed comparative advantages in low-technology products. Some European countries and the US might also be affected by the increasing presence of India in global markets whereas the Latin American and African countries were least affected.

Veeramani (2008) analysed the changing pattern of comparative advantage in India and China. Study concluded that in a number of products, India held a higher revealed comparative advantage than China, but her share in the world exports of these products was much lower than that of China. This was not surprising, as comparative advantage did not automatically translate into high market shares if there were certain impediments in the country in fully exploiting its comparative advantage. The study also found that China's exports and comparative advantage had undergone a greater degree of structural change over the years than that of India's. The findings of the study indicated that certain bottlenecks (such as poor physical infrastructure) and policy induced rigidities in the factor markets (such as those in the organised labour market) stood in the way of resource reallocation process and export activities in India.

Kowalski (2008) argued that despite the fact that India was relatively abundant in skilled labour and capital, its manufacturing exports were highly concentrated in low-technology goods and the share of high-technology manufactured goods in its total exports had barely changed since the mid-1990s and remained under five percent, as compared to thirty percent for China. Indeed, India's merchandise export structure was still heavily skewed towards petroleum products, jewellery, furniture, chemical products and textiles and wearing apparel, a structure that resembled to a certain extent the structure of China's exports at the beginning of the 1990s. The study, further, confirmed the still very traditional profile of India's merchandise trade. Most of the products in which India was estimated to have a revealed comparative advantage belong to the primary and labour-intensive sectors.

Máñez, et al. (2008) examined the extent to which the growth of India and China in world markets was affecting the patterns of trade specialisation in Latin American (LA) economies. The empirical analyses explored the correlation between the revealed comparative advantages of LA and the two Asian economies. Econometric estimates suggested that the specialisation pattern of LA, with the exception of Mexico, had been moving in opposite direction to the trade specialisation pattern of India and China. Labour-intensive sectors (both unskilled and skilled) probably had been negatively affected by the growing presence of India and China in world markets, while natural resource and scientific knowledge intensive sectors had probably benefited from India and China's growth since 1990.

Okamoto (2008) used revealed comparative advantage index to investigate competitiveness and complementarity of India and China for ASEAN countries. The rise of India and China as industrial powers was now regarded as an opportunity rather than as a threat for ASEAN countries. With respect to a Free Trade Area (FTA) between ASEAN and China, both Singapore and Malaysia seemed to gain through inter and intra-industry specialisation. Thailand appeared to gain significantly through intra-industry specialisation vis-à-vis China. Indonesia and the Philippines might not gain much through the formation of FTA unless substantial efforts were made in order to promote their industrial development. The promotion of economic cooperation between ASEAN and India, on the other hand, might make sense in the long run, but its immediate impact on both sides still seemed to be limited.

9.2 Revealed   Comparative   Advantage   and   its Measurement

It has been argued that Revealed Comparative Advantage (RCA) in goods or services refers to the potential advantage enjoyed by a country in specific skills, technology or know-how which together with natural factor endowments determines the competitive edge derived from the conduct of trade with the partner country. In simple words of Laursan (1998), RCA is an index that seeks to reveal whether a selected commodity or commodity group is more important for a country's total exports than it is for other trade partners, individually or collectively. The popularity of the RCA measure is its relative simplicity, its ability to utilise comparable data sets and its dependability as an indicator of actual changes in comparative advantage. The identification of commodities having RCA would enable policy makers to formulate an appropriate strategy which would help to accelerate exports of the specified commodities and allocate resources to develop those industries which have the potential to earn maximum foreign exchange for the country. Thus, RCA index considers the intrinsic advantage of a particular export commodity in world markets.

The study has used Balassa's index of RCA which compares the export share of a given sector/commodity in a country with the export share of that sector/commodity in the world market (Balassa, 1965, 1979 and 1986). In symbols;

$$RCA_{ij} = \frac{\dfrac{X_{ij}}{X_i}}{\dfrac{X_{wj}}{X_w}}$$

Where,

RCA_{ij} =   Revealed Comparative Advantage for country i of commodity j

X_{ij} = i^{th} country's export of commodity j

X_i =   total exports of country i

X_{wj} =   world exports of commodity j

X_w =   total world exports.

The index of value greater than unity indicates strong comparative advantage while a lower value would mean that the specified commodity is not particularly competitive in the world market. The advantage of using the RCA index is that it considers the intrinsic advantage of a particular export commodity and is consistent with changes in an economy's relative factor endowment and productivity. The disadvantage, however, is that it cannot distinguish improvements in factor endowments and pursuit of appropriate trade policies by a country.

This chapter, specifically, examines the structure of comparative advantage enjoyed by India and China in the global market, individually and in comparative framework. For this purpose, RCA indices have been computed for India and China by using the data 2-digit HS commodity classification. Further, RCA indices for India's major exports to China have also been computed by using the data at 6-digit HS commodity classification. The data are collected exclusively from UN Commodity Trade Statistics. For the comparative analysis, RCA indices have been calculated for the years 2001 and 2005.

9.3 The Analysis of Revealed Comparative Advantage (RCA): India

In year 2001, India enjoyed RCA>1 in 43 commodities. These commodities constituted 77 percent share of India's total exports.

Table 9.1 shows India's top ten commodities on the basis of RCA index in 2001. India enjoyed maximum comparative advantage in silk (i.e. 15.25). This was closely followed by two other commodities namely lac, gums, resins, vegetable

saps and extracts nes; and carpets and other textile floor
coverings. Pearls, precious stones, metals, coins, etc.; other
made textile articles, sets, worn clothing etc.; cotton; coffee,
tea, mate and spices; vegetable plaiting materials, vegetable
products nes; vegetable textile fibres nes, paper yarn, woven
fabric; and articles of leather, animal gut, harness, travel
goods, were other commodities that appear in the top ten
commodities ranked according to the value of RCA index.

Table 9.1: Top Ten Commodities with Highest Value of RCA in 2001: India

Rank	HS Code	Commodities	RCA
1	50	Silk	15.25
2	13	Lac, gums, resins, vegetable saps and extracts, nes	14.12
3	57	Carpets and other textile floor coverings	10.12
4	71	Pearls, precious stones, metals, coins, etc.	8.93
5	63	Other made textile articles, sets, worn clothing, etc.	8.67
6	52	Cotton	8.55
7	09	Coffee, tea, mate and spices	7.94
8	14	Vegetable plaiting materials, vegetable products, nes	5.53
9	53	Vegetable textile fibres nes, paper yarn, woven fabric	4.97
10	42	Articles of leather, animal gut, harness, travel goods	4.91

Source: Calculated from UN Commodity Trade Statistics.

In year 2005, India enjoyed RCA>1 in 40 commodities,
which constituted 67 percent share of India's total exports.
Table 9.2 reveals India's top ten commodities on the basis of
RCA in 2005. It shows almost the same picture as in 2001. In
2005, from rank one to rank six, there were same commodities
as in 2001. Only ores, slag and ash made its entry into the list

of top ten in 2005, while commodity namely articles of leather, animal gut, harness, travel goods, dropped out of the top ten set of 2001. In 2005, India enjoyed maximum comparative advantage in silk (i.e. 12.03). Hence, India's top ten exports on the basis of RCA did not reveal major changes over the period from 2001 to 2005.

Table 9.2: Top Ten Commodities with Highest Value of RCA in 2005: India

Rank	HS Code	Commodities	RCA
1	50	Silk	12.03
2	13	Lac, gums, resins, vegetable saps and extracts nes	11.38
3	57	Carpets and other textile floor coverings	9.63
4	71	Pearls, precious stones, metals, coins, etc	8.05
5	63	Other made textile articles, sets, worn clothing etc	7.03
6	52	Cotton	6.50
7	26	Ores, slag and ash	6.46
8	14	Vegetable plaiting materials, vegetable products nes	4.80
9	09	Coffee, tea, mate and spices	4.72
10	53	Vegetable textile fibres nes, paper yarn, woven fabric	4.71

Source: Calculated from UN Commodity Trade Statistics.

However, if we consider all the commodities whose RCA is greater than one, there can be seen some variations over the period from 2001 to 2005. The number of commodities for which India enjoyed comparative advantage was 43 in 2001 and this number declined to 40 in 2005. There were 35 commodities, which had comparative advantage in 2001 as well as in 2005. Five commodities namely inorganic chemicals, precious metal compound, isotopes; rubber and articles thereof; copper and articles thereof; ships, boats and other floating structures; and works of art, collectors pieces and antiques, gained comparative advantage in 2005, i.e. the value of RCA turned more than one. On the other hand, eight commodities namely products of animal origin, nes; milling products, malt, starches, insulin, wheat gluten; animal, vegetable fats and oils, cleavage products, etc; sugars and sugar confectionery; miscellaneous edible preparations; pharmaceutical products; miscellaneous manufactured articles; and commodities, not elsewhere specified, lost their comparative advantage in 2005, i.e. the value of RCA turned less than one.

Among the commodities that have retained comparative advantage, ores, slag and ash gained more than ten ranks, while special woven or tufted fabrics, lace, tapestry etc. lost more than ten ranks.

9.4 The Analysis of Revealed Comparative Advantage (RCA): China

In 2001, China enjoyed RCA>1 in 46 commodities, which constituted 65 percent share of China's total exports. Table 9.3 shows China's top ten export commodities on the basis of RCA index in 2001. China enjoyed maximum comparative advantage in manufactures of plaiting material, basketwork, etc. (i.e. 11.33). This was closely followed by commodities namely umbrellas, walking-sticks, seat-sticks, whips, etc; bird skin, feathers, artificial flowers, human hair; and silk. Articles of leather, animal gut, harness, travel goods; headgear and parts thereof; footwear, gaiters and the like, parts thereof; other made textile articles, sets, worn clothing, etc; toys, games, sports requisites; and tin and articles thereof, were other commodities that figured in the top ten commodities ranked according to the value of RCA index.

In 2005, China enjoyed RCA>1s in same number of commodities as in 2001, i.e. 46. However, the share of these commodities in China's total exports increased tremendously to 81 percent in 2005. As is true for India, top ten lists of commodities, on the basis of RCA index, remained almost the same between 2001 and 2005.

Table 9.3: Top Ten Commodities with Highest Value of RCA in 2001: China

Rank	HS Code	Commodities	RCA
1	46	Manufactures of plaiting material, basketwork, etc.	11.33
2	66	Umbrellas, walking-sticks, seat-sticks, whips, etc.	9.94
3	67	Bird skin, feathers, artificial flowers, human hair	8.45
4	50	Silk	8.29
5	42	Articles of leather, animal gut, harness, travel goods	6.42
6	65	Headgear and parts thereof	4.86
7	64	Footwear, gaiters and the like, parts thereof	4.82
8	63	Other made textile articles, sets, worn clothing, etc.	4.81
9	95	Toys, games, sports requisites	4.70
10	80	Tin and articles thereof	4.54

Source: Calculated from UN Commodity Trade Statistics.

Only one commodity namely fur skins and artificial fur, manufactures thereof made its entry into the list of top ten in 2005, while tin and articles thereof got dropped out of the top ten set of 2001. In 2005, China enjoyed maximum comparative advantage in manufactures of plaiting material, basketwork, etc., i.e. 8.12. Umbrellas, walking-sticks, seat-sticks, whips, etc.; bird skin, feathers, artificial flowers, human hair; silk; headgear and parts thereof; fur skins and artificial fur, manufactures thereof; articles of leather, animal gut, harness, travel goods; other made textile articles, sets, worn clothing etc.; toys, games, sports requisites; and footwear, gaiters and the like, parts thereof, were other commodities that figured in the top ten commodities ranked according to the value of RCA index (Table 9.4). Thus, China's top ten exports on the basis of

RCA did not reveal major changes over the period, 2001 to 2005.

**Table 9.4: Top Ten Commodities with Highest
Value of RCA in 2005: China**

Rank	HS Code	Commodities	RCA
1	46	Manufactures of plaiting material, basketwork, etc.	8.12
2	66	Umbrellas, walking-sticks, seat-sticks, whips, etc.	7.78
3	67	Bird skin, feathers, artificial flowers, human hair	6.07
4	50	Silk	5.54
5	65	Headgear and parts thereof	4.50
6	43	Fur skins and artificial fur, manufactures thereof	4.43
7	42	Articles of leather, animal gut, harness, travel goods	4.27
8	63	Other made textile articles, sets, worn clothing, etc.	4.12
9	95	Toys, games, sports requisites	4.10
10	64	Footwear, gaiters and the like, parts thereof	3.83

Source: Calculated from UN Commodity Trade Statistics.

However, as done in case of India, if we consider all the commodities whose RCA is greater than one, there can be seen some variations over the period 2001-2005. The number of commodities for which China enjoyed comparative advantage was same in both the years, i.e. 46. Like India, China also retained its comparative advantage in 35 commodities, during 2001 to 2005. Four commodities namely impregnated, coated or laminated textile fabric; glass and glassware; nuclear reactors, boilers, machinery, etc; and optical, photo, technical, medical, etc apparatus, gained comparative advantage in 2005, i.e. the value of the RCA turned more than one.

Similarly, in 2005, China lost comparative advantage (i.e.

value of RCA turned less than one) for four commodities namely coffee, tea, mate and spices; oil seed, oleagic fruits, grain, seed, fruit, etc, nes; zinc and articles thereof; and tin and articles thereof. Among the commodities that have retained comparative advantage, three commodities namely fur skins and artificial fur, manufactures thereof; manmade filaments; and special woven or tufted fabric, lace, tapestry etc., gained more than ten ranks. On the other hand, in case of two commodities namely lead and articles thereof; and clocks and watches and parts thereof, China lost more than ten ranks.

9.5 India-China: A Comparative Analysis of RCA

For the comparative analysis, both the tables have been viewed together. There were 25 commodities where India and China both enjoyed comparative advantage in 2001. However, their figure was 22 commodities in 2005. The number of commodities where India enjoyed more RCA than China declined from 13 in 2001 to 10 in 2005. Similarly, the number of commodities where China enjoyed more RCA than India declined from 8 in 2001 to 7 in 2005. However, the number of commodities, where both the countries had equal RCA, increased from 4 in 2001 to 5 in 2005.

In case of special woven or tufted fabric, lace, tapestry etc., India had a higher comparative advantage relative to China in 2001 but lost this in 2005. India and China were equally advantageously placed in edible vegetables and certain roots and tubers; articles of apparel, accessories, not knit or crochet; and articles of iron or steel for 2001 and 2005. India was more advantageously placed than China in the world market in products such as fish, crustaceans, molluscs, aquatic invertebrates nes; vegetable plaiting materials, vegetable products nes; salt, sulphur, earth, stone, plaster, lime and cement; silk; cotton; vegetable textile fibres nes, paper yarn, woven fabric; carpets and other textile floor coverings; other made textile articles, sets, worn clothing etc.; and stone, plaster, cement, asbestos, mica, etc., in both 2001 and 2005.

China was more advantageously placed than India in the world market in products like explosives, pyrotechnics, matches, pyrophorics, etc.; articles of leather, animal gut, harness, travel goods; articles of apparel, accessories, knit or crochet; footwear, gaiters and the like, parts thereof; bird skin, feathers, artificial flowers, human hair; and tools, implements, cutlery, etc. of base metal, in both 2001 and 2005.

India's comparative advantage lied predominantly in the agriculture and allied products category in both the years. In this category, India maintained comparative advantage in edible fruit, nuts, peel of citrus fruit, melons; cereals; lac, gums, resins, vegetable saps and extracts nes; residues, wastes of food industry, animal fodder; and tobacco and manufactured tobacco substitutes. Similarly,

India also held its comparative advantage in categories of mineral and mineral fuels; and chemicals and plastics. Though India's comparative advantage in resource based manufactures; and miscellaneous manufactures also increased, yet not up to the mark. China, on the other hand, was relatively advantageously placed in the global market for both resource based manufactures as well as machinery and equipments, with the former comprising larger number of commodities than the later. New gains in resource based manufactures were also acquired by China between 2001 and 2005. In the category of resource based manufactures, China gained comparative advantage in commodities like impregnated, coated or laminated textile fabric; and glass and glassware, while lost comparative advantage in zinc and articles thereof; and tin and articles thereof, in 2005. In categories of machinery and equipments; and miscellaneous manufactures, China attained comparative advantage in nuclear reactors, boilers, machinery, etc.; optical, photo, technical, medical, etc. apparatus; and miscellaneous manufactured articles in 2005.

However, in the categories of agriculture and allied products; and chemicals and plastics, India outscores China. Among these categories, China was advantageously placed in the world market vis-à-vis India for only inorganic chemicals, precious metal compound, isotopes in 2001; however, it lost this comparative advantage in 2005. Thus, it can be said that in the world market, India's comparative advantage lies in categories of agriculture and allied products; mineral and mineral fuels; and chemicals and plastics. While, on the other hand, China's comparative advantage lies in the categories of resource based manufactures; machinery and equipments; and miscellaneous manufactures.

After analysing RCA of India and China at aggregate level (i.e. 2-digit HS classification), it is also important to view the RCA of India's exports to China at disaggregate level (i.e. 6-digit HS classification). For this purpose, India's top twenty exports to China were selected at 6-digit HS classification for the years 2001 and 2005. Then, their market share and RCAs were calculated for both the years. These twenty exports constituted 63 percent share of India's total exports to China. Among these selected exports, India had comparative advantage in thirteen products.

While in the remaining seven products, India's RCA was less than one. India enjoyed the maximum comparative advantage for the commodity namely worked human hair, wool or animal hair, for wig making (i.e. 27.94), which was closely followed by chromium ores and concentrates (i.e. 26.21). India held good market share in China for all the commodities, in which its RCA was greater than one, except three commodities namely polypropylene in primary forms; cotton yarn (except sewing thread) >85 percent cotton, retail; and 6-hexanelactam (epsilon-captolactam). India had good market share in China for two commodities namely shrimps and prawns, frozen; and antibiotics nes, in bulk, but their RCA indices were less than one.

Twenty exports constituted 79 percent share in India's total exports to China. Among these selected exports, India had comparative advantage in fifteen products, while in the remaining five products, India's RCA index was less than one.

In 2005, India had maximum comparative advantage in the same commodity as in 2001, i.e. worked human hair, wool or animal hair, for wig making and its RCA index was 26.30. India held good market share in China for all the commodities, in which its RCA was greater than one, except three commodities namely ethylene glycol (ethanediol); organic compounds, nes; and o-xylene. India had good market share in China for commodities namely polyethylene-specific gravity >0.94 in primary forms; and flat rolled i/nas, coated with zinc, width >600mm, nes, but its RCA indices were less than one.

It could also be noted that all the commodities in which India's RCA was greater than one were primary products and natural resource based or low technology manufacturing products. Out of these natural resource based products, some of them were exhaustible in nature like iron ore, granite crude, etc. Therefore, increase in exports of these products may not be desirable to India in the long run.

To sum up, the above analysis reveals that at the aggregate level of data (i.e. 2-digit HS classification) neither India's nor China's RCA index showed big alterations during 2001 and 2005. Top ten commodities on the basis of RCA>1 for India and China remained same during 2001 and 2005, with minor exceptions. During the above years, India's RCA was highest for silk, while China's RCA was highest in case of manufacturing of plaiting material, basketwork, etc.

In both the years (i.e. 2001 and 2005), the number of those commodities whose $RCA_I > RCA_C$ was greater than the number of those commodities whose $RCA_C < RCA_I$. Similarly, for both the years, India's comparative advantage lied predominantly in agriculture and allied products category. India also held comparative advantage in categories of mineral and mineral fuels; and chemicals and plastics. Though India's comparative advantage in resource based manufactures and miscellaneous manufactures also increased, yet not up to the standard of the Chinese market. On the other hand, China was relatively advantageously placed in the global market for both resource based manufactures as well as machinery and equipments, with the former comprising larger number of commodities than the later.

The analysis of RCA at disaggregate level (i.e. 6-digit HS classification) shows that in 2001, out of the top twenty Indian exports to China India had comparative advantage in thirteen products, while in the remaining seven products India's RCA index was less than one. Similarly, in 2005, out of top twenty Indian exports to China, India had comparative advantage in fifteen products, while in the remaining five products India's RCA index was less than one. Further, it was also be noted that most of the products in which India's RCA was greater than one fall in the category of natural resource based products. However, some of these products are exhaustible in nature like iron ore, granite crude, etc. Therefore, increase in exports of these products may not be desirable to India in the long run. To increase the complementarities with China, there is an urgent need to diversify the export basket towards technologically advanced products. However, with given industrial structure and advancement, it seems highly difficult in the immediate future.

10

India-China Economic Cooperation: The Road Ahead

Over the past three decades, the Asian economies have consistently outperformed other developing regions and become the new growth pole of the world economy. This is the case with both India and China, which are emerging as economic powerhouses not only in Asia but also in the world. With their high growth rates and huge markets, these two Asian giants have attracted the attention of international business mangers to take a fresh look at the rapidly emerging opportunities in the two countries. Hence, the importance of India and China in international business is becoming apparent with each passing day. So, it is an important subject to examine their economic interactions, for the simple reason that both are close neighbours and enjoy unbounded cultural affinity.

Moreover, there are possibly few issues that academics, policy makers and market participants regard as new chapters in the history. The emergence of India and China is probably one of them. From a domestic perspective, both constitute unprecedented stories of economic development. Owing to vibrant growth rates in the last two decades, they have already reached heavyweight status in the global economy. It is also held that with the rapid growth of India and China, Asia is expected to regain its place as a centre of gravity of the world economy. Any attempt for strengthening their economic ties would, therefore, be most rewarding for their rapid development.

India's relations with China over the past fifty years have traversed the entire spectrum: the initial phase of amity and camaraderie, jolted by outright hostility, followed by a protracted period of mutual suspicion and antagonism, gradual thawing, to a phase of 'uncomfortable co-existence'. However, the relations between the two countries have been developing and diversifying in a steady manner since 1991. During this period, there have been series of high level officials' visits from both sides that have further helped the process of mutual understanding and laid the foundation for cooperation in a diverse set of sectors.

Today, the economic and trade interactions between India and China are at the driving seat for the development of their overall relationship. Both the sides have recognised the importance of trade and economic relations for strengthening bilateral relations. Important progress has been made in this direction. Bilateral trade has grown at fast pace, mutual investment is set to grow in various sectors, viz. civil aviation, customs cooperation, agriculture, tourism and so forth.

In fact, India and China are perceived as leaders amongst developing countries with immense potential and prospects of emerging as global economic players in economic and diplomatic spheres in the foreseeable future. Both the countries have attained high economic growth rates with the considerably opening up of their economies. India began relaxing its rigidly controlled economy in a piecemeal fashion in the 1980s, but its significant opening to the world economy and deeper domestic reforms did not begin until after the severe macroeconomic crisis of 1991. On the other side, China began its economic reforms and opening to the world economy in 1978. Both India and China initiated the process of economic reforms to bring out their respective economies from the socio-economic crisis. However, the performance of both the countries was not equal.

In fact, since the 1980s, China had far outstripped India in economic performance in terms of growth of GDP, agriculture, industry, savings, investment, foreign trade, foreign direct investment, international reserves, living standard of its population and integration of its economy with the world. The fact that China initiated reforms more than a decade earlier than India explains only a small part of this difference, since India also liberalised its economy to a limited extent in the 1980s. It is argued that China's success in achieving such high economic growth is due to the huge investments of overseas Chinese, an advantage that India does not have as its non-resident Indians are mostly professionals. Further China, being an authoritarian society, did not budge to the pressure groups that stood to gain or lose from the reforms. The dominance of communist party also helped in keeping the bureaucratic apparatus intact and reasonably efficient while the pro-market policies of its paramount leader, Deng Xiaoping, took hold.

After negotiating for over fifteen years, China joined the WTO on December 11, 2001. Given the potential size of the Chinese market, its accession to the WTO may have been a watershed event in the history of world trade. China's entry into the WTO was viewed in India as a mixed blessing. On one hand, it helped India to voice its concerns in the WTO on the issues of domestic interest, but there were also large downsides as our exports, especially labour-intensive manufactures, became less competitive. There were also concerns that Chinese goods would flood the Indian markets and spell doom for the domestic producers. However, China's entry into the WTO also presented significant trade opportunities to India as it gained access to the largest market in the world.

At the start of the reform process in 1978, China was not evidently better placed to attract large amounts of FDI than India, which at that time shared a number of characteristics with China. Both countries had relatively closed economies, with low average incomes and a large share of the population dependent on agriculture. Neither China nor India was then receiving significant amount of FDI. However, this picture has since changed dramatically and both have emerged as the most favoured destinations for a major part of world's FDI inflows. But, there are significant differences in their FDI performance.

In fact, China is well ahead of India in terms of attracting the FDI inflows. However, it is believed that as compared to China, India's FDI inflows appear to be under estimated. Many economists have estimated India's real FDI to be at least double of India's current official figures. But, hard facts still remain too stark to ignore and gap of India and China in this segment remains far too wide to be bridged by adopting different methods of calculation. This is well evident from UNCTAD's Inward FDI Performance Index which has placed China on 62nd rank and India on 121st rank in 2005.

Though the FDI inflows in the India and China have been increasing sharply, yet the mutual investment between the two is quite small. Further, there are also a lot of discrepancies in the data available regarding their mutual investment and, hence, there is need for reconciling the statistics of FDI inflows in both the countries. Since the last few years, many Indian companies have entered into the Chinese market, which include pharmaceutical companies like Ranbaxy Laboratories, Aurobindo Pharmaceuticals, Dr. Reddy's Laboratories; manufacturing companies like Sundram Fasteners Ltd., Aditya Birla Group, Mahindra; and IT software companies like Aptech, NIIT, Tata Consultancy Services (TCS), Infosys, etc. The number of Indian companies in China has increased significantly, but it is not true for Chinese companies in India. According to many Chinese companies, it is very hard to find profits in India. Tax barriers everywhere are eroding cost advantages. Corruption is rampant, adding another layer of difficulty.

Since nineties, trade in services has emerged as a major area in international trade. The share of India and China in world's service trade has been increasing continuously, which indicates that both have bilateral trade potential in services. The two countries have signed a number of service sector related agreements, including education, human resources, auditing, consultancy, tourism, marine transportation, environment and technology. However, even then, the scale of their mutual investments and trade in service sector is not large.

Amongst the economic relations, the trade relations between India and China are developing by good momentum and dynamism. During 1950-90, their trade relations were seriously affected by their political relations and remained at a very low level. However, since the 1991, the mutual trade between the two countries rose tremendously. The value of their merchandise trade was just ₹ 96.17 crore in 1990-91 which shot up to ₹ 57,125.28 crore in 2004-05. During the same period, the growth rates of India's exports to and imports from China also remained well above than that of its overall exports and imports. Since the mid-nineties, the values of intensity indices and integrity indices have increased substantially which shows the growing orientation and integration between the two countries in terms of their trade.

China emerged as the second largest trade partner of India in 2005, as the former's share in the latter's total trade increased from 0.13 percent in 1990-91 to 6.52 percent in 2004-05. Though India's share in China's foreign trade also increased from 0.19 percent in 1991 to 1.32 percent in 2005, yet it remained well below than that of China's share in India's foreign trade. The same trend has also been found in case of exports and imports. However, one major problem, from the Indian perspective, found to be its rising trade deficit with China. Most of the years, India experienced adverse balance of trade with China and the deficit of trade widened substantially due to the higher growth rate of imports from her. The other major problem identified was the narrowness of India's export basket to China. Indian exports were mainly dominated by exports of ores, slag and ash. Importantly, this commodity alone constituted about 52.13 percent of India's exports to China in 2004-05. Moreover, during the same year, out of India's total world exports of ores, slag and ash, nearly 78.31 percent was exported to China alone. The rapid depletion of China's iron ore reserves, thereby, has made its front-running steel industry dependent on imports from India in order to meet the growing demand for steel for its construction and defence industries.

It has been found that China has paid higher unit values to India in case of ores, slag and ash than rest of the world. Besides, ores, slag and ash, the list of India's other major exports to China consisted of iron and steel; organic chemicals; plastic; inorganic chemicals; salt, sulphur, earths and stone; cotton; and fish and crustaceans. On the other side, Chinese exports to India were found to be more diversified and the bulk of the Indian imports from China constitute manufactured goods, with electronic machinery alone constituting about 25.04 percent of the total Indian imports from China in 2004-05. Except the electronic machinery, India's major imports from China were nuclear reactors and boilers; mineral fuels and oils; organic chemicals; silk; inorganic chemicals; articles of iron or steel; natural or cultured pearls, precious or semiprecious stones; optical, photographic cinematographic measuring; man-made filaments; and impregnated, coated, covered or laminated textile fabrics.

The analysis shows that Indian exports to China were mainly dominated by raw material and semi-manufactured products while Chinese exports to India were more diversified and include resource based manufactures, and low and medium technology products. The Hirschman Index also revealed that Chinese exports to India were more diversified than the Indian exports to China. Therefore, it appears that Chinese exports to India are more sustainable than India's exports to China. The various statistical methods employed, namely Grubel-Lloyd Intra-Industry Trade Index, Complementarity Index and Trade Overlap Index showed that during the recent years in India-China bilateral trade, the inter-industry trade recorded a strong growth, but the role of intra-industry trade remained on the lower side. Further, the indices namely Economic Distance Index, Coefficient of Specialisation and Coefficient of Conformity revealed that the extent of competition between the exports of the two countries had declined over time.

India experienced favourable terms of trade with China as compared to its overall adverse terms of trade. The prices of India's exports to China increased quite faster than the prices of India's overall exports. On the other side, during 1992-93 to 1998-99, the prices of India's overall imports remained below that of the prices of India's imports from China. However, since 1999-00, India's import unit value index with China remained much below India's overall import unit value index. That's why during that period, India's terms of trade with China improved significantly as compared to India's overall terms of trade. However, on the export side, it was found that Indian exports to China were mainly based on one or two major commodities whose share reached nearly half of the total exports to China. For example, in 2004-05, the share of iron ore and concentrates (both agglomerated and non-agglomerated) reached to 47.71 percent of India's total exports to China. Further, with the sharp rise in the demand, the unit values of these commodities also rose surprisingly. This sudden rise in the unit value of few commodities made the terms of trade index in India's favour. Similarly, on imports side, it is also argued that the unit values of Chinese products were lower not because of any genuine price differences but because of low quality of the products. This made the terms of trade index to move in India's favour.

Further, the analysis of unit values revealed that the export unit values realised from China were more favourable vis-à-vis from Rest of the World (RoW). Similarly, the imports from China cost less than the imports from RoW. In other words, on the basis of export ratio and import ratio, it can be concluded that India is gaining more if it exports to China rather RoW and its losses can be minimum if it imports from China rather RoW. The Relative Terms of Trade Index (RTTI) also revealed the same that during the study period India's trade with China remained more superior as compared to its trade with RoW. Hence, like the NBTT, the RTTI also revealed that during the period 1990-91 to 2004-05, India experienced favourable terms of trade with China.

The Coppock's instability analysis established that India's export earnings from China were subject to strong variations. Out of the fifteen commodities (selected as a sample), China had stabilised the overall value and unit value of seven commodities and volume of eight commodities. In terms of value, the seven commodities for which China had a stabilising effect constituted 11.73 percent of the total value of India's exports to China and rest of the eight commodities for which China had a destabilising effect, constituted 37.06 percent of the total exports. Thus, China had more of destabilising effect on India's exports than the stabilising effect. Further, the instability in India's export earnings from China was primarily due to the volume instability. The index of instability for volume was uniformly higher than that for unit value of all the selected commodities. This implied that the instability in value of exports was more due to the instability in volume of the commodity groups exported than due to the fluctuations in unit values obtained, because value of a commodity would be its volume multiplied by its unit value.

To analyse the competitiveness, the total change in India's exports to China has been decomposed into three different effects, viz. demand effect, competitiveness effect and product-diversification effect. The influence of competitiveness on India's exports to China has declined in recent years. During the period 1996-2000, the competitiveness effect played a leading role in augmenting Indian exports to China. The role of diversification factor was also important one, while the increase in Chinese import demand played a least role in augmenting Indian exports to China. On the other side, during 2001-05, Indian exports to China rose mainly due to the increase in Chinese global import demand. In fact, the rapid growth of India's overall merchandise exports, since 2002, was mainly driven by a buoyant world economy.

The competitiveness and product diversification effects, though positive, were not the major contributing factors to the acceleration in the growth of merchandise exports in the same period. This analysis was confined to those products whose individual share was more than 0.50 percent in India's total exports to China. However, the more disaggregative analysis of market shares and unit values of India's exports of China showed that the commodities namely iron ore, concentrate, not iron pyrites, unagglomerated; aluminium oxide, except artificial corundum; hot rolled stainless steel coil, w >600mm, t <3mm; polyethylene-specific gravity >0.94 in primary forms; and flat rolled i/nas, coated with zinc, width >600mm, nes were getting more competitive in Chinese market. On the other side, few commodities had lost their competitive position in the Chinese market namely chromium ores and concentrates; iron ore, concentrate, not iron pyrites, agglomerated; cotton yarn >85 percent single combed 714-232 dtex, not retail; fish nes, frozen, whole; and polyethylene-specific gravity <0.94 in primary forms.

The aggregative analysis of revealed comparative advantage showed that India's comparative advantage lied predominantly in the categories of agriculture and allied products; mineral and mineral fuels; chemicals; and plastics. Though India's comparative advantage in resource based manufactures and miscellaneous manufactures also increased, yet were not up to the standard of the Chinese market. On the other hand, China was relatively advantageously placed in the global market for both resource based manufactures as well as machinery and equipments.

At the disaggregative level, out of the top twenty Indian exports to China in 2001, India had comparative advantage in thirteen products, while in the remaining seven products India's RCA index was less than one. Similarly, in 2005, out of top twenty Indian exports to China, India had comparative advantage in fifteen products, while in the remaining five products India's RCA index was less than one. Further, it was also found that most of the products in which India's RCA was greater than one fall in the category of natural resource based products. However, some of these products are exhaustible in nature like iron ore, granite crude, etc. Therefore, increase in exports of these products may not be desirable to India in the long run. To increase the complementarities with China, there is an urgent need to diversify the export basket towards technologically advanced products. However, with given industrial structure and advancement it seems highly difficult in the immediate future.

Policy Implications

The present study is useful to find out the prospects to enhance economic cooperation between India and China and to identify sub-sectors where potential exists for mutual economic cooperation. On the basis of the study, following policy recommendations are suggested.

It is assumed that greater cooperation between the two countries can help them to understand their problems and seek their solutions better. The future options may be different, both because of systematic differences and because the resource endowments of the two countries are now different. However, both countries face the same task of removing obstacles to growth, ensuring optimum utilisation of resources and correcting the earlier misallocations. Consequently, both have a lot to learn from each other. Management techniques of China have their own uniqueness which plays a critical role in the development issues. Similar to China, India is combining a market economy with planned development though their ratios are different.

However, a crucial fact which needs to be taken into account is that India and China have different political systems and their economies cannot be examined in isolation. It is not always similarity alone but occasionally differences too offer inputs for a viable development strategy. China's entry into the

WTO has presented both opportunities and challenges for the Indian economy, but it seems that the challenges are much more than the opportunities. These Chinese challenges can be overcome only if we further strengthen the competitiveness of our economy by undertaking additional reforms and improving infrastructure. In other words, to maximise its gains, India must adopt a forward looking strategy aimed both at neutralising Chinese competition by making Indian goods more competitive as well as pushing Indian exports into Chinese market.

The mutual investment between the two countries is the most neglected part of their economic interactions. Comparing the performance of their mutual investments with their overall performance in attracting FDI both the countries have fared better which shows that the pace of their mutual investments still continues to be guided by their politico-strategic equations. Though the mutual investment between the two countries is still low, yet there exists a vast potential for further cooperation. Chinese enterprises may find fruitful opportunities for investment in India in many sectors like power generation projects, infrastructure, manufacture of electronic hardware, food processing, etc., for which there is a growing market in India.

Aiming to develop the bilateral economic and trade relations, Chinese government is also encouraging Chinese enterprises to invest in India in fields such as crop planting, coal, iron ore, manufacturing of apparatus, meters and office equipment, electric power machines as high-press and low-press switch and dynamotor, mechanical manufacturing of refrigeration equipment and air conditioners etc., electric equipment such as TV sets, plastic products, pharmacy, trade, software, construction, transportation, tourism, infrastructure and generation and supply of electricity etc. Indian enterprises, on the other side, may also find attractive investment opportunities in China in the areas of pharmaceuticals, automobile components, light engineering goods, automotives, financial services besides IT software and training. Moreover, India has also signed Bilateral Investment Promotion and Protection Agreement (BIPA) with China on 21st November, 2006. The Agreement came into force from August 1, 2007. This agreement will surely provide a propitious entourage for the mutual investment inflows.

Similarly, in the service sector, the two countries have a vast potential for mutual cooperation. India can provide services to China in the fields of software, consultancy, financial services such as auditing and accountancy, legal services, environment, education and health. On the other side, Chinese construction enterprises have experience in acquiring contracts for overseas projects in areas like electric power, telecommunications and highways, and might become strong bidders for Indian projects. Further, comprehensive economic cooperation will increase the international competitiveness of the two countries in the services sector. Indian and Chinese economies are complementary not only in the goods sector but also in the services sector. Through cooperation between industries and enterprises, it is possible to benefit from this complementarity. For example, while China has comparative advantage in manufacturing hardware of computers and electronics and telecommunications equipment, India has comparative advantage in software development and R&D. Combining these advantages will greatly improve the international competitiveness of the two countries in this sector.

India is facing rising trade deficits with China, which can be checked only by diversifying its export basket. The product diversification is high in case of Chinese exports to India but it is not true in case of Indian exports to China. In Chinese exports to India, medium and high-tech products dominate but Indian export basket to China is dominated by primary and resource based products. Further, Indian export basket is highly concentrated around one or two products, which needs an immediate policy intervention. To enhance trade complementarities, India needs to diversify into medium and high-technology products. Moreover, attempts must also be made to strengthen the intra-industry trade between the two countries.

In the context of terms of trade, India had favourable terms of trade with China. However, it is noteworthy that iron ore and concentrates (non-agglomerated) is one commodity which played a dominant role in deciding about India's terms of trade with China. With the growing demand of China, the prices of this commodity rose quite rapidly and had a positive impact on India's terms of trade with China. But, these favourable terms of trade cannot be sustained for long because this commodity is exhaustible in nature. So, India needs to think twice before further encouraging the exports of this commodity. The analysis of instability implies that India's export earnings from China were unstable primarily due to their volume instability. Apparently, India has no control over the movement of international prices, thus an appropriate action on the supply side would certainly be helpful in reduction of the fluctuations in overall export earnings. Attempts must be made to explore the possibilities of shifting the exports from the higher instable commodities to lower ones.

Though Indian exports to China rose rapidly during the recent few years, yet there exists a vast potential to enhance them further by improving their competitiveness. There is a need to control the unit values of major exports to China, so that India can get maximum market share in Chinese world imports. India should learn from the cost competitiveness of China which appears to help latter's exports in negotiating large distances. In India, duties and taxes are still on the higher side as compared to world standards, and they need to be reduced further, as higher duties and taxes lead to higher unit prices and reduced market size by reducing domestic consumption as well as foreign consumption and hence deprive economies of scale and make Indian firms less competitive.

Thus, low tariff rates have strong signalling effects on competitiveness of Indian firms. Further, by promoting higher FDI inflows; reducing the intensive industrial reservation; and improving the quality of public infrastructure, including power and transport, India can reduce the cost (and hence unit value) and improve the quality of its exports. India would then be in position to corner a higher market share for a large range of commodities in the Chinese economy as well as in the world economy.

In a number of products, India does hold a higher revealed comparative advantage, but its share in the world export of these products is much lower than that of China. China has been quite successful in exploiting the opportunities that arise from the growing international fragmentation of the production process in manufacturing industries. India, so far, has failed to take full advantage of such opportunities. India can take the advantage of these opportunities only by inducing foreign direct investment in major sectors of the economy, which will augment the process of integrating Indian industry with the fragmented structure of global production activities.

Hence, the study has specified certain lines of action which would be helpful in gaining the maximum benefit from mutual economic interaction between India and China. Further, the two countries are also looking for free trade arrangement, which will boost the economic ties between the two. Both stand to gain significantly by striking synergies in trade and business. By coming together and drawing on their advantages, India and China can not only make a strong regional impact but also make a mark in the world, by giving shape to a new economic world order and thereby making the 21st Century a truly Asian one.

Bibliography

Bibliography

Acharya, A. (2000). India-China Relations: An Overview, in K. Bajpai and A. Mattoo (ed.), *The Peacock and the Dragon: India-China Relations in the 21st Century*, Har-Anand Publications Pvt. Ltd., New Delhi, Pp. 168-198.

Agarwal, M.R. (1982). Export Earning Instability and Economic Development in Less Developed Countries: A Statistical Verification, *The Indian Economic Journal*, Vol. 29, No. 3, Pp. 61-70.

Agarwal, R. (2002). WTO, India and Emerging Global Trade Challenges in Higher Education, *Foreign Trade Review*, Vol. 37, No. 1 & 2, April-September, Pp. 35-46.

Agrawal, P. and P. Sahoo (2003). China's Accession to WTO: Implications for China and India, *Economic and Political Weekly*, Vol. 38, No. 25, June 21, Pp. 2544-2551.

Agrawal, P. and P. Saibaba (2001). Improving India's Exports of Textiles and Garments, *Economic and Political Weekly*, Vol. 36, No. 41, October 13, Pp. 3886-3888.

Ahluwalia, I.J. (1999). Industrial and Trade Reforms in India, in R. Shand (ed.), *Economic Liberalisation in South Asia*, Macmillan India Ltd., New Delhi, Pp. 254-269.

Al-Rfough, F.O. (2003). Sino-Indian Relations: From Confrontation to Accommodation (1988-2001), *China Report*, Vol. 39, No.1, Pp. 21-38.

Ambegaokar, N. (1974). India's Trade with East European Countries: Trends and Problems, *Reserve Bank of India Bulletin*, March Issue.

Ardeni, G. and B. Wright (1992). The Prebish-Singer Hypothesis: A Reappraisal Independent of Stationary Hypothesis, *Economic Journal*, Vol. 102, Pp. 803-812.

Askari, H. and G. Weil (1974). Stability of Export Earnings of Developing Nations, *Journal of Development Studies*, Vol. 11, No. 1, Pp. 85-90.

Bajpai, N. and N. Dasgupta (2004). *What Constitutes Foreign Direct Investment? Comparison of India and China*, Centre on Globalisation and Sustainable Development (CGSD), Working Paper No. 1, January.

234 India and China

Balassa, B. (1962). *Recent Developments in the Competitiveness of American Industry and Prospects for the Future Factors Affecting the United States Balance of Payments*, U.S. Government Printing Office, Washington.

Balassa, B. (1965). Trade Liberalisation and Revealed Comparative Advantage, *The Manchester School*, Vol. 33, No. 2, Pp. 99-123.

Balassa, B. (1979). The Changing Pattern of Comparative Advantage in Manufactured Goods, *The Review of Economics and Statistics*, Vol. 61, No. 2, May, Pp. 259-266.

Balassa, B. (1986). Comparative Advantage in Manufactured Goods: A Reappraisal, *The Review of Economics and Statistics*, Vol. 68, No. 2, May, Pp. 315-319.

Ball, R.J., J.R. Eaton and M.D. Steuer (1966). The Relationship between United Kingdom Export Performance in Manufactures and the Internal Pressure of Demand, *The Economic Journal*, September, Pp. 501-518.

Banerjee, P.K. (1994). Planned Development in India and China, *Foreign Trade Review*, Vol. 29, No. 2 and 3, July-December, Pp. 204-213.

Batra, A. (2007). Structure of Comparative Advantage of China and India: Global and Regional Dynamics, *China and World Economy*, Vol. 15, No. 6, Pp. 69-86.

Batra, A. and Z. Khan (2005). *Revealed Comparative Advantage: An Analysis for India and China*, Working Paper No. 168, Indian Council for Research on International Economic Relations (ICRIER), New Delhi.

Bender, S. and K.W. Li (2002). *The changing Trade and Revealed Comparative Advantages of Asian and Latin American Manufacture Exports*, Discussion Paper Series No. 843, Economic Growth Center, Yale University, Yale.

Bhagwati, J.N. (1970). The Tying of Aid, in J.N. Bhagwati and R.S. Eckaus (ed.), *Foreign Aid*, Penguin Books, Middle-Sex, England, Pp. 235-293.

Bhagwati, J.N. and T.N. Srinivasan (1976). *Foreign Trade Regime and Economic Development: India*, Macmillan Company of India, New Delhi.

Bhalla, A.S. and S. Qiu (2004). *The Employment Impact of China's WTO Accession*, Routledge Curzons, Taylor and Francis Group, London and New York.

Bhat, T.P., A. Guha and M. Paul (2006). *India and China in WTO:*

Building Complementarities and Competitiveness in the External Trade Sector, A Report prepared by Institute for Studies in Industrial Development (ISID), New Delhi.

Biandara, J.S. and C. Smith (2002). Trade Policy Reforms in South Asia and Australia-South Asia Trade: Intensities and Complementarities, *South Asia Economic Journal*, Vol. 3, No. 2, Pp. 177-199.

Biyum, H. (2005). A Bright Future for China-India Economic Cooperation based on Equality and Mutual Benefit, in C.V. Ranganathan (ed.), *Panchsheel and the Future Perspectives on India-China Relations*, Samskriti Press, New Delhi, Pp. 271-285.

Bleaney, M. and D. Greenaway (1993). Long Run Trends in Relative Price of Primary Commodities and in the Terms of Trade of Developing Countries, *Oxford Economic Papers*, No. 45, Oxford University Press, Pp. 349-363.

Bradsher, K. (2009). Downturn in Factories Sows Fear across Asia, *International Herald Tribune*, 22nd January, Paris.

Brar, J.S. (1996). *India and European Union: Issues in Economic Relations*, Vision & Venture, Patiala and New Delhi.

Bussiere, M. and A. Mehl (2008). *China's and India's Roles in Global Trade and Finance: Twin Titans for the New Millennium?*, Occasional Paper Series No. 80, January, European Central Bank, Euro System.

Cairncross, A.K. (1962). *Factors in Economic Development*, Praeger Publishers, New York.

Cashin, P. and J. McDermott (2002). The Long-Run Behaviour of Commodity Prices: Small Trends and Big Variability, *IMF Staff Papers*, Vol. 49, No. 2, Pp. 175-199.

Cerra, V., S.A. Rivera and S.C. Saxena (2005). *Crouching Tiger, Hidden Dragon: What Are the Consequences of China's WTO Entry for India's Trade?*, IMF Working Paper, No. 2005/101, International Monetary Fund (IMF), Washington, D.C.

Chadha, A. (2006). Destination India for the Pharmaceutical Industry, *Delhi Business Review*, Vol. 7, No. 1, January-June, Pp. 1-8.

Chandra, N.K. (1999). FDI and Domestic Economy: Neo-liberalisation in China, *Economic and Political Weekly*, Vol. 34, No. 45, November 6-12, Pp. 3195-3212.

Chishti, S. (1973). *India's Terms of Trade with East Europe*, Indian

Institute for Foreign Trade of India, New Delhi.

Chishti, S. (1974). *India's Terms of Trade: 1930-1968*, Orient Longman, New Delhi.

Chishti, S. (2002). Globalisation, Income Inequalities, Terms of Trade and Developing Countries, *Foreign Trade Review*, Vol. 37, No. 1 and 2, April-September, Pp. 21-34.

Chittle, C.R. and K.H. Kim (1999). Foreign Direct Investment in China and India, in S. Dazver and J. Jaussuad (ed.), *China and India Economic Performance and Business Strategies of Firms in the Mid-1990's*, Macmillan Press, Houndmills, Pp. 3-15.

Cohen, B. (1964). The Stagnation of Indian Exports: 1951-1961, *Quarterly Journal of Economics*, November, Pp. 604-620.

Coppock, J.D. (1962). *International Economic Instability*, McGraw Hill, New York.

Cuddington, J.T. (1992). Long-Run Trends in 26 Primary Commodity Prices: A Disaggregated Look at the Prebisch-Singer Hypothesis, *Journal of Development Economics*, Vol. 39, Pp. 207-227.

Cuddington, J.T. and C. Urzúa (1989). Trends and Cycles in the Net Barter Terms of Trade: A New Approach, *The Economic Journal*, Vol. 99, No. 396, Pp. 426-442.

Da Costa, G.C. (1983). India's Terms of Trade: An Alternative Method, *The Indian Economic Journal*, Vol. 30, No. 3, Pp. 119-130.

Das, S.K. and M. Pant (1989). On Export Diversification and Earning Instability: Theory and Evidence, *The Indian Economic Journal*, Vol. 36, No. 3, Pp. 65-71.

Dash, S. (2006). *Services Outsourcing: Evaluating Changes in Revealed Comparative Advantage - The Case of the US and India*, Working Paper Series, MarketRx India Pvt. Ltd., February, available at http://papers.ssrn.com/sol3/papers.cfm?abstract_id =887690.

Deaton, A. and G. Laroque (1992). On the Behaviour of Commodity Prices, *Review of Economic Studies*, Vol. 59, Pp. 1-23.

Debroy, B. (1989). China's External Trade-A Review, *Foreign Trade Review*, Vol. 24, No. 1, April-June, Pp. 1-36.

Debroy, B. (1990). The Terms of Indo-Soviet Trade Revisited, *Foreign Trade Review*, January-March, Vol. 24, No. 4, Pp. 377-398.

Deepak, B.R. (2001). *India-China Relations: In the First Half of the*

Bibliography   237

20th Century, A.P.H. Publishing Corporation, New Delhi, Pp. 1-35.

Deshpande, G.P. and A. Acharya (2001). Introduction, in G.P. Deshpande and A. Acharya (ed.), *50 Years of Crossing a Bridge of Dreams: India-China*, Tulika Press, New Delhi, Pp. 1-17.

Devi, L.K. (2006). India's Terms of Trade: A Commodity Group-Wise Analysis, *The ICFAI Journal of Financial Economics*, March, Vol. 4, No. 1, Pp. 54-68.

Dimaranan, B., E. Ianchovichina and W. Martin (2007). *China, India and the Future of the World Economy: Fierce Competition or Shared Growth*, The World Bank, Policy Research Working Paper, No. 4304, Washington, DC.

Dyer, G. (2009). China becomes the Third Largest Economy, *Financial Times*, 15th January, Pp. 5, London.

Eastern Economist (1974). *Annual Number*, December.

Economic Survey (2009-10). *Industry*, Government of India, Ministry of Finance, Economic Division, Pp. 208-232.

Economic Survey (2004-05). *Industry*, Government of India, Ministry of Finance, Economic Division, Pp. 161-162.

Economic Survey (2006-07). *Statistical Tables*, Government of India, Ministry of Finance, Economic Division, Pp. S-96.

Economic Times (2006). *Nathu La to Open for Indo-China Trade After 44 Years*, July 5.

Elbehri, A., T. Hertel and W. Martin (2003). Estimating the Impact of WTO and Domestic Reforms on the Indian Cotton and Textile Sectors: A General-Equilibrium Approach, *Review of Development Economics*, Vol. 7, No. 3, Pp. 343-359.

Ellsworth, P.T. (1956). The Terms of Trade between Primary Producing and Industrial Countries, *Inter-American Economic Review*, Vol. 10, Pp. 47-65.

Evans, D. (1987). The Long-Run Determinants of North-South Terms of Trade and Some Recent Empirical Evidence, *World Development*, Vol. 15, No. 5, Pp. 657-671.

Fertö, I. and L.J. Hubbard (2002). *Revealed Comparative Advantage and Competitiveness in Hungarian Agri-Food Sectors*, Discussion Papers, New Series No. 2002/8, Institute of Economics, Hungarian Academy of Sciences, Budapest.

FICCI (2003). *FICCI's FDI Survey 2003: The Experience of Foreign Direct Investment in India*, Federation of Indian Chambers of Commerce and Industry, Executive Summary, May, New Delhi.

Fude, W. (2004). Sino-Indian Economic Cooperation under WTO Framework, in B. Debroy and M. Saqib (ed.), *Future Negotiation Issues at WTO: An India-China Perspective*, Globus Books, New Delhi, Pp. 477-486.

Gang, P. (2010). *Enhancing Economic Cooperation for a Win-Win Situation*, Economic and Commercial Counsellor's Office of the Embassy of People's Republic of China (PRC) in Republic of India, available at http://in2.mofcom. gov.cn/aarticle.

Ganguli, B.N. (1956). *India's Economic Relations with the Far Eastern and Pacific Countries in the Present Century*, Orient Languages Pvt. Ltd., Calcutta, Bombay and Madras, Pp. 162-177.

Garnaut, R. (1999). Economic Reform in India and China, in R. Shand (ed.), *Economic Liberalisation in South Asia*, Macmillan India Ltd., New Delhi, Pp. 320-338.

Ghosh, D.N. (2005). FDI and Reform: Significance and Relevance of Chinese Experience, *Economic and Political Weekly*, Vol. 40, No. 51, December 17, Pp. 5388-5392.

Ghuman, R.S. (1986). *Indo-Pakistan Trade Relations*, Deep and Deep Publication, New Delhi.

Gill, S.S. (1983). *Political Economy of Indo-Soviet Relations: 1947-80*, Rajesh Publications, New Delhi.

Glezakos, C. (1973). Export Instability and Economic Growth: A Statistical Verification, *Economic Development and Cultural Change*, Vol. 21, No. 4, Pp. 670-679.

GOI, (2009). *Export-Import Data Bank*, Ministry of Commerce and Industry, Government of India, available at http://commerce.nic.in.

GOI (2005). *Report of the India-China Joint Study Group on Comprehensive Trade and Economic Cooperation*, available at http://www.hinduonnet.com/thehindu/ nic/0041/report.pdf.

Goud, R.S. (2003). Impact of FDI on Emerging Economies: Comparative Analysis of India and China, in V. Suguna, G.R. Krishna and A.G. Moss (ed.) *Economic Reforms in India: Retrospects and Prospects*, Himalaya Publishing House, New Delhi, Pp. 435-447.

Grilli, E. and M.C. Yang (1988). Primary Commodity Prices, Manufactured Goods Prices and Terms of Trade of Developing Countries: What Does the Long-Run Show?, *The World Bank*

Economic Review, Vol. 2, Pp. 1-48.

Guha, A. and A.S. Ray (2000). *Multinational Versus Expatriate FDI: A Comparative Analysis of Chinese and Indian Experience*, Working Paper No. 56, Indian Council for Research on International Economic Relations (ICRIER), New Delhi.

Gupta, S.P. and A. Singh (1995). Economic Reforms in China and India: A Comparison, in S.P. Gupta, N. Stern and A. Hussain (ed.), *Development and Institutional Structures: China and India*, London School of Economics, London and ICRIER, New Delhi.

Gyimah-Brempong, K. (1991). Export Instability and Economic Growth in Sub-Saharan Africa, *Economic Development and Cultural Change*, Vol. 39, July, Pp. 815-828.

Hadass, Y. and J. Williamson (2001). *Terms of Trade Shocks and Economic Performance 1870-1940: Prebisch and Singer Revisited*, Working Paper No. 8188, National Bureau of Economic Research (NBER).

Hindustan Times (2011). *Chinese Imports Hit Indian Silk*, January 05, New Delhi.

Hosamane, M.D. and S Bisaliah (2006). Export Performance of India during Post-Reform Period: Constant Market Share Analysis, *Indian Journal of Economics and Business*, June.

Hu, V. (2005). *The Chinese Economic Reforms and Chinese Entrepreneurship*, A Lecture, available at www.uoc.edu/ symposia/calxaresa/jomadaeconomia/2005/ eng/vicky_hu.pdf.

ITPO (2003). *A Strategy for Enhanced Economic Cooperation between India and China*, A Report, Trade Information Department, Indian Trade Promotion Organisation, July, New Delhi.

Javalgi, R.G., V.S. Talluri and O. Lee (1997). India and China as Emerging Giants in the Global Economy: A Comparative Outlook, *Foreign Trade Review*, Vol. 32, No. 1 and 2, April-September, Pp. 1-15.

Kapur, S.N. (1991). The Structure and Competitiveness of India's Exports, *Indian Economic Review*, Vol. 26, No. 2, Pp. 221-237.

Katrak, H. (1973). Commodity Concentration and Export Fluctuations: A Probability Analysis, *Journal of Development Studies*, Vol. 9, No. 4, Pp. 556-565.

Kaur, N. (1993). *India's Exports: An Analysis of Instability and Performance*, Ph.D. Thesis, Department of Business

Management, Punjabi University, Patiala.

Kaur, N. and K.C. Singhal (1989). India's Export Instability, *The Indian Economic Journal*, Vol. 36, No. 3, Pp. 72-79.

Kazi, S.S. (2007). Hu's Visit to India: A Step Forward in Bilateral Ties, *Civil Services Chronicle*, January, Pp.9-12.

Kennen, P.B. and C.S. Voivodas (1972). Export Instability and Economic Growth, *Kyklos*, Vol. 25, No. 4, Pp. 791-804.

Khatkhate, D. (1991). Trade Policies and Business Opportunities in Southern Asia, *Economic and Political Weekly*, Vol. 26, No. 49, December 7, Pp. 2815-2820.

Kilduff, P. and T. Chi (2006). Longitudinal Patterns of Comparative Advantage in the Textile Complex, *Journal of Fashion Marketing and Management*, Vol. 10, No. 2, Pp. 134-149.

Kindleberger, C.P. (1956). *Terms of Trade: An European Case Study*, John Wiley Press, New York.

Kingston, J.L. (1973). Export Instability in Latin America: The Post-War Statistical Record, *Journal of Developing Area*, Vol. 7, Pp. 381-395.

Knudsen O. and A. Parnes (1975). *Trade Instability and Economic Development: An Empirical Study*, Lexington Books, Lexington, Mass.

Kojima, K. (1964). The Pattern of International Trade Among Advanced Countries, *Hitosubashi Journal of Economics*, Vol. 5, No. 1, June.

Kongsamut, P.P., S.T. Rebelo and D. Xie (2001). *Beyond Balanced Growth*, IMF Working Paper No. 01/85, International Monetary Fund.

Kowalski, P. (2008). *China and India: A Tale of Two Trade Integration Approaches*, Indian Council for Research on International Economic Relations (ICRIER), Working Paper No. 221, August.

Krueger, A. (1980). Trade Policy as An Input to Development, *The American Economic Review*, Vol. 70, No. 2, Pp. 288-292.

Krueger, A. (1998). Why Trade Liberalisation is Good for World?, *The Economic Journal*, Vol. 108, September.

Kumar, G. and S.A. Singh (2008). Growth and Forecasts of Foreign Direct Investment Inflows to South and East Asia–An Empirical Analysis, *Asian Economic Review*, Vol. 50, No. 1, April, Pp. 16-31.

Kumar, N. (2005a). Liberalisation, Foreign Direct Investment

Bibliography 241

Inflows and Development: Indian Experience in the 1990's, *Economic and Political Weekly*, Vol. 40, No. 14, April 2, Pp. 1459-1469.

Kumar, N. (2005b). Towards an Asian Economic Community a Longer-Term Vision of Sino-Indian Partnership, in C.V. Ranganathan (ed.), *Panchsheel and the Future Perspectives on India-China Relations*, Samskriti Press, New Delhi, Pp. 349-368.

Kumar, N. and K.J. Joseph (2007). *International Competitiveness and Knowledge-Based Industries in India*, Oxford University Press, New Delhi.

Kwatra, V. (2005). India-China Trade and Economic Relations Current Status and Prospects, in C.V. Ranganathan (ed.), *Panchsheel and the Future Perspectives on India-China Relations*, Samskriti Press, New Delhi, Pp. 237-270.

Lal, D. (1995). India and China: Contrasts in Economic Liberalization?, *World Development*, Vol. 23, No. 9, Pp. 1475-1494.

Lanceiri, E. (1987). Export Instability and Economic Development: A Reappraisal, in H.W. Singer, N. Hatti and R. Tondon (ed.), *International Commodity Policy-Part II*, Ashish Publishing House, New Delhi, Pp. 567-593.

Lanchovichina, E and W. Martin (2001). *Trade Liberalisation in China's Accession to the World Trade Organisation*, Policy Research Working Paper No. 2623, The World Bank, Washington.

Lardy, N.R. (2002). *Integrating China into the Global Economy*, Brooking Institution Press, Washington, D.C.

Laursan, K. (1998). *Revealed Comparative Advantage and the Alternatives as Measures of International Specialisation*, Working Paper No. 98-30, December, Danish Research Unit for Industrial Dynamics, Denmark.

Lee, S.C. (2003). *Patterns Of Canada's Revealed Comparative Advantage in the United States*, Discussion Paper No. 104, December, Department of Economics, University of Regina, Regina, Canada.

Lehman Brothers (2007). India: Everything to Play for, *Business Standard*, Thursday, February 05.

León, J. and R. Soto (1995). *Structural Breaks and Long-Run Trends in Commodity Prices*, Policy Research Working Paper, No.

1406, The World Bank, January.

Leonard, A.G., SJ (1993). *India's Trade Relations With Japan: An Economic Analysis*, Indus Publishing Company, New Delhi.

Leu, G.J.M. (1998). *Changing Comparative Advantage in East Asian Economies*, Working Paper No. 3-98, School of Accountancy and Business Research Centre, Nanyang Technological University.

Loke, W.H. (2007). *Assessing Malaysia's and China's Comparative Advantages in Selected Manufacturing Goods*, Working Paper No. 2007-3, Institute of China Studies, University of Malaya, Kuala Lumpur, Malaysia.

Love, J. (1979). A Model of Trade Diversification based on Markowitz Model of Portfolio Selection, *Journal of Development Studies*, Vol. 15, No. 2, Pp. 233-241.

Love, J. (1992). Export Instability and Domestic Economy: Questions of Casualty, *Journal of Development Studies*, Vol. 28, No. 4, Pp. 735-742.

Lutz, M. (1999). A General Test of the Prebisch-Singer Hypothesis, *Review of Development Economics*, Vol. 3, Pp. 44-57.

Macbean, A.I. (1966). *Export Instability and Economic Development*, George Allen and Unwin Ltd., London.

Madaan, D.K. (1998). *Indo-Bangladesh Economic Relations and SAARC*, Deep and Deep Publication, New Delhi.

Maizels, A. (1968). Review of Export Instability and Economic Development, *American Economic Review*, Vol. 58, No. 3, Pp. 183-201.

Máñez J.A., M.E. Rochina-Barrachina and J.A. Sanchis (2008). Trade Specialization in Latin America: The Impact of China and India, *Review of World Economics*, Vol. 144, No. 2, Pp. 272-294.

Marjit, S. and A. Raychaudhuri (1997). *India's Exports: An Analytical Study*, Oxford University Press, New Delhi.

Massell, B.F. (1964). Export Concentration and Fluctuations in Export Earnings: A Cross Section Analysis, *American Economic Review*, Vol. 54, No. 2, Pp. 47-63.

Massell, B.F. (1970). Export Instability and Economic Structure, *American Economic Review*, Vol. 60, No. 4, Pp. 618-630.

Mathur, A.B.L. (1973). India's Terms of Trade with USA: 1951-52 to 1968-69, *The Indian Economic Journal*, Vol. 21, No. 2, Pp. 73-90.

Mathur, V. (2006). *Foreign Trade of India 1947-2007: Trends, Policies and Prospects*, New Century Publication, New Delhi.

McGeehan, J.M. (1968). Competitiveness: A Survey of Recent Literature, *The Economic Journal*, June, Pp. 243-262.

Meier, G.M. (1963). *International Trade and Development*, Harper and Row Press, New York.

Meier, G.M. and R.E. Baldwin (1957). *Economic Development: Theory, History and Policy*, John Wiley Press, New York.

Michaely, M. (1962). *Concentration in International Trade*, North-Holland Publishing Co., Amsterdam.

Mishra, S.K. and V.K. Puri (2007). *Indian Economy: Its Development Experience*, Himalaya Publishing House, Delhi.

Mitra, A. and A. Roy (2005). An Overview of India-China Trade and Investment, in C.V. Ranganathan (ed.), *Panchsheel and the Future Perspectives on India-China Relations*, Samskriti Press, New Delhi, Pp. 286-302.

Moran, C. (1983). Export Fluctuations and Economic Growth: An Empirical Analysis, *Journal of Development Economics*, February-April, Vol. 12, Pp. 195-218.

Mukherjee, N. and A. Mukherjee (1980). Secularly Deteriorating Terms of Trade Myth or Reality: India 1952-77, *Foreign Trade Review*, Vol. 15, No. 1, Pp. 85-97.

Mukherjee, S. (1987). Export Instability and Economic Development 1950-51 to 1980-81: The Indian Case, *The Indian Journal of Economics*, Vol. 67, No. 266, Pp. 375-397.

Myrdal, G. (1956). *An International Economy*, Harper and Row, New York.

Nayyar, D. (1976). *India's Exports and Export Policy in 1960*, Cambridge University Press, Cambridge.

Nurkse (1953). *Problems of Capital Formation in Underdeveloped Countries*, Basil Blackwell Press, Oxford.

Ocampo, J.A. (1993). Terms of Trade and Center-Periphery Relations, in Osvaldo Sunkel (ed.), *Development from Within: Toward a Neo-Structuralist Approach for Latin America*, Lynne Rienner Publishers, Boulder and London.

Ohlin, B. (1952). *Interregional and International Trade*, Cambridge University Press, Harvard, Pp. 29.

Okamoto, Y. (2008). *ASEAN, China and India: Are They More Competitive to Each Other?*, available at http://elib.doshisha.ac.jp/cgibin/retrieve/sr_bookview.cgi/   U_CHARSET.utf-

8/BD00011652/Body/040000010 008.pdf.

Ozler, S. and J. Harrigan (1988). *Export Instability and Growth*, Working Paper No. 486, Department of Economics, University of California, Los Angeles.

Pappu, S. and S. Kumar (2002). *Impact of China's Entry into the WTO on India*, Working Paper Series, Social Science Research Network, available at http://ssrn.com/abstract=303439.

Patnaik, P. (2009). The Economic Crisis and Contemporary Capitalism, *Economic and Political Weekly*, Vol. 64, No.13, Pp. 47-54.

Paul, S. and V.L. Mote (1970). Competitiveness of Exports: A Micro Level Approach, *The Economic Journal*, Vol. 80, No. 320, Pp. 895-909.

Peiyong, G. (2004). Sino-Indian Economic and Trade Relations in the Background of China's Entry into WTO, in B. Debroy and M. Saqib (ed.), *Future Negotiation Issues at WTO: An India-China Perspective*, Globus Books, New Delhi, Pp. 123-139.

Powell, A. (1991). Commodity and Developing Country Terms of Trade: What Does the Long Run Show?, *Economic Journal*, Vol. 101, Pp. 1485-1496.

Prebisch, R. (1950). The Economic Development of Latin America and its Principal Problems, *Economic Bulletin for Latin America*, Vol. 7, No. 1, 1962, Pp. 1-22.

Purushottam, S. (1999). Chinese Economic Reforms and Their Relevance to India, in M. Dubey and N. Jettly (ed.), *South Asia and Its Eastern Neighbours: Building Relationship in the 21st Century*, Konark Publishers Pvt. Ltd., New Delhi, Pp. 128-161.

Qureshi, M.S. and G. Wan (2008). *Trade Expansion of China and India: Threat or Opportunity*, Research Paper No. 2008/08, February, World Institute for Development Economics Research, United Nations University.

RNCOS, (2009). *Indian Iron Ore Exports Shine, 2009 Forecast Re-Evaluated*, RNCOS Industry Research Solutions, February 07, available at www.rncos.com.

Rajesh, P. (2003). Economic Reforms and Foreign Direct Investments in India: Emerging Trends and Patterns, in V. Suguna, G.R. Krishna and A.G. Moss (ed.), *Economic Reforms in India: Retrospects and Prospects*, Himalaya Publishing House, New Delhi, Pp. 448-461.

Reddy, J.M. (2003). Economic Reforms and Foreign Direct

Investment: The Case of India, in V. Suguna, G.R. Krishna and A.G. Moss (ed.) *Economic Reforms in India: Retrospects and Prospects*, Himalaya Publishing House, New Delhi, Pp. 420-434.

Reinhart, C. and P. Wickham (1994). Commodity Prices: Cyclical Weakness or Secular Decline?, *IMF Staff Papers*, No. 41, Pp. 175-213.

Richardsan, D.J. and C. Zhang (1999). *Revealing Comparative Advantage Chaotic or Coherent Patterns across Time and Sector and U.S. Trading Partner*, Working Paper No. 25, National Bureau of Economic Research (NBER).

Rodrick, D. (2006). *What's So Special about China's Exports?*, Research Working Paper No. 06-001, January, Kennedy School of Government, Harvard University, Harvard.

Roy, P.C. (1986). *Indo-U.S. Economic Relations*, Deep and Deep Publications, New Delhi.

Ruisheng, C. (1999). China and South Asia in 21st Century, in M. Dubey and N. Jettly (ed.), *South Asia and It's Eastern Neighbours: Building Relationship in the 21st Century*, Konark Publications Pvt. Ltd. Pp. 115-127.

Ruisheng, C. (2001). China and India: Transforming Historical Sino-Indian Relations, *World Affairs*, Vol. 5, No. 4, Pp. 18-26.

Ruixiang, Z. (2000). India and China: A Chinese Overview, in M.D. David and T.R. Ghoble (ed.), *India, China and South-East Asia: Dynamics of Development*, Deep and Deep Publications Pvt. Ltd., New Delhi, Pp. 4-7.

Rumbaugh, T. and N. Blancher (2004). International Trade and the Challenges of WTO Accession, in E. Parsad (ed.), *China's Growth and Integration into the World Economy Prospects and Challenges*, Occasional Paper No. 232, IMF, Washington, D.C., Pp. 5-13.

Saksena, K.D. (2005). *Economic Reforms: The Indian Experience*, Shipra Publications, New Delhi.

Sapsford, D. (1985). The Statistical Debate on the Net Barter Terms of Trade between Primary Commodities and Manufactures: A Comment and Some Additional Evidence, *The Economic Journal*, Vol. 95, September, Pp. 781-788.

Sarkar, P. (1986). The Singer-Prebisch Hypothesis: A Statistical Evaluation, *Cambridge Journal of Economics*, Vol. 10, Pp. 37-58.

Savvidos, A. (1984). Export Instability and Economic Growth: Some New Evidence, *Economic Development and Cultural Change*, Vol. 32, No. 3, Pp. 607-614.

Scandizzo, P.L. and D. Diakosavvas (1987). Instability in the Terms of Trade of Primary Commodities, 1900-1982, *FAO Economic and Social Development Paper*, No. 64.

Schiavo-Campo and G.F. Erb (1969). Export Instability, Level of Development and Economic Size of Less Developed Countries, *Bulletin of Oxford University Institute of Economics and Statistics*, Vol. 31, No. 11, Pp. 263-283.

Schott, P. (2008). The Relative Sophistication of Chinese Exports, *Economic Policy*, Vol. 23, No. 53, January, Pp. 5-49.

Sebastian, A.M. (1988). A New Approach to the Relationship between Export Instability and Economic Development, *Economic Development and Cultural Change*, Vol. 36, January, Pp. 217-236.

Shafaeddin, S.M. (2004). Is China's Accession to the WTO Threatening Exports of Developing Countries?, *China Economic Review,* Vol. 15, No. 2, Pp. 109-144.

Sharan, V. (1986). Instability in Export Earnings, Export Concentration and India, *Foreign Trade Review*, Vol. 19, No. 1, Pp. 143-150.

Shen, G. and Y. Gu (2007). Revealed Comparative Advantage, Intra-Industry Trade and the US Manufacturing Trade Deficit with China, *China & World Economy*, Vol. 15, No. 6, Pp. 87-103.

Shetty, S.V. (1976). India's Trade with the Socialist Countries of East-Europe under Bilateral Trade and Payment Agreement, *Indian Economic Journal*, Vol. 24, No. 2, Pp. 327-347.

Shirk, L.S. (2004). One-Sided Rivalry: China's Perception and Policies towards India, in F.R. Frankel and H. Harding (ed.), *The India-China Relations: Rivalry and Engagement*, Oxford University Press, New Delhi, Pp. 75-100.

Singer, H.W. (1950). The Distribution of Gains between Investing and Borrowing Countries, *American Economic Review Papers and Proceedings*, Vol. 40, Pp. 473-485.

Singh, A. (2000). Sino-Indian Economic Relations: An Analysis of Recent Trends in Bilateral Trade, *China Report*, Vol. 36, No. 3, Pp. 397-410.

Singh, L. (1999). *Globalisation and Economic Growth in Asian Economies*, Report submitted to Directorate Planning and

Monitoring, August, Department of Economics, Punjabi University, Patiala.

Singh, M. (1964). *India's Export Trends*, Oxford University Press, London.

Singh, S. (2001). China-India: Expanding Economic Engagement, *Strategic Analysis*, Vol. 24, No. 10, Pp. 1813-1831.

Singh, S. (2005). *China-India Economic Engagement: Building Mutual Confidence*, CSH Occasional Paper, No.10, Rajdhani Arts Press, New Delhi.

Singhal, K.C. and N. Kaur (1986). Destination Wise Export Instability in India, *Margin*, Vol. 18, No. 3, Pp. 61-71.

Singla, S.K. and J.S. Brar (2008). *India's Exports during Post Reform Period with Special Reference to China*, Journal of Agricultural Development and Policy, Punjab Agricultural University, Ludhiana, Punjab (forthcoming).

Singla, S.K. and K. Singh (2008). India and China: Growing Trade Ties in New Era, *Third Concept-An International Journal of Ideas*, Vol. 22, No. 255, May, Pp. 11-20.

Sinha, D. (1999). *Export Instability, Investment and Economic Growth in Asian Countries: A Time Series Analysis*, Center Discussion Paper No. 799, Economic Growth Center, Yale University, April.

Soutar, G.N. (1977). Export Instability and Concentration in the Less Developed Countries, *Journal of Development Economics*, Vol. 4, No. 3, Pp. 279-297.

Spraos, J. (1980). The Statistical Debate on the NBTT between Primary Commodities and Manufactures, *The Economic Journal*, Vol. 90, Pp. 107-128.

Spraos, J. (1983). *Inequalising Trade?*, Oxford University Press, Oxford.

Srinivasan, T.N. (1990). External Sector in Development: China and India 1950-89, *American Economic Review*, Vol. 80, No. 2, Pp. 113-117.

Srinivasan, T.N. (2004). Economic Reforms and Global Integration, in F.R. Frankel and H. Harding (ed.), *India-China Relationship: Rivalry and Engagement*, Oxford University Press, New Delhi, Pp. 219-266.

Srinivasan, T.N. (2006). China, India and the World Economy, *Economic and Political Weekly*, Vol. 61, No. 34, August 26, Pp. 3716-3727.

Strategic Digest (2005). India-China: Joint Statement of Republic of India and the People's Republic of China, *Strategic Digest*, Vol. 35, No. 5, Pp. 491-507.

Strategic Digest (2008). Prime Minister's Visit to China, *Strategic Digest*, Vol. 38, No. 3, Pp. 138-154.

Swamy, S. (2001). *India's China Perspective*, Konark Publishers Pvt. Ltd., New Delhi.

Tandon, J.K. (1978). *Indo-German Economic Relations*, National Publishing House, New Delhi.

Tandon, R. (1985). *Prebisch-Singer Hypothesis and Terms of Trade: Periphery Capitalism in the 1980s*, Ashish Publishing House, New Delhi.

Tandon, R. and N. Hatti (1987). *Exports and Development: The Indian Experience*, Ashish Publishing House, New Delhi.

Tendulkar, S.D. and Bhavani (2007). *Understanding Reforms: Post 1991 India*, Oxford University Press, New Delhi.

The Tribune (2008). *PM's China Visit: Focus to be on Trade and Energy Security*, Vol. 128, No. 12, January 12, Chandigarh, Pp. 1 and 10.

Thiruvenkatachari, K. (1976). Indo-Soviet Trade: A Perspective, *The Indian Economic Journal*, Vol. 24, No. 2, Pp. 295-308.

Tiwari, R.S. (1986). *India's Export Performance*, Deep and Deep Publication, New Delhi.

Tiwari, R.S. (1998-99). Export Competitiveness and Trade Cooperation among NICs, *Foreign Trade Review*, Vol. 33, October-March, Pp. 73-102.

Tseng, W. and H. Zebregs (2003). Foreign Direct Investment in China: Some Lessons for Other Countries, in W. Tseng and M. Rodlauer (ed.), *China Competing in the Global Economy*, International Monetary Fund (IMF), Washington, D. C., USA, Pp. 68-88.

United Nations (1950). *The Economic Development of Latin America and its Principal Problems*, Lake Success, New York.

Utkulu, U. and D. Seymen (2004). *Revealed Comparative Advantage and Competitiveness: Evidence for Turkey vis-à-vis the EU/15*, presented at European Trade Study Group 6th Annual Conference, Nottingham, available at http://www.etsg.org/ETSG2004/Papers/ seymen.pdf.

Veeramani, C. (2007). Sources of India's Export Growth in Pre- and Post-Reform Periods, *Economic and Political Weekly*, Vol. 62,

No. 25, June 23, Pp. 2419-2427.

Veeramani, C. (2008). India and China: Changing Patterns of Comparative Advantage, in R. Radhakrishna (ed.), *India Development Report 2008*, Oxford University Press, New Delhi, Pp. 145-156.

Viner, J. (1937). *Studies in Theory of International Trade*, Harper and Brothers, New York, Pp. 436-40.

Wei, L. (2004). A Road to Common Prosperity: Relevance of an FTA between India and China, in N. Kumar (ed.), *Towards an Asian Economic Community: Vision of a New Asia*, Research and Information System for Developing Countries (RIS), New Delhi, and Institute of Southeast Asian Studies (ISEAS), Singapore, Pp. 75-106.

WIR (2002). Transitional Corporations and Export Competitiveness, *World Investment Report 2002*, United Nations Conference on Trade and Development (UNCTAD), UN, New York and Geneva.

WIR (2003). FDI Policies for Development: National and International Perspectives, *World Investment Report 2003*, United Nations Conference on Trade and Development (UNCTAD), UN, New York and Geneva.

World Bank (2003). *Sustainable Development in Dynamic World-Transforming Institutions: Growth and Quality of Life*, World Bank Publications, Washington, D.C. and New York.

World Bank (2008). *Trade Indicators and Indices*, Data and Statistics, The World Bank Group, available at http://web.world bank.org.

WTO (2001). *WTO Successfully Concludes Negotiations on China's Entry*, WTO News, World Trade Organisation (WTO), Geneva.

Yang, Y. (2005). Deepening Investment and Economic Relations between China and India, in J.K. Ray and Parbir De (ed.), *India and China in an Era of Globalisation: Essays on Economic Cooperation*, Bookwell, New Delhi, Pp. 77-84.

Yin, X. (2004). China's Trade Reform and Economic Development, *China Report*, Vol. 40, No. 4, Pp. 407-417.

Yongtu, L. (2007). China's WTO Accession: Implications and Key Lessons Learned, in I. Gill, Y Huang and H. Kharas (ed.) *East Asian Visions: Perspectives on Economic Development*, World Bank and Institutes of Policy Studies (IPS).

Zanias, G. (2005). Testing for Trends in the Terms of Trade between

Primary Commodities and Manufactured Goods, *Journal of Development Economics*, Vol. 78, No. 1, Pp. 25-46.

Index

Index